Exploration

Food

Geography

Native Americans   **Oceans**   **Polar Regions**

Universe

Weather

Zoos

The Kids' FUN-FILLED ENCYCLOPEDIA A to Z

Written by Kerry Acker
Illustrated by Tony Tallarico

kidsbooks
Incorporated

ABOUT THIS BOOK
Note to Parents and Teachers

GETTING CHILDREN'S ATTENTION

The Kid's Fun-Filled Encyclopedia has been specially created to stimulate and educate young children. The book's humorous, informative illustrations and wealth of fascinating facts will draw children into the world of learning—and keep them there!

HELPING THEM ENJOY LEARNING

The Kids' Fun-Filled Encyclopedia is designed to encourage as well as satisfy a child's curiosity. As young readers explore topics that interest them, the book's fun format will inspire them to read other entries, fostering a love of learning. Children will enjoy returning to this resource again and again to answer questions that arise as they do schoolwork, watch TV, and read other books.

THE ENTRIES IN THIS ENCYCLOPEDIA

The 96 main entries in *The Kids' Fun-Filled Encyclopedia* cover many of the same key topic areas as reference books for older children, at a level that young children can understand and enjoy. The entries support all the main educational content areas: history, science, the arts, mathematics, civics, and sports and recreation. Within entry text, words likely to be unfamiliar to young readers appear in **boldface** type, followed by a brief definition in parentheses. Cross-references (the "see-also" list under each entry title) help readers discover other relevant information, teaching them valuable research skills in the process.

BUILDING AN AT-HOME LIBRARY

An at-home library is best when it contains informational resources that are both educational and fun to read. *The Kids' Fun-Filled Dictionary*, *The Kids' Fun-Filled Encyclopedia*, and *The Kids' Fun-Filled Question & Answer Book* do just that. They keep kids learning—and laughing!

Africa

(see also AFRICAN WILDLIFE ● WORLD)

Africa is the world's second-largest continent. It is so big that the U.S., Europe, India, and Japan could all fit into it—with room to spare! Its many kinds of terrain include deserts, savannas (grasslands), and tropical forests. The world's largest desert (the Sahara) covers one third of Africa. The continent also is home to the world's longest river (the Nile), and one of the most spectacular waterfalls (Victoria Falls). Most of the continent gets quite hot, but some of Africa's mountains are so high that they are snowcapped year-round.

MOST NATIONS HERE WON INDEPENDENCE AFTER 1956.

Ancient Africa

Africa's most powerful kingdoms grew wealthy from mining metals and gold, and trading with other African kingdoms, Asia, and Europe. The Songhai Empire (8th-16th centuries) was the greatest in West Africa. It spread across what is now Gambia and parts of present-day Senegal, Guinea, Guinea-Bissau, Mauritania, Mali, Niger, and Nigeria. The kingdoms of Mali and Ghana were also powerful. The kingdom of Zimbabwe was one of the richest cultures of southern Africa. Its height of power was in the early 1400s, when its people traded gold and ivory for glass, porcelain, and beads from Asia.

TIMBUKTU, A CITY OF THE SONGHAI KINGDOM, WAS A CENTER OF CULTURE AND LEARNING IN THE 15TH AND 16TH CENTURIES. (TODAY, IT IS CALLED TOMBOUCTOU, IN THE NATION OF MALI.)

DURING THE LATE 1800s AND EARLY 1900s, EUROPEAN COUNTRIES COLONIZED MUCH OF AFRICA.

MOST OF AFRICA'S LARGE CITIES ARE NEAR THE COASTS.

FROM THE 13TH TO THE 15TH CENTURY, WHEN THEIR WEALTHY KINGDOM WAS AT ITS HEIGHT, THE SHONA PEOPLE OF SOUTHERN AFRICA BUILT GREAT ZIMBABWE, A STONE CITY.

THE BENIN PEOPLE OF WEST AFRICA (ABOUT A.D. 900) WERE HIGHLY SKILLED METALWORKERS WHO MADE BEAUTIFUL BRONZE FIGURINES.

NOW THIS IS WHAT I CALL A SCHOOL OF FISH!

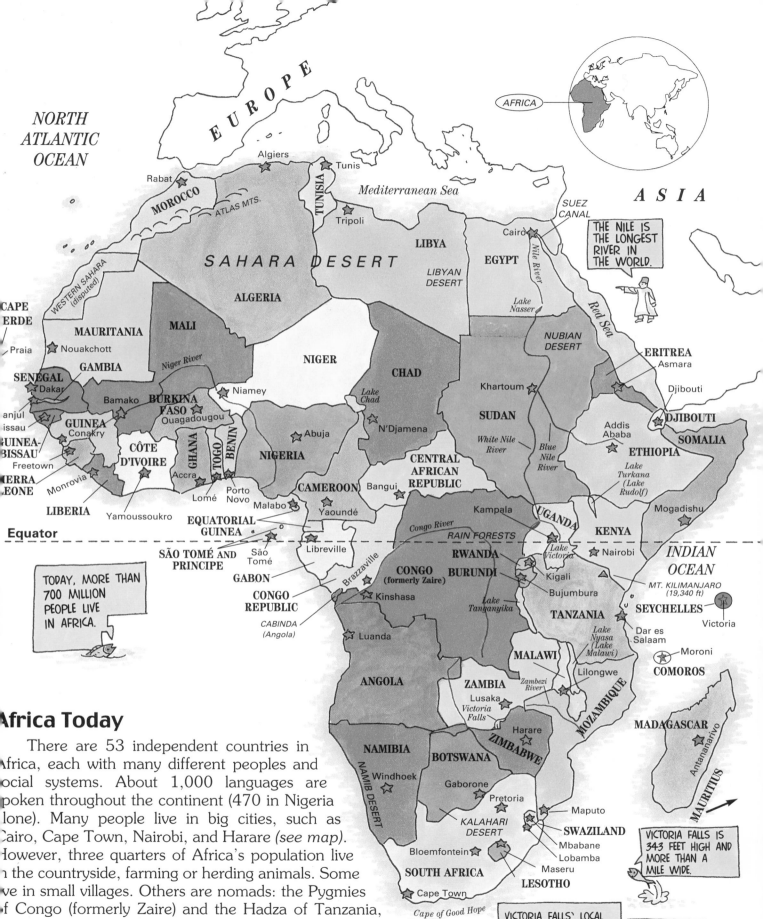

NORTH ATLANTIC OCEAN

E U R O P E

Mediterranean Sea

A S I A

AFRICA

Algiers
Tunis
Rabat
MOROCCO
ATLAS MTS.
TUNISIA
Tripoli
LIBYA
EGYPT
SUEZ CANAL
Cairo

Nile River

THE NILE IS THE LONGEST RIVER IN THE WORLD.

S A H A R A   D E S E R T

LIBYAN DESERT

Lake Nasser

Red Sea

CAPE VERDE
WESTERN SAHARA (disputed)
Praia

ALGERIA

MAURITANIA
Nouakchott
MALI

NIGER

CHAD

NUBIAN DESERT

ERITREA
Asmara

GAMBIA
Niger River
Khartoum
Djibouti

SENEGAL
Dakar
Bamako
BURKINA FASO
Niamey
SUDAN

anjul
issau
GUINEA
Conakry
Ouagadougou
Abuja
N'Djamena
Lake Chad
White Nile River
Blue Nile River
Addis Ababa
DJIBOUTI

GUINEA-BISSAU
Freetown
CÔTE D'IVOIRE
GHANA
TOGO
BENIN
NIGERIA
CENTRAL AFRICAN REPUBLIC
Bangui
ETHIOPIA
Lake Turkana (Lake Rudolf)
SOMALIA

ERRA
EONE
Monrovia
Accra
Lomé
Porto Novo
CAMEROON
Yaoundé
Mogadishu

LIBERIA
Yamoussoukro
Malabo
Kampala
UGANDA
KENYA

EQUATORIAL GUINEA
Congo River
RAIN FORESTS
Lake Victoria
Nairobi
INDIAN OCEAN

Equator

SÃO TOMÉ AND PRINCIPE
São Tomé
Libreville
RWANDA
Kigali
MT. KILIMANJARO (19,340 ft)
SEYCHELLES
Victoria

TODAY, MORE THAN 700 MILLION PEOPLE LIVE IN AFRICA.

GABON
CONGO REPUBLIC
Brazzaville
CONGO (formerly Zaire)
BURUNDI
Bujumbura
Lake Tanganyika
TANZANIA
Dar es Salaam

CABINDA (Angola)
Kinshasa
Luanda
Lake Nyasa (Lake Malawi)
Moroni
COMOROS

MALAWI
Lilongwe

ANGOLA
ZAMBIA
Zambezi River
MOZAMBIQUE
MADAGASCAR

Lusaka
Victoria Falls
Harare
Antananarivo

Africa Today

There are 53 independent countries in Africa, each with many different peoples and social systems. About 1,000 languages are spoken throughout the continent (470 in Nigeria alone). Many people live in big cities, such as Cairo, Cape Town, Nairobi, and Harare (see map). However, three quarters of Africa's population live in the countryside, farming or herding animals. Some live in small villages. Others are nomads: the Pygmies of Congo (formerly Zaire) and the Hadza of Tanzania, for instance. They move from place to place in small groups, seeking water and food.

NAMIBIA
Windhoek
NAMIB DESERT
BOTSWANA
Gaborone
ZIMBABWE
MAURITIUS

VICTORIA FALLS IS 343 FEET HIGH AND MORE THAN A MILE WIDE.

Pretoria
Maputo
SWAZILAND
Mbabane
Lobamba

KALAHARI DESERT
Bloemfontein
Maseru
SOUTH AFRICA
LESOTHO
Cape Town
Cape of Good Hope

VICTORIA FALLS' LOCAL NAME MEANS "THE SMOKE THAT THUNDERS."

THE FALLS ARE FED BY THE ZAMBEZI RIVER.

9

African Americans

(see also NORTH AMERICA ● UNITED STATES ● UNITED STATES HISTORY ● WOMEN, FAMOUS)

By the end of the 20th century, there were more than 35 million Americans of African descent in the U.S. That was nearly 13 percent of the population, making African Americans the largest racial minority in the country.

The Beginning

People of African descent have lived in this country since 1619, when a group of about 20 Africans were sold as servants in Virginia. From 1619 to 1808, European slave traders and rival African groups kidnapped more than 10 million Africans from their homelands and took them to the Americas to serve as slaves. (Most of today's African Americans are descended from those slaves.) Captives who survived the harsh conditions during the long passage across the Atlantic Ocean were sold at public slave markets and put to work. Families were often split apart by the slave trade.

DID YOU KNOW . . . ?
In 1630, the black population of the American colonies was 100. By 1861, when the Civil War began, there were four million slaves—three million of them in the South.

Many people fell ill or died on crowded slave ships.

Family being broken up and sold into slavery

The End of Slavery

The question of whether slavery should be allowed was debated from the earliest days of the nation. The Founding Fathers argued over whether to ban it in the Declaration of Independence (1776). Over time, the split between supporters and opponents of slavery deepened, especially as the nation expanded westward. By 1804, slavery was illegal in the North but still legal in the South. This split was one of the reasons for the U.S. Civil War (1861-1865). Slavery was **abolished** (banned) by the Thirteenth Amendment in 1865. After the war, southern states passed unfair laws, known as Jim Crow laws, that denied African Americans many rights of U.S. citizens, such as the right to vote.

Most slaves worked as field hands on plantations or small farms. Others were skilled laborers or house servants.

African Americans joined the Union Army to fight slave states during the Civil War.

Many African Americans were denied the right to vote, even after the Constitution guaranteed it.

VOTE

The Civil–Rights Movement

In the late 1950s and the 1960s, Martin Luther King Jr. and many other Americans worked to overturn Jim Crow laws, end discrimination, and achieve equality for African Americans. This campaign, known as the civil-rights movement, was a largely nonviolent effort. Protesters took part in peaceful marches and rallies, held **boycotts** (refused to use certain stores or services) and sit-ins, and encouraged African Americans to insist on their right to vote. In 1964 and 1965, Congress passed new laws that banned discrimination on the basis of race or religion in employment, voting, and education. Today, civil-rights leaders campaign for better education, job training, health care, and other services for people who have been disadvantaged by racial inequality.

Notable African Americans in History

Jean Baptiste du Sable
(1745?-1818)
Known as the Father of Chicago, this Haitian-born fur trader founded a settlement in the 1770s that later grew into the city of Chicago, Illinois.

Phillis Wheatley
(1753-1784)
A slave in Boston, Massachusetts, who was taught by her owners to read and write, she became a noted poet and, in 1773, the first African American to publish a book.

Frederick Douglass
(1817-1895)
As a slave in Maryland, he secretly learned to read and write—then escaped to freedom. He became a famous antislavery speaker and newspaper publisher, and his autobiography was a popular book.

Harriet Tubman
(about 1820-1913)
An escaped slave herself, she led more than 300 African Americans to freedom by way of the Underground Railroad, a secret organization that helped slaves escape north to free states or to Canada.

Booker T. Washington
(1856-1915)
Born into slavery, he became a noted scientist and educator. He also founded the Tuskegee Institute, one of the first high-level educational institutions for African Americans.

Matthew Henson
(1866-1955)
A skilled navigator, survivalist, and explorer who, in 1909, was a member of the team (with Admiral Robert E. Peary and four Eskimos) that became the first to reach the North Pole.

W. E. B. Du Bois
(1868-1963)
A noted author and publisher, he helped organize the National Association for the Advancement of Colored People (NAACP), and was an influential leader in the campaign for black liberation.

Ida B. Wells-Barnett
(1869-1931)
A journalist and speaker, she was a major crusader against lynchings (murder by mob action) and other harsh injustices suffered by African Americans in the South during the 19th and 20th centuries.

Thurgood Marshall
(1908-1993)
As a lawyer, he won *Brown* v. *the Board of Education*, the 1954 Supreme Court ruling that declared segregation in U.S. schools unconstitutional. In 1967, he became the first African-American Supreme Court justice.

Martin Luther King Jr.
(1929-1968)
World-famous for his powerful, eloquent speeches, he helped organize peaceful protests against racial discrimination. He won the Nobel Peace Prize in 1964.

African Wildlife

(see also AFRICA ● ANIMAL KINGDOM ● DESERTS ● ECOSYSTEMS ● RAIN FORESTS)

There are more different kinds of animals living on the continent of Africa than anywhere else in the world. Africa's **savannas** (grasslands) are home to zebras, lions, and cheetahs. Some of the largest animals in the world live on the savannas, eating grass—or other animals. Towering, 18-foot-tall giraffes eat from parts of trees that other animals can't reach. Lions doze under trees, ostriches scout for food, and gazelles graze, while elephants cool off by spraying water over themselves.

DURING THE SERENGETI MIGRATION, ZEBRA, WILDEBEEST, AND GAZELLE GATHER AND SEARCH HUNDREDS OF MILES FOR GRASS AND WATER.

I'M A CHEETAH, THE WORLD'S FASTEST ANIMAL. I CAN RUN AS FAST AS 65 MPH!

THE NGORONGORO CRATER IN TANZANIA, THE WORLD'S LARGEST COLLAPSED VOLCANO, IS HOME TO MORE THAN 100 BIRD SPECIES AND 25,000 LARGER ANIMALS.

Water Wildlife

In Africa's wetlands, four-foot-tall flamingos use their beaks to filter insects, algae, and small fish from the water. (Their pink color comes from the pigments in their food.) Crocodiles—so still that they look like logs—wait for prey, with just their eyes, ears, and nostrils above water. Two-ton hippos flop in the mud, and secretary birds run over the plain, searching for snakes to eat.

I LOVE MUD!

SSSS!

I LOOK GOOD!

I'M NOT A LOG.

Desert Denizens

Africa's Sahara, Namib, and Kalahari deserts are among the driest places on Earth. Yet many animals thrive there. The addax, a type of antelope, gets water from the plants it eats. The camel, a hardy species that can survive dry conditions and high temperatures, is also at home there. In fact, camels have played an important role in helping traders make long journeys across the desert.

Frolicking in the Forest

Africa's dense rain forests are home to gorillas, chimps, and monkeys, as well as bright-colored birds and insects. Before going to sleep at night, gorillas build themselves nests to lie down in—a different nest every night!

Air
(see also ENVIRONMENT ● WEATHER)

Air is made of different gases. We can't see, smell, or taste air, but it contains the gases that we need in order to survive: oxygen, carbon dioxide, and nitrogen, among others. Human beings and other animals breathe in oxygen, use it to turn food into energy, then breathe out carbon dioxide. Plants take in carbon dioxide, use it to make foods that help them grow, then give off oxygen. What teamwork!

BREATHE IN OXYGEN

BREATHE OUT CARBON DIOXIDE

The Wonders of Wind

When air moves, it is called wind. Moving air can be as gentle as a light breeze that rustles leaves, or as powerful as a hurricane that can flip over cars and wreck buildings. Wind is what makes kites fly and sailboats move. It also turns windmills, generating electricity.

Nice Atmosphere!

Earth is surrounded by the atmosphere—a layer of air about 400 miles thick. This protects Earth from extreme heat and cold. The atmosphere has five layers: the troposphere, stratosphere, mesosphere, thermosphere, and exosphere.

Hot-air balloons float because the heated air inside is lighter than the cool air outside. Hence, the balloon rises into the sky.

The higher you go on Earth, the thinner the air gets. That is why people climbing high mountains (such as Mount Everest) carry oxygen tanks.

Mercury spacecraft

Meteors

X-15 manned rocket plane

EXOSPHERE
(300-400 miles above ground)

THERMOSPHERE
(50-300 miles above ground)

MESOSPHERE
(30-50 miles above ground)

The Human Factor

What humans do changes the air around us. Smoke from factories and exhaust from motor vehicles create **smog** (smoke + fog), which pollutes the air.

STRATOSPHERE
(7-30 miles above ground)

Manned balloon

Cirrus clouds
Cumulus clouds

Mt. Everest (29,802 ft)

TROPOSPHERE
(0-7 miles above ground)

Alphabets

(see also ANCIENT CIVILIZATIONS ● COMMUNICATION)

Alphabet Soup

In writing, we use an alphabet—symbols or letters that represent sounds. By rearranging those letters in different ways, we spell out words. Many written languages have an alphabet. The Phoenicians developed the first modern alphabet about 3,000 years ago. Ancient Greeks based their alphabet on the Phoenicians'; ancient Romans adapted the Greek alphabet. The Latin alphabet, which has 26 letters, is the one we're using right now.

THE WORD ALPHABET COMES FROM THE FIRST TWO LETTERS OF THE GREEK ALPHABET: ALPHA AND BETA.

ENGLISH SPEAKERS READ FROM LEFT TO RIGHT, BUT NOT EVERYONE DOES. FOR INSTANCE, JAPANESE READERS GO FROM RIGHT TO LEFT, AND START AT THE TOP AND READ DOWN.

THE CYRILLIC (SUH-**RIL**-IK) ALPHABET, WHICH WAS INFLUENCED BY THE GREEK ALPHABET, IS USED IN RUSSIAN, SERBIAN, UKRAINIAN, BELORUSSIAN, AND BULGARIAN.

Braille, an alphabet for the blind, uses raised dots arranged in different combinations.

Chinese and Japanese are the only major languages that use symbols, called characters, ideographs, or pictograms. Each character (there are about 50,000 in Chinese) represents an object or an idea.

When people first wrote, they used small pictures to represent objects, people, or ideas. Egyptians began using such pictures, called hieroglyphics, about 5,000 years ago.

Some Hieroglyphics

- hand
- seated
- noose
- plants
- snake
- house

In 1799, an ancient stone was found near Rosetta, Egypt. It was carved with writing in two kinds of hieroglyphics, as well as with Greek. It said the same thing using three different alphabets. Scholars were able to use the Rosetta Stone's Greek section to figure out how to read the hieroglyphics.

Until the Middle Ages, the Latin alphabet had no letter for *U* or *W*. It used a *V* instead. It also used an *I* for the letter *J*.

VI

Ancient Civilizations

(see also ALPHABETS ● ARCHAEOLOGY ● ARCHITECTURE ● ANCIENT EMPIRES ● MUMMIES ● MYTHOLOGY)

Mesopotamia

Mesopotamia is a name used for the area between the Tigris and Euphrates rivers of the Middle East. Sumer, one of the world's first civilizations, began there 6,000 years ago. It was followed by the Assyrian and Babylonian empires. Babylon, the capital of Babylonia, was a religious and trading center, and the people were prosperous. Babylon—founded about 2000 B.C.—was most glorious around 600 B.C., with its grand palaces and **ziggurats** (stepped pyramids).

THE SUMERIANS WERE THE FIRST PEOPLE TO USE THE WHEEL.

THEY ALSO DEVELOPED ONE OF THE FIRST FORMS OF WRITING.

BLACK SEA

CASPIAN SEA

TIGRIS RIVER

MEDITERRANEAN SEA

BABYLONIA

EUPHRATES RIVER

RED SEA

PERSIAN GULF

THE HANGING GARDENS OF BABYLON WERE ONE OF THE SEVEN WONDERS OF THE ANCIENT WORLD.

Ancient Egypt

The civilization of ancient Egypt, in northeastern Africa, began about 3000 B.C. Its beautiful temples and pyramids, and its people's understanding of agriculture, medicine, and science, are why many historians consider Egypt to be the birthplace of great ideas. Egyptians believed that their **pharaohs** (rulers) were sons of the sun god. They honored the pharaohs by building them spectacular, treasure-filled tombs, such as the famous pyramids. Ancient Egypt lasted for more than 3,000 years.

PHARAOHS WERE BURIED WITH FOOD, WEAPONS, AND JEWELRY IN PYRAMID TOMBS.

THE BODIES OF PHARAOHS AND OTHER EGYPTIANS (AS WELL AS ANIMALS CONSIDERED SACRED) WERE PRESERVED BY EMBALMING.

EGYPTIANS BELIEVED THAT WHEN PEOPLE DIED, THEY MOVED ON TO THE NEXT WORLD.

EGYPTIANS BELIEVED THAT THE PHARAOH'S SPIRIT WOULD CLIMB UP THE PYRAMID STEPS AND JOIN THE SUN GOD AT THE TOP.

ALL ORGANS EXCEPT THE HEART WERE REMOVED AND PUT IN JARS.

THE BODIES WERE COVERED WITH PRESERVATIVES AND WRAPPED IN STRIPS OF LINEN.

MEDITERRANEAN SEA

EGYPT

Ancient China

China has been inhabited for about 500,000 years—first by human ancestors, then by modern humans. Villages appeared around 5000 B.C., and the first Chinese city was built about 3500 B.C. The ancient Chinese contributed much to the world, including writing, paper, gunpowder, and many ideas about nature, life, and art. Confucius (551-479 B.C.) was one of ancient China's most famous thinkers—people still quote his ideas today.

FOR CENTURIES, CHINA WAS RULED BY ROYAL FAMILIES CALLED DYNASTIES.

EMPEROR SHIH HUANG-TI WAS FAMOUS FOR HIS HARSH RULE AND FOR UNITING MANY CHINESE KINGDOMS.

WHEN SHIH HUANG-TI DIED AROUND 209 B.C., SLAVES MADE LIFE-SIZE TERRA-COTTA SCULPTURES OF SOLDIERS AND BURIED THEM NEAR HIS TOMB TO GUARD HIM.

THIS "CLAY ARMY" WAS DISCOVERED IN 1975.

CHINA

SHIH HUANG-TI'S WORKERS COMPLETED CONSTRUCTION OF THE GREAT WALL OF CHINA.

Ancient Greece

Ancient Greece flourished between 750 and 200 B.C. At that time, Athens was the Mediterranean world's most important city, and the center of culture and thought. **Democracy** (rule by the people)—an important foundation of many present-day governments—began there. Ancient Greece's architecture, theater, and philosophy remain influential today.

THE OLYMPIC GAMES WERE HELD EVERY FOUR YEARS AT OLYMPIA IN HONOR OF ZEUS, KING OF THE GODS.

TRAGEDY AND COMEDY—TWO FORMS OF DRAMA—WERE BORN IN GREECE.

THE GREEKS BELIEVED IN MANY DIFFERENT GODS AND GODDESSES.

THEY BELIEVED THAT THE DEITIES WERE ALL RELATED AND THAT MANY LIVED ON TOP OF MOUNT OLYMPUS.

FROM 336 TO 323 B.C., ALEXANDER THE GREAT CONQUERED MOST OF THE KNOWN WORLD—SPREADING GREEK CULTURE AS HE WENT.

SOCRATES (469-399 B.C.) WAS ONE OF THE WORLD'S MOST IMPORTANT THINKERS ON ETHICS—HOW WE SHOULD LIVE. PEOPLE STILL READ AND DISCUSS HIS IDEAS TODAY.

Europe

Asia

GREECE

Africa

Red areas on this map were part of the Greek Empire at its peak.

Ancient Empires

(see also ANCIENT CIVILIZATIONS ● ARCHAEOLOGY ● ARCHITECTURE ● MYTHOLOGY)

JULIUS CAESAR, A BRILLIANT, POWERFUL LEADER OF ANCIENT ROME, RULED THE EMPIRE FROM 46 B.C. TO 44 B.C. THIS MAP SHOWS THE EMPIRE AT ITS HEIGHT.

Roman Empire

More than 2,000 years ago, western Europe, the Middle East, and northern Africa were united by a single government—that of the very powerful and advanced Roman Empire. At its most extensive—around A.D. 200—the Empire stretched from what is now England to the Middle East. The Romans had highly organized cities and towns, all planned the same way. A system of roads connected every town to Rome, and water was transported by aqueducts. Every Roman city had sewers, a central marketplace where traders sold their wares, and baths with steam rooms and warm and cold pools.

The Inca Empire

The Inca Empire began in the 12th century A.D., in present-day Peru. At its height, in the 15th century, more than 10 million people were living in the Inca Empire, which had grown to include present-day Bolivia, Chile, Ecuador, and Peru.

The Inca worshipped their chief as a god. They had a powerful army, and vast road and communications networks. (Messages were carried by fleet-footed runners.) The Inca carved cities and farms into the steep sides of the Andes Mountains.

The ruins of Machu Picchu, a city of the Inca Empire, were found in 1911. The city sits more than 2,000 feet above sea level, on land straddling two taller peaks. Its streets and buildings were built on different levels connected by more than 3,000 steps!

SOUTH AMERICA

Inca Empire

ALREADY WEAKENED BY CIVIL WAR, THE INCA EMPIRE WAS CONQUERED BY SPANISH SOLDIERS WHO ARRIVED IN 1532.

Mongol Empire

In the early 13th century, Genghis Khan (JENG-gis KHAN) united the many feuding Mongol tribes of Asia and built a huge, invincible army that helped him build a vast empire. By 1260, it included all of China and reached westward through most of Asia. The Mongols' brutal battle tactics made them feared throughout Asia and into Europe.

MONGOL WARRIORS—FAMED FOR THEIR HORSEMANSHIP AND SPEED—BURNED DOWN BUILDINGS AND TERRORIZED PEOPLE IN THE LANDS THEY INVADED.

I'M GENGHIS KHAN.

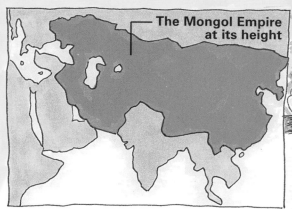

The Mongol Empire at its height

THE NOMADIC (WANDERING) MONGOLS LIVED IN YURTS—TENTS MADE OF FELT.

Descendants of the Mongols established later empires, including India's Mogul Empire. A Mogul emperor, Shah Jahan, built the world-famous Taj Mahal (left) as a tomb for his beloved wife.

The Aztec Empire

The Aztec were the last Native American rulers of Mexico. At its height, the Aztec Empire had 12 million people. Its capital was Tenochtitlán (where Mexico City now stands), a "floating city" built on a huge lake.

The Aztec built towering temples and pyramids to take them closer to the sun, and believed that the sun would refuse to move unless they sacrificed people to the sun god. The empire fell in 1521, when the Aztec were defeated by Spanish conquistadors.

THE AZTEC THOUGHT THAT HERNÁN CORTÉS, A SPANISH EXPLORER, WAS A GOD. MONTEZUMA II, THE AZTEC EMPEROR, GREETED CORTÉS WITH MUCH CEREMONY, BUT THE SPANISH SOON CONQUERED THE EMPIRE. MONTEZUMA WAS CAPTURED AND KILLED BY HIS OWN PEOPLE.

THIS IS AN AZTEC SACRIFICIAL ALTAR.

Tenochtitlán

The Aztec Empire at its height

ROMAN EMPIRE: 509 B.C.-A.D. 476	INCA EMPIRE: c. 1200-1532
MONGOL EMPIRE: c. 1213-c.1382	AZTEC EMPIRE: c. 1325-1521

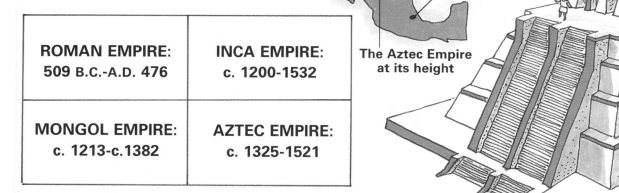

Animal Kingdom

(see also AFRICAN WILDLIFE ● ASIAN WILDLIFE ● COLORS ● DINOSAURS ● FLIGHT ● NORTH AMERICAN WILDLIFE ● OCEANS AND SEA LIFE ● PLANT KINGDOM ● SOUTH AMERICAN WILDLIFE ● ZOOS)

Animals are multicelled, living things that breed, eat other living things to get energy, and can sense and react to their surroundings. There are millions of animal species, and they come in countless shapes and sizes. Animals range from microscopic creatures (like those pictured at left) to blue whales, the largest animals on Earth.

I'M BIGGER THAN YOU!

The largest dinosaurs, once the largest animals on Earth, would have been dwarfed by the blue whale.

Invertebrates

Most animal species (about 97 percent) have no backbone. Animals without backbones are called invertebrates. Some invertebrates have hard shells that protect their soft bodies—snails, clams, scallops, and abalone are some examples. Other invertebrates—insects, spiders, and crabs, for example—have tough outer skeletons (called exoskeletons) and flexible joints. Other invertebrates—such as jellyfish, octopus, and earthworms—have no shell or hard covering.

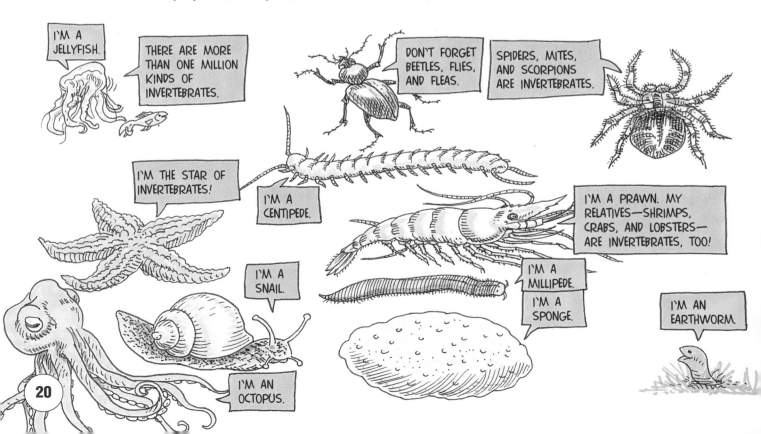

I'M A JELLYFISH.

THERE ARE MORE THAN ONE MILLION KINDS OF INVERTEBRATES.

DON'T FORGET BEETLES, FLIES, AND FLEAS.

SPIDERS, MITES, AND SCORPIONS ARE INVERTEBRATES.

I'M THE STAR OF INVERTEBRATES!

I'M A CENTIPEDE.

I'M A PRAWN. MY RELATIVES—SHRIMPS, CRABS, AND LOBSTERS—ARE INVERTEBRATES, TOO!

I'M A SNAIL.

I'M A MILLIPEDE.

I'M A SPONGE.

I'M AN EARTHWORM.

I'M AN OCTOPUS.

20

Vertebrates

The other three percent of animal species have a backbone. They are called vertebrates. The five types of vertebrates are fish, amphibians, reptiles, birds, and mammals.

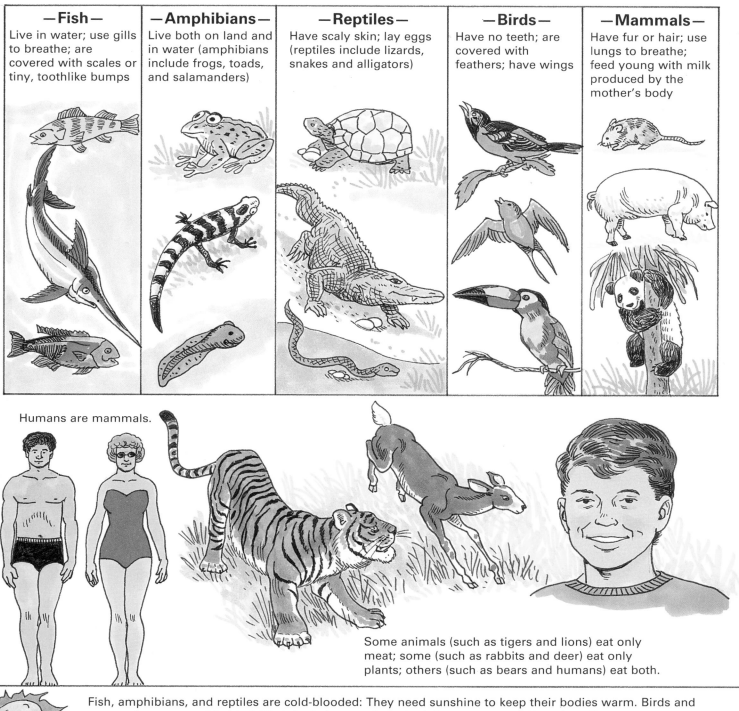

—Fish—	—Amphibians—	—Reptiles—	—Birds—	—Mammals—
Live in water; use gills to breathe; are covered with scales or tiny, toothlike bumps	Live both on land and in water (amphibians include frogs, toads, and salamanders)	Have scaly skin; lay eggs (reptiles include lizards, snakes and alligators)	Have no teeth; are covered with feathers; have wings	Have fur or hair; use lungs to breathe; feed young with milk produced by the mother's body

Humans are mammals.

Some animals (such as tigers and lions) eat only meat; some (such as rabbits and deer) eat only plants; others (such as bears and humans) eat both.

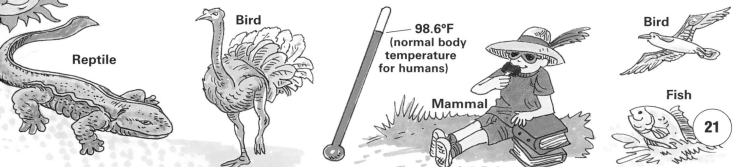

Fish, amphibians, and reptiles are cold-blooded: They need sunshine to keep their bodies warm. Birds and mammals are warm-blooded: Their body temperature stays the same, no matter where they are.

Reptile

Bird

98.6°F (normal body temperature for humans)

Mammal

Bird

Fish

Animation

(see also ART AND ARTISTS ● MOVIES AND TELEVISION ● TECHNOLOGY)

It is amazing what some cartoon characters can do! When Scooby-Doo yelps, the Road Runner blazes off into the sunset, or the Little Mermaid swooshes her tail, there was a whole team of artists who made it happen, using animation.

It works like this: A painter paints a background, and an illustrator draws a series of images, each at a slightly different stage, on clear plastic pages called cels. Then the pages are photographed. When these images are shown one after another, quickly, on a screen, they look as if they are moving. (One million drawings may be needed for one full-length film!) Animation can now be done with computers, which help plan the cartoon, add color, and make some amazing special effects possible.

ANIMATION TABLE
(before computers)

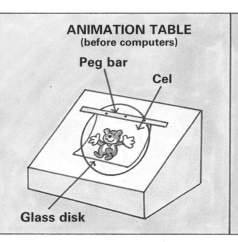

- Peg bar
- Cel
- Glass disk

A Short–Short History of Animation

1645: Athanasius Kircher, a Jesuit scholar, describes a new invention called the magic lantern. He later explains how it was used: a series of images was painted on a glass disk, which was revolved before a lantern. The images projected on the wall seemed to move!

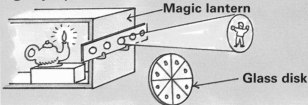

- Magic lantern
- Glass disk

1911: Winsor McCay completes his first animated film, *Little Nemo* **(A)**—with more than 4,000 drawings. In **1914,** he releases his most famous film, *Gertie the Dinosaur* **(B)**. His animated **1918** editorial film *The Sinking of the Lusitania* **(C)** required more than 25,000 drawings!

A **B** **C**

1920s: *Felix the Cat*, created by Otto Messmer, is the most popular cartoon.

1928: Mickey Mouse is born! He stars in Walt Disney's *Steamboat Willie*, often called the first animated cartoon with sound. But Max Fleischer's *Song Car-Tunes* (1924) and Paul Terry's *Dinner Time* (early 1928) put sound with a cartoon even earlier.

1937: Walt Disney's *Snow White and the Seven Dwarfs* is the first full-length animated film.

1995: *Toy Story* (released by Disney) is the first animated feature film made entirely by computer.

(see also ANCIENT CIVILIZATIONS ● ANCIENT EMPIRES ● DINOSAURS ● FOSSILS ● MUMMIES)

Archaeology is the study of the remains of the past. Archaeologists use science to examine weapons, buildings, bones, artwork, and other objects so that we may understand how ancient people lived. When archaeologists find an area that might provide clues to an ancient civilization, they start a dig, or excavation, to gather those clues. On a dig, scientists measure, examine, and record what they find. Their hard work and careful study have given us a great deal of information about our past and, therefore, some insights into our future.

The Dirt on Digs

On a dig, archaeologists use different techniques to discover what is underground without disturbing important clues. They may use aerial photographs—photos taken from high above that may reveal evidence of ancient roads or buildings. They also may use computers or old maps to figure out where to dig.

Archaeologists divide the area into squares, then remove the soil carefully. Next, they may sieve the soil to make sure that they haven't missed any tiny fragments. Then experts study the finds from each square, sorting and numbering each object by its age, type, and other features.

Bone fragments might reveal how old people and animals were when they died—perhaps even how they died!

Bits of seeds can give scientists information about what people ate, and clues to how they may have used the land.

Archaeologists use small brushes to remove dirt from delicate pieces.

Archaeologists can figure out the age of vases, ceramic pieces, and tools if their style is typical of a certain period.

Some objects and bone fragments are dated by the use of X rays.

Archaeologists can sometimes date wooden objects by studying growth rings in the wood.

Eugène Dubois (1858-1940) discovered the remains of Java man, the first important fossil of an early human.

Archaeologist Richard Leakey (1944-), son of famous archaeologists Louis and Mary Leakey, has found many human fossils in Africa—including a skull piece dating back 1.9 million years.

In 1922, Howard Carter found the treasure-filled tomb of Tutankhamen, the boy-king of Egypt who lived 3,500 years ago.

Architecture

(see also ART AND ARTISTS ● MONUMENTS ● RENAISSANCE)

Architecture is the art and science of designing and building structures—including bridges, castles, churches, houses, and office buildings. Throughout history, people have designed structures for different purposes. Some were built to provide shelter from weather, some as places of worship, and some for leaders of government to assemble in. Many temples, monuments, and tombs have been built to honor gods and powerful people.

FUTURISTIC HOUSE

PYRAMID

JAPANESE PAGODA

Doric

Ionic

COLUMNS

Corinthian

GOTHIC CATHEDRAL

History Highlights

● Much of modern architecture is influenced by the classical style, in which everything was simple, even, and elegant. Classical architecture was developed in ancient Greece and Rome. It uses columns, sculpture, and straight, flat beams.
● In ancient Japan, pagodas were built to honor Buddha. Designed to withstand earthquakes, they have several tiers (levels) that curve upward.
● Another important architectural era began in western Europe during the Middle Ages. The Gothic style (12th through 15th centuries) featured enormous cathedrals designed with stained glass, pointed arches, and beautiful stone sculptures.
● In the baroque period (17th and 18th century), architects used elaborate designs and stonework, domes, and other ornaments for palaces and churches.

GREEK TEMPLE
(PARTHENON)

DOME OF THE U.S. CAPITOL
(Washington, D.C.)

TIPI (TEPEE)

CAPE COD-STYLE HOUSE

CASTLE

EIFFEL TOWER
(Paris, France)

TAJ MAHAL
(Agra, India)

EMPIRE STATE BUILDING
(New York, New York)

WOW! I JUST LIVE IN A HOLE IN THE GROUND.

24

Bridges

The first bridges were probably made of tree trunks placed across rivers. Now there are many different types of bridges, with many levels of roadway, so hundreds of cars can travel over them at once. Beam bridges are held up by piers. Suspension bridges are supported by heavy steel cables hung between tall towers.

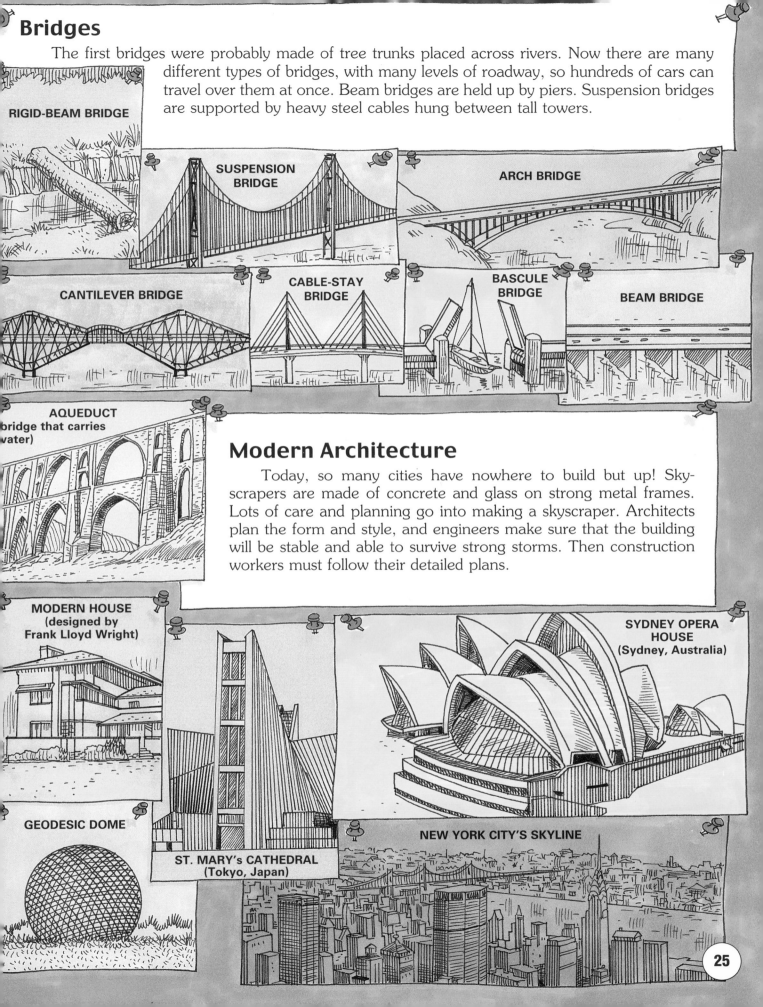

RIGID-BEAM BRIDGE

SUSPENSION BRIDGE

ARCH BRIDGE

CANTILEVER BRIDGE

CABLE-STAY BRIDGE

BASCULE BRIDGE

BEAM BRIDGE

AQUEDUCT (bridge that carries water)

Modern Architecture

Today, so many cities have nowhere to build but up! Skyscrapers are made of concrete and glass on strong metal frames. Lots of care and planning go into making a skyscraper. Architects plan the form and style, and engineers make sure that the building will be stable and able to survive strong storms. Then construction workers must follow their detailed plans.

MODERN HOUSE (designed by Frank Lloyd Wright)

SYDNEY OPERA HOUSE (Sydney, Australia)

GEODESIC DOME

ST. MARY's CATHEDRAL (Tokyo, Japan)

NEW YORK CITY'S SKYLINE

25

Arms and Weapons

(see also ANCIENT CIVILIZATIONS ● TECHNOLOGY ● WAR)

When human beings realized that they couldn't do everything with their bare hands, they used sticks, stones, and animal bones as tools and weapons. When hunting, they hurled stones at wild animals to slow them down (slingshots were very effective for this), or injured them with rocks made into knives.

During the Stone Age, which began about two million years ago, humans experimented with stone tools, using the sharp edges of broken rocks to make all sorts of new weapons. Then humans started to work with metal: The Bronze Age began about 5,500 years ago in Mesopotamia, when people began making **bronze** (a mixture of copper and tin). Bronze made good weapons because it is harder than other metals. During the Iron Age, which started about 2,350 years ago, people realized that daggers and spears made of iron were even better than those made of bronze.

Spears and harpoons could be thrown from far away.

The first-known swords were made out of bronze.

With the invention of the bow and arrow at least 50,000 years ago, people could hit faraway targets with great force. It was the most effective weapon—especially for armies in Middle Ages Europe—until gunpowder was invented.

Gunpowder and Guns

After gunpowder (invented in China) became widely available in the late 1200s, muskets and cannons joined the bow and arrow as tools of warfare. Gunpowder exploded with a force that could launch iron balls from cannon or bullets from guns with tremendous speed. The machine gun, invented in the late 1800s, made it possible for soldiers to fire many bullets rapidly and to reload less often.

Armor

Ever since humans began fighting one another, they have tried to protect themselves, using armor—clothing or tools that would prevent injury or death. At first, they wore leather. But as weapons became more powerful, so did armor. The ancient Romans used strong metal armor up through the 5th century. Viking warriors from Norway and Sweden carried wooden shields, and wore helmets and chain-mail armor. In 15th-century Europe, knights wore elaborate suits of armor that weighed 70 pounds.

In the 20th century, gas masks were developed to protect World War I troops from a new weapon, poison gas. Today, lightweight bulletproof vests help protect police officers, as well as soldiers.

Roman armor

Viking armor

Middle Ages armor

Gas mask

Bullet-proof vest

Modern Weaponry

Today's weapons are more powerful—and deadlier—than ever. Armored tanks can move over many kinds of terrain, firing their guns while protecting the soldiers inside. Warships, submarines, and combat aircraft can launch missiles powerful enough to cause great destruction. Nuclear weapons can destroy entire cities.

Art and Artists

(see also ANIMATION ● ARCHITECTURE ● DANCE ● LITERATURE AND WRITERS ● MOVIES AND TELEVISION ● MUSIC ● RENAISSANCE ● THEATER ● WOMEN, FAMOUS)

The oldest known paintings—from 40,000 to 10,000 B.C.—are pictures of animals and hunters painted on cave walls in southern France.

Ancient Greeks painted scenes from myths and everyday life on pottery and on the walls of houses.

Ancient Romans decorated tombs and temples with figures of gods and goddesses.

For many centuries, many African peoples have created art often used in religious ceremonies, as well as for adornment.

Art is something decorative or creative made by a person. Artists make art for different reasons: for religious purposes, to record a special event, tell a story, describe an idea, amuse a viewer, or just create something. Artists use color, shape, and texture—as well as many different tools and styles of working—to create their individual visions of people, places, things, and ideas. Art includes painting, drawing, photography, pottery, sculpture, jewelry, and weaving.

Some Artistic Movements

In Europe, artists before the 14th century often portrayed scenes from Christianity, painting on wooden panels and on the inside walls of churches. In the 16th century, Renaissance painters—mainly in Italy—began to paint what they saw around them, creating realistic views of buildings and landscapes. In the Romantic period (18th and 19th centuries), Europeans and Americans painted scenes from nature that were filled with light, color, and emotion, while Chinese artists decorated silk scrolls with breathtaking views of forests, rivers, and mountains. In the late 19th century, French Impressionists shocked the world with their nonrealistic paintings, made with many dabs of color. Following their lead, modern artists of the 20th century experimented with many styles and mediums, such as plastics, film, and videotape.

Leonardo da Vinci
(Italian, 1452-1519)
He painted the *Mona Lisa* and *The Last Supper*, two of the world's most famous paintings.

Michelangelo
(Italian, 1475-1564)
He created the marble statue *David* and painted the ceiling of the Sistine Chapel in Rome.

Diego Velázquez
(Spanish, 1599-1660)
He celebrated Spain's grandeur with paintings of royalty, nobility, and famous battles.

Rembrandt
(Rembrandt Harmenszoon van Rijn)
(Dutch, 1606-1669)
His portraits revealed the inner lives of his subjects.

Katsushika Hokusai
(Japanese, 1760-1849)
He created beautiful wood-block prints of scenes from nature.

Auguste Rodin
(French, 1840-1917)
Known for his expressive sculptures made of bronze or marble, Rodin was also known for portraits and monuments.

Mary Cassatt
(American, 1844-1926)
She is best-known for her Impressionist paintings of mothers and children.

Vincent van Gogh
(Dutch, 1853-1890)
With bold, swirling brush strokes, van Gogh painted brilliant landscapes and vivid portraits.

Pablo Picasso
(Spanish, 1881-1973)
This giant of 20th-century art (along with fellow painter Georges Braque) invented a style called cubism—a new way of seeing the world.

Georgia O'Keeffe
(American, 1887-1986)
O'Keeffe is best known for her large, colorful still-life paintings, especially those of desert flowers, sun-bleached cow's skulls, and other desert scenes.

Frida Kahlo
(Mexican, 1907-1954)
She is known for her haunting and colorful self-portraits.

Jackson Pollock
(American, 1912-1956)
He stretched his canvases on the floor and dripped, splashed, and poured paint over them, creating dramatic swirls and patterns.

Romare Bearden
(American, 1914-1988)
His large collages, made with photos clipped from magazines and newspapers, often showed black Americans' struggle for equal rights.

Andy Warhol
(U.S., 1928-1987)
This central figure of the pop art movement used soup cans, soda bottles, and faces of celebrities in his images.

Asia

(see also ASIAN WILDLIFE ● GEOGRAPHY ● RELIGIONS ● WORLD)

Asia, Earth's largest continent, takes up one third of the world's landmass. Its widely varied terrain includes forests, grasslands, deserts, rivers, and the world's tallest mountains. It has 47 independent countries in five main regions: Southwest Asia (the Middle East); the eastern part of Russia and other former Soviet republics; South Asia (India, Pakistan, others); Southeast Asia (Thailand, Laos, Cambodia, Vietnam, Indonesia, the Philippines, others); and the Pacific Coast (China, North Korea, South Korea, Japan).

Rice is mostly grown in terraces— flat, wide rows of dirt built into hillsides and flooded with water.

Asian Peoples and Religions

More than 60 percent of the world's population lives in Asia. The two most populous countries, China and India, are in Asia. However, much of the continent is uninhabited: The far north is a frozen land of ice, while parts of the Middle East are hot, dry desert. Well over 2,000 languages and dialects are spoken throughout the continent. (In Madhya Pradesh, which is just one state in central India, an estimated 375 languages or dialects are spoken!) Asia is the birthplace of the world's five major religions: Hinduism and Buddhism in India, and Judaism, Christianity, and Islam in the Middle East.

DID YOU KNOW . . . ?

The Middle East has two thirds of the world's oil supply.

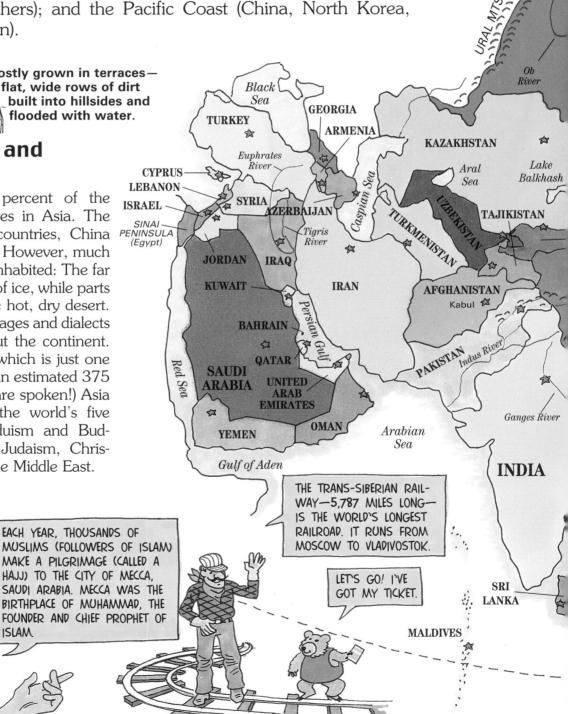

EACH YEAR, THOUSANDS OF MUSLIMS (FOLLOWERS OF ISLAM) MAKE A PILGRIMAGE (CALLED A HAJJ) TO THE CITY OF MECCA, SAUDI ARABIA. MECCA WAS THE BIRTHPLACE OF MUHAMMAD, THE FOUNDER AND CHIEF PROPHET OF ISLAM.

THE TRANS-SIBERIAN RAILWAY—5,787 MILES LONG—IS THE WORLD'S LONGEST RAILROAD. IT RUNS FROM MOSCOW TO VLADIVOSTOK.

LET'S GO! I'VE GOT MY TICKET.

Kara
Sea

Laptev
Sea

KOLYMA MTS.

Bering
Sea

Lena River

Arctic Circle

RUSSIA

STANOVOY MTS.

Sea of
Okhotsk

SAKHALIN
ISLANDS
(Russia)

KURIL
ISLANDS
(Russia)

SAYAN MTS.

Lake
Baikal

ALTAI MTS.

MONGOLIA

KYRGYZSTAN

KUNLUN
MTS.

CHINA

Huang He River

Mekong River

HIMALAYA
MTS.

Chang Jiang River

BHUTAN

EPAL

INDIA

Mekong River

MYANMAR
(BURMA)

LAOS

BANGLADESH

THAILAND

Bay of
Bengal

VIETNAM

CAMBODIA

INDIAN
OCEAN

MALAYSIA

SINGAPORE

JAPAN

NORTH
KOREA

SOUTH
KOREA

Sea
of
Japan

East
China
Sea

TAIWAN

Hong
Kong

South
China
Sea

PHILIPPINES

BRUNEI

INDONESIA

ASIA

SOUTH
PACIFIC
OCEAN

Equator

OCEANIA

COUNTRY	CAPITAL CITY
Afghanistan	Kabul
Armenia	Yerevan
Azerbaijan	Baku
Bahrain	Manama
Bangladesh	Dhaka
Bhutan	Thimphu
Brunei	Bandar Seri Begawan
Cambodia	Phnom Penh
China	Beijing
Cyprus	Nicosia
Georgia	Tbilisi
India	New Delhi
Indonesia	Jakarta
Iran	Tehran
Iraq	Baghdad
Israel	Jerusalem
Japan	Tokyo
Jordan	Amman
Kazakhstan	Astana
Kuwait	Kuwait
Kyrgyzstan	Bishkek
Laos	Vientiane
Lebanon	Beirut
Malaysia	Kuala Lumpur
Maldives	Malé
Mongolia	Ulaanbaatar (Ulan Bator)
Myanmar (Burma)	Yangon (Rangoon)
Nepal	Kathmandu
North Korea	Pyongyang
Oman	Muscat
Pakistan	Islamabad
Philippines	Manila
Qatar	Doha
Saudi Arabia	Riyadh
Singapore	Singapore
South Korea	Seoul
Sri Lanka	Colombo
Syria	Damascus
Taiwan	Taipei
Tajikistan	Dushanbe
Thailand	Bangkok
Turkey	Ankara
Turkmenistan	Ashgabat
United Arab Emirates	Abu Dhabi
Uzbekistan	Tashkent
Vietnam	Hanoi
Yemen	Sanaa

Asian Wildlife

(see also ANIMAL KINGDOM ● ASIA ● DESERTS ● ECOSYSTEMS ● FORESTS ● RAIN FORESTS)

The landscapes of Asia—including forests, mountains, **steppes** (dry, treeless areas), and deserts—are home to thousands of different animal and plant species. Many Asian forests and other areas have been cleared for farming, which destroys animals' habitats. Some animal species are hunted for their furs and skins, which also endangers their survival.

Steppes and Deserts

A wide variety of animal species lives in the steppes of Asia. Cobras, grass snakes, and deer share space with Dorcas gazelles, short-legged Pallas's cats, birds, and lizards.

The hot, dry, sandy deserts of the Middle East and India may seem like harsh places, but lizards, snakes, scorpions, beetles, and burrowing creatures (such as gophers in the Gobi Desert) make these areas home—and thrive there.

Forests

The forests of Japan and southeast Asia provide food and shelter for some of the world's most fascinating animals and birds. Some Indian elephants—smaller than their African cousins—still live wild in the forests. Others are used as work animals. Gibbons—a type of ape—swing from tree to tree, while birds of paradise show off their lovely plumage. The Asiatic black bear and the sun bear live in forests.

Teak trees, sought after for their beautiful wood—very hard with a rich, yellowish-brown color—are native to India, Myanmar, and Thailand.

Mountain Wildlife

Roaming the Himalaya and other Asian mountain ranges are yaks, mongooses, deer, brown bears, tigers, and wild goats. The giant panda lives in China's Szechuan Mountains. Most mountain animals dwell in the lower slopes, but mammals with thick, furry coats—such as the rare snow leopard—can withstand the cold of higher areas. Vultures soar on their large wings, looking for animal carcasses to feed on. Except for spiders, mites, and insects, few animals live high above the tree line.

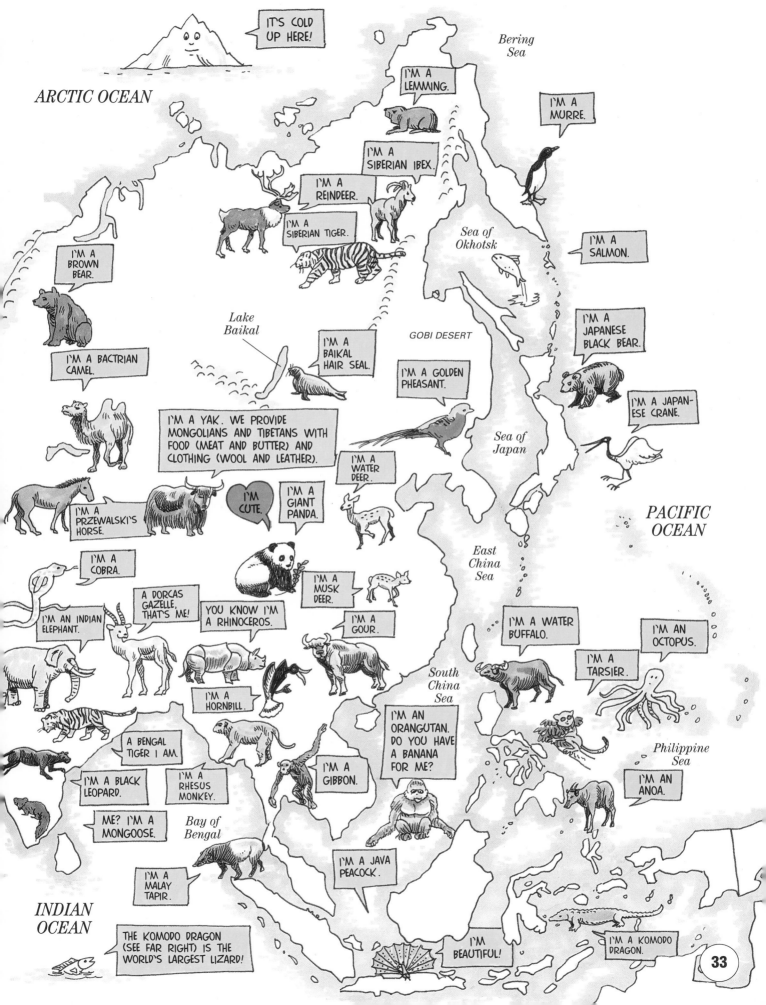

Australia and Oceania
(see also AUSTRALIAN WILDLIFE ● ECOSYSTEMS ● WORLD)

Oceania is the name of a region that includes Australia—the world's smallest, flattest, and driest continent—and the many islands scattered from the Indian Ocean across the South Pacific. Among the many South Pacific islands of Oceania are 14 independent countries: Australia, Fiji, Kiribati, the Marshall Islands, Micronesia, Nauru, New Zealand, Palau, Papua New Guinea, Samoa, the Solomon Islands, Tonga, Tuvalu, and Vanuatu. (Some of them are quite tiny!)

Oceania's climate varies from wet and tropical in the outer Pacific islands to hot and dry in central Australia's outback region. Australia's interior is barren. Most Australians live in cities on the coasts, including Sydney, Canberra, and Melbourne.

Australia's History and Peoples

Aboriginal peoples—also known as Aborigines—were the first inhabitants of Australia. (The word *aborigine* means *from the beginning*.) They arrived from Southeast Asia more than 40,000 years ago. Today, there are about 160,000 Aborigines. Most live in cities, but some still live in the outback—a vast, rural, scarcely populated region of Australia. There, they hunt with spears, gather plants and fruits, and make homes and clothing from the plants and animals of the region, as their ancestors did.

In 1770, Great Britain claimed Australian lands. The first Europeans to live in Australia were convicts sent to British prison camps located there. As convicts were released and other Europeans arrived to farm and settle the land, the white population grew. In the 1940s through the 1960s, two million Europeans moved to Australia, lured by the government's offer to pay for part of their passage.

PALAU
Koror ☆

> **DID YOU KNOW . . . ?**
> The tropical rain forests of Papua New Guinea and northern Australia are home to more than 600 different types of trees.

AUSTRALIA

Ayers Rock, a huge sandstone rock in the outback, is a sacred site for Aborigines.

AYERS ROCK

AUSTRALIA EXPORTS WOOL!

● Perth

IN THE LATE 18TH CENTURY, BRITISH SETTLERS TOOK MUCH OF THE ABORIGINES' SACRED LANDS. IN RECENT YEARS, AFTER LONG LEGAL BATTLES, MOST OF THE LAND WAS RETURNED.

SURFING IS ONE OF AUSTRALIA'S POPULAR PASTIMES.

I'M A GREAT WHITE SHARK. I LIVE HERE.

EIGHTY-SIX PERCENT OF AUSTRALIANS LIVE IN CITIES.

AUSTRALIA PROVIDES ABOUT ONE THIRD OF THE WORLD'S URANIUM (NECESSARY FOR NUCLEAR POWER).

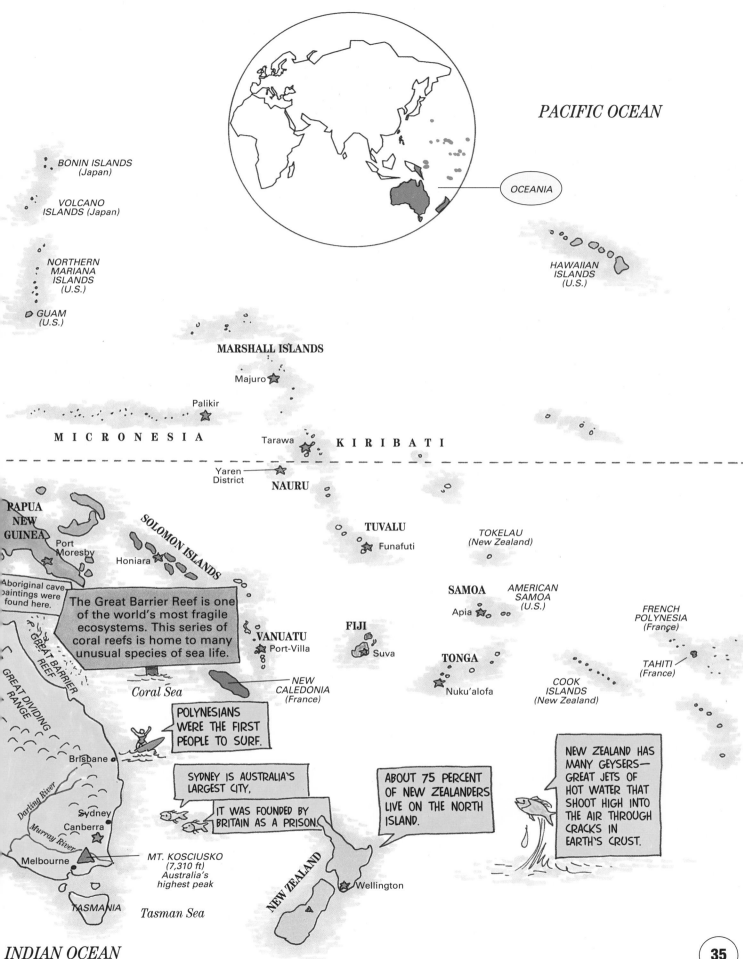

PACIFIC OCEAN

OCEANIA

BONIN ISLANDS
(Japan)

VOLCANO
ISLANDS (Japan)

HAWAIIAN
ISLANDS
(U.S.)

NORTHERN
MARIANA
ISLANDS
(U.S.)

GUAM
(U.S.)

MARSHALL ISLANDS

Majuro

Palikir

M I C R O N E S I A

Tarawa

K I R I B A T I

Yaren
District

NAURU

PAPUA
NEW
GUINEA

Port
Moresby

SOLOMON ISLANDS

Honiara

TUVALU

Funafuti

TOKELAU
(New Zealand)

Aboriginal cave
paintings were
found here.

The Great Barrier Reef is one
of the world's most fragile
ecosystems. This series of
coral reefs is home to many
unusual species of sea life.

SAMOA

Apia

AMERICAN
SAMOA
(U.S.)

FRENCH
POLYNESIA
(France)

VANUATU

Port-Villa

FIJI

Suva

GREAT BARRIER REEF

GREAT DIVIDING RANGE

Coral Sea

NEW
CALEDONIA
(France)

TONGA

Nuku'alofa

COOK
ISLANDS
(New Zealand)

TAHITI
(France)

POLYNESIANS
WERE THE FIRST
PEOPLE TO SURF.

Brisbane

Darling River

SYDNEY IS AUSTRALIA'S
LARGEST CITY.

IT WAS FOUNDED BY
BRITAIN AS A PRISON.

ABOUT 75 PERCENT
OF NEW ZEALANDERS
LIVE ON THE NORTH
ISLAND.

NEW ZEALAND HAS
MANY GEYSERS—
GREAT JETS OF
HOT WATER THAT
SHOOT HIGH INTO
THE AIR THROUGH
CRACKS IN
EARTH'S CRUST.

Sydney

Canberra

Murray River

Melbourne

MT. KOSCIUSKO
(7,310 ft)
Australia's
highest peak

NEW ZEALAND

Wellington

TASMANIA

Tasman Sea

INDIAN OCEAN

Australian Wildlife

(see also AUSTRALIA AND OCEANIA • ECOSYSTEMS •
RAIN FORESTS)

THE KANGAROO'S VERY STRONG BACK,
LEGS, AND TAIL MAKE IT A GREAT
JUMPER. THE RED KANGAROO CAN
GROW TO MORE THAN SIX FEET TALL!

The continent of Australia is home to some of the world's most unusual plants and animals.

Grasslands, the Bush, and Shrub Lands

Australia's grasslands, bush, and shrub lands are home to many marsupials, a type of mammal that carries its young in a body pouch. Marsupials include the kangaroo, bandicoot, possum, and koala. Other resident creatures of these areas are dingos (a wild dog), wombats, and many kinds of snakes, some poisonous (especially the taipan and the death adder).

DID YOU KNOW . . . ?

Some Australian animals are found nowhere else in the world! The continent is so isolated from other large land areas that the animals there evolved in different ways.

I'M A CUTE KOALA.

THERE ARE MANY DIFFERENT TYPES OF KANGAROO, INCLUDING THE WALLABY, PADEMELON, AND QUOKKA. I'M A TREE KANGAROO!

I'M A WALLABY.

I'M A WOMBAT.

I'M AN ECHIDNA.

I'M A PLATYPUS. THE ECHIDNA AND I ARE THE ONLY TYPES OF MAMMALS THAT LAY EGGS.

I'M A TASMANIAN DEVIL.

WE FIERCE DINGOS HUNT KANGAROOS, WALLABIES, RABBITS, SHEEP, AND BIRDS.

WE ALSO HUNTED THE TASMANIAN DEVIL UNTIL THERE WERE NONE LEFT ON THE MAINLAND.

I'M A KOOKABURRA.

Rain Forests and Swamps

The green, misty rain forests of New Guinea and northern Australia have many different types of trees, and gorgeous orchids that thrive in the warm air. Colorful cockatoos, lorikeets, and eclectus parrots chatter and suck nectar from flowers. The swamps are home to crocodiles (and the fish and frogs they eat), turtles, and tortoises. Wading birds poke their beaks into mud to pluck and eat worms.

Orchids grow high up in the trees, getting nourishment from the air.

THE EMU IS THE SECOND-LARGEST BIRD IN THE WORLD. WE CAN GROW TO 6.5 FEET TALL!

I'M A CROCODILE.

I'M A BROLGA CRANE.

I'M A LYREBIRD. WE LOOK LIKE PEACOCKS.

Coral Reefs

Australia's Great Barrier Reef is the largest structure in the world built by living creatures. It is 1,250 miles long! The reef was created by polyps, tiny sea animals that build skeletons—called corals—around themselves. After the polyps die, the corals grow together, creating an extraordinary sight. Jellyfish, anemones, and vibrantly colored fish add to the coral reef's beauty. These waters teem with life. Barracuda, tuna, and Australian salmon are caught by fishers. Blue whales and killer whales can be found, along with dolphins and sharks—including the great white shark, which can grow to 40 feet long. Blue-ringed octopus and box jellyfish live near the coasts.

Desert Life

Australia's deserts, located in the interior, cover more than half the continent. They are extremely hot during the day, so most desert dwellers are active only at night. Many different types of lizards live there, including frill-necked lizards, which show their frilly ruffles like an umbrella when scared, and thorny devils. The desert scorpion, another desert denizen, uses the sting from the poisonous tip of its tail as a defense.

Clothing

(see also ENVIRONMENT ● SOCIETY AND CULTURE)

Clothing is what a person wears to cover and protect his or her body. Clothing styles vary from country to country, and from job to job. The type of clothing that people wear often indicates where and how they live. Some people who live in very cold climates, such as the Inuit (Eskimos), wear warm animal skins and furs. In hot, desert climates, such as Saudi Arabia, people wear long robes and scarves to protect themselves from the blazing heat. People also choose clothing styles to express their personality or moods.

Work Clothes

What people do for a living often affects the type of clothing they wear. Someone who works in a factory is likely to wear comfortable clothes that are easy to move around in and keep clean. Firefighters wear clothing that protects them from heat and smoke. Some workers wear uniforms to make them easy to recognize, such as police officers and nurses. Soldiers' uniforms protect them against weather, while camouflage helps them hide from the enemy. Athletes' outfits are easy to move around in, and reinforce team spirit with colors and symbols.

Some people wear particular clothing for religious reasons. Many Muslim women, for example, keep their heads and legs covered when they are in public.

Astronauts wear helmets, gloves, and a special spacesuit equipped with an air supply, since there is no air to breathe in space.

Astronaut

Nun

Chef

Firefighter

Student

Baseball player

Police officer

Style and Fashion

Clothing fashions are constantly changing. Sometimes, people wear certain clothing to show their status in society. From the 16th through the 19th centuries, women wore corsets—tight underclothing made of whalebone that made their waists look tinier. In the 1920s, women wore straight **shifts** (dresses) and short skirts that reflected the freedom and fun of the era. Clothing became less formal in the 1960s, 1970s, 1980s, and 1990s. Since the 1960s, blue jeans—first made for miners during the California gold rush of 1850—have been popular all over the world. There has always been a great deal of experimentation in fashion. Designers from Europe and the U.S. have been in the forefront in recent years.

Europe, A.D. 800

1600s Europe

Puritan of the 1600s

European child of the 1770s

American child of the1800s

1800s

1850s (bloomers)

1900s

1920s

1950s

Today

Tomorrow?

All over the world, a bride's clothing reflects her religion and culture. A Hindu bride wears flower necklaces around her neck. A Western bride wears white to symbolize innocence.

Bathing suits of the 1900s . . .

. . . and today

39

Colors

The world is filled with colors. In order to see those colors, light is needed. Light is made of invisible waves, each in a different length. Each wavelength is a different color. When light from the sun hits Earth's atmosphere and scatters in many different directions, our eyes see different colors. The longest wavelength of light that human eyes can see is red; the shortest is blue.

RED   BLUE

The Color Spectrum

When light passes through a triangular glass called a prism, the glass bends the light, splitting it into its different wavelengths. The light that comes out shows all the colors of the spectrum: red, orange, yellow, green, blue, indigo, and violet. (The colors always appear in the same order.)

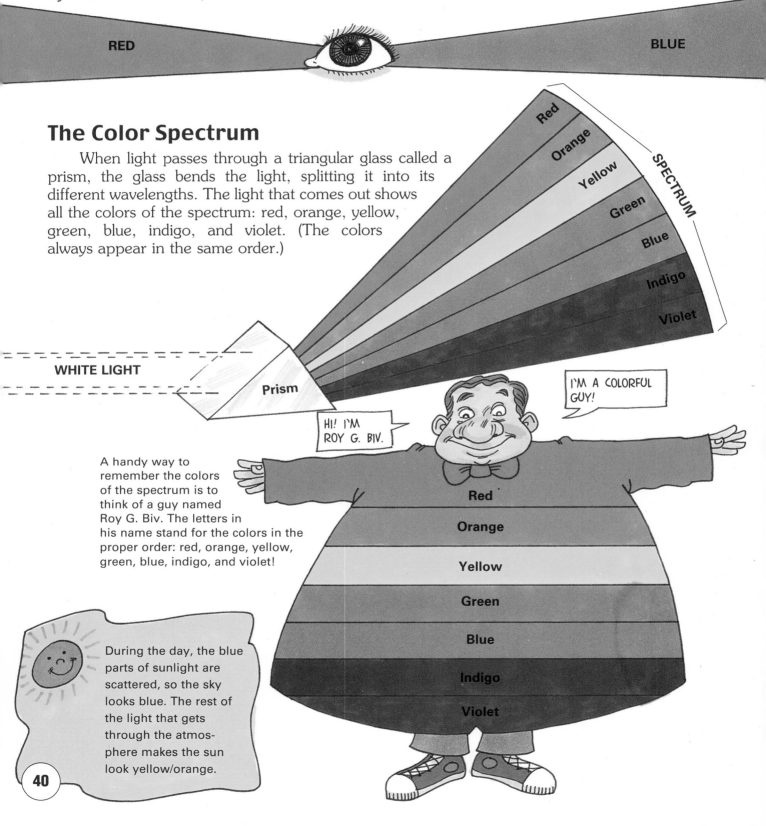

SPECTRUM

Red
Orange
Yellow
Green
Blue
Indigo
Violet

WHITE LIGHT

Prism

HI! I'M ROY G. BIV.

I'M A COLORFUL GUY!

A handy way to remember the colors of the spectrum is to think of a guy named Roy G. Biv. The letters in his name stand for the colors in the proper order: red, orange, yellow, green, blue, indigo, and violet!

Red
Orange
Yellow
Green
Blue
Indigo
Violet

During the day, the blue parts of sunlight are scattered, so the sky looks blue. The rest of the light that gets through the atmosphere makes the sun look yellow/orange.

Colors in Nature

Many animals have camouflage—colors on their fur or skin that help them blend into their environment. This helps them hide from enemies or surprise their prey.

Some animals use color to attract mates. The male peacock displays his beautiful plumage, while the bird of paradise hangs upside down, revealing bright blue feathers.

Other animals use color as a warning. For example, some butterfly wings have colorful spots that look like big eyes, to scare off enemies.

The bright colors of some flowers and plants attract birds and insects to their sweet nectar.

Humans can't see ultraviolet light, but some animals can. Bees see some flowers as very bright—they can detect the ultraviolet light given off by the flowers' petals.

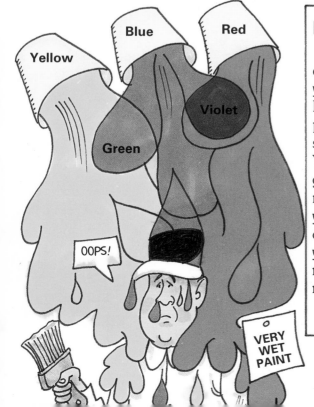

Primary Colors

The primary colors of paint are yellow, blue, and red. Mixing any two primary colors creates secondary colors: Yellow and blue make green, blue and red make violet, and yellow and red make orange. If you mix red, yellow, and blue in the right proportions, the result is black.

The primary colors of light are red, green, and blue. When you mix them in the proper amounts . . .

. . . white light is created.

Communication

(see also ALPHABETS ● COMPUTERS ● FLAGS ● INVENTORS AND INVENTIONS ● MACHINES ● MOVIES AND TELEVISION ● LITERATURE AND WRITERS ● SOCIETY AND CULTURE ● TECHNOLOGY)

Communication is the exchange of information and ideas. Humans communicate with each other in many different ways—most often, through spoken or written language. Written language began about five thousand years ago, when people began scratching pictures into stone. The earliest long-distance written communications were probably letters sent by way of travelers, then by postal services.

Newspapers, magazines, and films also convey information. Technology has developed newer, faster ways of communicating, changing the way we live.

WHAT PAGE IS FOR HOMEWORK?

PAGE SEVEN!

Telecommunications

Telecommunications systems allow people to exchange information instantly over long distances, using phones, fax machines, computers, TVs, and many other devices. Messages are sent as signals in the form of electric currents, by way of telephone lines or communications satellites. (A satellite is a man-made object that is sent into space orbit above Earth to beam down signals from one part of the world to another.) Fiber-optic cables, which are made of thin strands of glass, are able to carry telephone and other types of signals—in the form of light waves—at high speeds.

MORSE CODE

The telegraph, using Morse code, was one of the earliest forms of telecommunication. Electric current was used to send series of short and long signals—dots and dashes—over wire. Each combination of signals spelled out a message. The alphabet in International Morse Code is shown at right.

A	• —	N	— •
B	— • • •	O	— — —
C	— • — •	P	• — — •
D	— • •	Q	— — • —
E	•	R	• — •
F	• • — •	S	• • •
G	— — •	T	—
H	• • • •	U	• • —
I	• •	V	• • • —
J	• — — —	W	• — —
K	— • —	X	— • • —
L	• — • •	Y	— • — —
M	— —	Z	— — • •

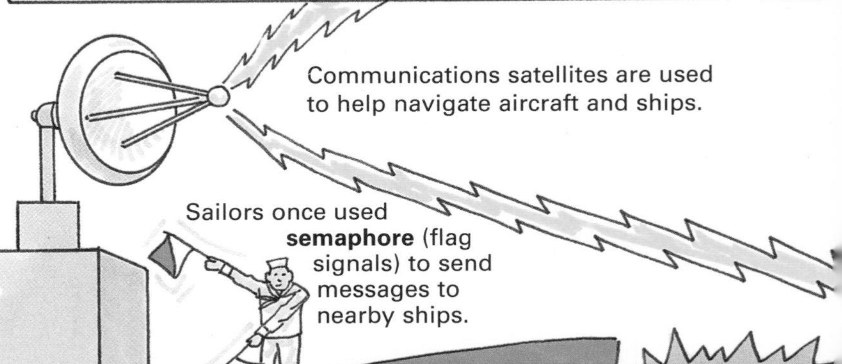

Communications satellites are used to help navigate aircraft and ships.

Sailors once used **semaphore** (flag signals) to send messages to nearby ships.

WHAT PAGE IS FOR HOMEWORK?

PAGE SEVEN!

THIS IS THE HARD WAY TO COMMUNICATE!

Important Dates in Communications History

A.D. 868: The Chinese print the earliest-known book, using wooden blocks.

1438: Johannes Gutenberg (Germany) develops movable type.

1837: Samuel F. B. Morse (U.S.) invents Morse code.

1875: Alexander Graham Bell (U.S.) invents the telephone.

1895: Guglielmo Marconi (Italy) invents wireless telegraphy (radio).

1895: The Lumière brothers (France) show the first motion picture.

Early 1900s: Television is invented.

1901: Marconi receives and sends the first transatlantic radio signals.

1927: The first film with sound is shown.

1951: UNIVAC (Universal Automatic Computer) is invented. It is the first business computer able to process both alphabetical and numerical data.

The Internet allows many different computers to share information and enables users to communicate with each other by **e-mail** (electronic mail).

During a videoconference, participants speak through microphones and—thanks to video cameras—they can see one another on a screen.

Computers

(see also COMMUNICATION • GAMES • INVENTORS AND
INVENTIONS • MACHINES • TECHNOLOGY)

I'M ENIAC, THE FIRST MAIN-
FRAME COMPUTER. I WAS
INTRODUCED IN 1945. I WAS
SO BIG, I WEIGHED MORE
THAN 30 TONS AND FILLED AN
ENTIRE ROOM! (ENIAC STANDS
FOR ELECTRONIC NUMERIC
INTEGRATOR AND CALCULA-
TOR.) THE FIRST DESKTOP-
SIZED PERSONAL COMPUTERS
WERE SOLD IN THE 1970s.

A computer is an electronic device that can store and process information quickly and accurately. Computers can keep files, solve problems, play games, control other machines, and convey countless types of information. Humans write detailed sets of instructions, called programs, that tell a computer how to perform various tasks.

Computers have transformed how people work, as well as how many other everyday tasks are performed. They have made our lives much easier and safer. They are used to plan and design safer and more efficient cars, buildings, and machinery, and many other products. They help doctors treat all sorts of medical problems, help navigate ships and planes, and make getting all kinds of information faster and simpler than ever before.

Computer Components

Monitor

CPU
(hard drive)

Printer

Keyboard

CD-ROM drive

Zip disk drive

Floppy disk drive

Mouse

DID YOU KNOW . . . ?
It took ENIAC two hours to complete its first calculation. But the same physics problem would have taken 100 engineers a whole year to figure out!

What Makes It Go

A computer's **CPU** (central processing unit) calculates and processes data, based on instructions from a program. The "brains" of the computer are its **microchips**—tiny devices on which huge amounts of information can be stored. The CPU has two different kinds of memory: **ROM** (read-only memory) and **RAM** (random-access memory). Data is stored in different ways: on the CPU's built-in hard disk, and on removable, portable diskettes, compact disks (CDs) and other types of disks, and magnetic tapes.

Each **microchip** has thousands of components that make it work. A huge amount of information can be programmed onto its tiny space, making ever-smaller computers, telephones, and other electronic equipment possible.

The **mouse** is a device used to enter data into a computer. It is made of a ball and buttons. It must be used on a smooth, flat surface. Some computers have a device built into the keyboard area—a trackball or trackpad—to be used instead of a mouse.

A **keyboard** is used to enter data into a computer. It is used much like a typewriter: When a key is pressed, information is fed into the computer and appears on the screen.

A **joystick** can be used for playing games or controlling data.

HELLO, THERE!

Computers communicate with each other using a modem and telephone lines, or by exchanging wireless signals.

HI, YOURSELF!

Virtual Reality

Virtual reality is a type of computer program that simulates real life. Such programs can create complex, lifelike images, including weather patterns and flight or road conditions—making them helpful in training pilots and astronauts, or designing buildings and cars.

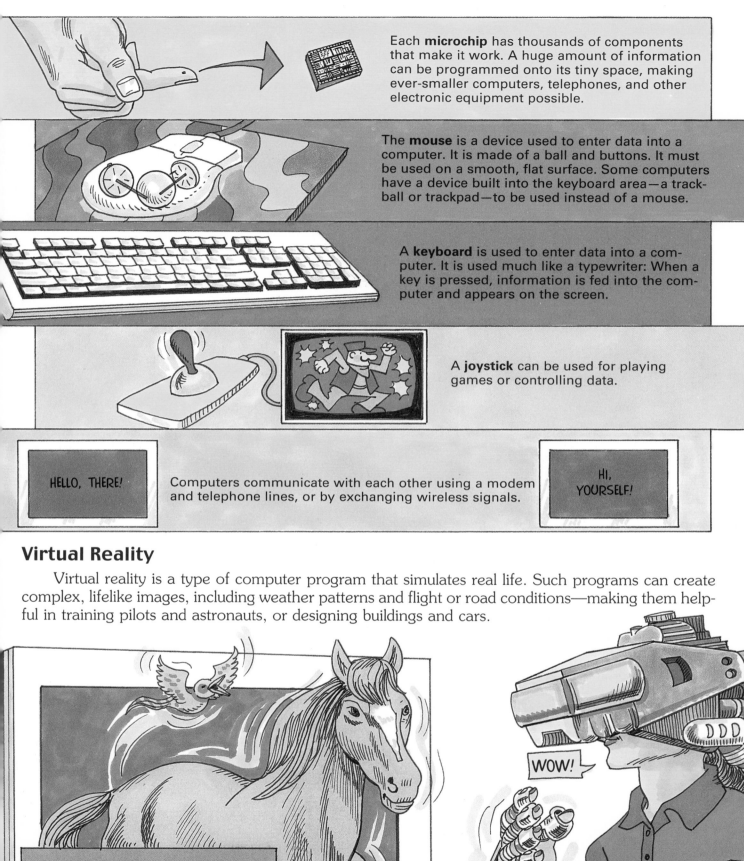

WOW!

Virtual-reality users wear special gloves and a helmet, which send signals (such as eye and body movements) to the computer. The computer responds by producing 3-D pictures and sounds that fit the users' movements.

45

Dance

(see also ART AND ARTISTS ● LITERATURE AND WRITERS ● MOVIES AND TELEVISION ● MUSIC ● SOCIETY AND CULTURE ● THEATER)

Dance is the movement of the body in time to music. Dancing may be body-twirling, foot-stomping, making motions with hands, or following a pattern of steps. People have been dancing since prehistoric times. Stone Age cave paintings show people dancing—way back then! Many styles of dance have developed since then, from formal steps to wild and crazy hip-shaking. Dance can be used to tell a story, to worship nature or gods, as art, or just to have fun.

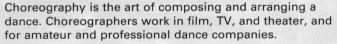

Choreography is the art of composing and arranging a dance. Choreographers work in film, TV, and theater, and for amateur and professional dance companies.

Ballet is a formal combination of music, mime, and dance. Often, it is dancing that tells a story. *The Nutcracker* and *Swan Lake* are two of the most famous ballets.

Tap, a lively style of dance influenced by Irish and African styles, was popularized in 1930s movies by Fred Astaire, Ginger Rogers, and other stars. Broadway star Savion Glover is one of today's leading dancers and scholars of tap.

In the early 20th century, Isadora Duncan broke away from formal ballet and created modern dance—a looser, freer style. Other leading choreographers of modern dance include Martha Graham, Twyla Tharp, Katherine Dunham, and Merce Cunningham.

Isadora Duncan

Fred Astaire and Ginger Rogers

Savion Glover

Every ballet dancer must learn five basic body positions: first, second, third, fourth, and fifth.

1st   2nd   3rd

4th   5th

Traditional Dances

In most cultures, dance is part of long-followed traditions. Some Native Americans dance to praise ancestors or spirits, following the steps in a specific order. Hawaiian hula dancers use hand, foot, and hip motions to tell stories. Some Africans dance to worship the sun, or for fertility, rain, or war. In India, female dancers move their hands and fingers to tell a story. In Spanish flamenco, dancers stamp and tap their heels to guitar music. Some traditional dances—such as the hora, a circle dance of Romania and Israel—are group dances. Most cultures have some form of folk or traditional dance.

YEE-HA!

Square dancing

Social Dancing

Through the centuries, the way people have danced to enjoy themselves has changed often. New political and social ideas, as well as art styles and other fashions, often influenced changes in dance styles. Ballroom dancing started in Europe in the 1300s. The waltz was popular there in the 1800s. In the U.S. in the 1920s, people danced the Charleston, a lively dance. Dancing became even livelier in the 1930s and 1940s, as the jitterbug became popular. In the 1950s and 1960s, rock and roll ruled, with freer dance styles, while disco was the rage in the 1970s. In the 1980s and 1990s, popular dances included break-dancing, moshing, the running man, and line dances or group dances, such as the electric slide and the macarena.

Minuet 1740s

Jitterbug 1940s

Disco 1970s

Deserts

(see also AFRICAN WILDLIFE ● ASIAN WILDLIFE
● AUSTRALIAN WILDLIFE ● ECOSYSTEMS ● ENVIRONMENT ●
NORTH AMERICAN WILDLIFE ● WATER ● WEATHER)

A desert is very dry land—an area where fewer than 10 inches of rain fall per year. Temperatures are usually very high during the day, cooler at night. Only certain plants can survive in dry desert soil, which tends to be rocky or sandy.

About twenty percent of Earth's land surface is desert, and that percentage has been growing. Some areas dry out due to changes in climate; others, because so many trees are cut down that there is nothing to hold moisture in the soil. Sometimes, land is overgrazed by farm animals. However, deserts have also been turned into fertile land. Farmers can use irrigation—water brought from elsewhere, using pipes, trenches, or sprinklers—to turn dry earth into fertile soil.

Types of Deserts

In Africa's Sahara Desert, the air is so hot that any moisture is burned away before it can form rain clouds. Asia's Gobi Desert is too far from the sea for winds to bring rain. Rainshadow deserts, such as California's Death Valley, form near large mountains, which block winds that would otherwise bring rain. There are cold-weather deserts, too: In Antarctica, for instance, the ground is dry because all moisture is permanently frozen.

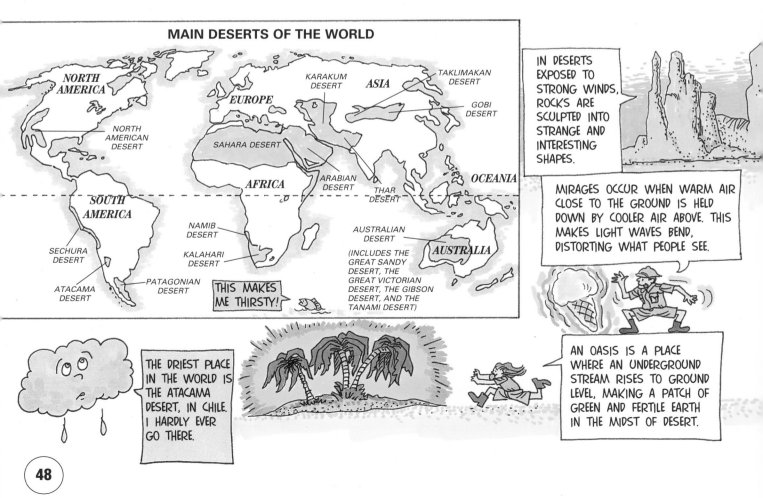

MAIN DESERTS OF THE WORLD

NORTH AMERICA

KARAKUM DESERT

TAKLIMAKAN DESERT

ASIA

EUROPE

GOBI DESERT

NORTH AMERICAN DESERT

SAHARA DESERT

ARABIAN DESERT

AFRICA

THAR DESERT

OCEANIA

SOUTH AMERICA

SECHURA DESERT

NAMIB DESERT

KALAHARI DESERT

AUSTRALIAN DESERT

(INCLUDES THE GREAT SANDY DESERT, THE GREAT VICTORIAN DESERT, THE GIBSON DESERT, AND THE TANAMI DESERT)

AUSTRALIA

ATACAMA DESERT

PATAGONIAN DESERT

THIS MAKES ME THIRSTY!

IN DESERTS EXPOSED TO STRONG WINDS, ROCKS ARE SCULPTED INTO STRANGE AND INTERESTING SHAPES.

MIRAGES OCCUR WHEN WARM AIR CLOSE TO THE GROUND IS HELD DOWN BY COOLER AIR ABOVE. THIS MAKES LIGHT WAVES BEND, DISTORTING WHAT PEOPLE SEE.

THE DRIEST PLACE IN THE WORLD IS THE ATACAMA DESERT, IN CHILE. I HARDLY EVER GO THERE.

AN OASIS IS A PLACE WHERE AN UNDERGROUND STREAM RISES TO GROUND LEVEL, MAKING A PATCH OF GREEN AND FERTILE EARTH IN THE MIDST OF DESERT.

Desert Life

Some animals and plants have adapted to life in a desert. Many desert animals are nocturnal, which means that they sleep or hide out of the sun during the day, coming out at night, when it is cooler. Cactuses store water in their thick stems. Their tough, spiny stems protect them from animals that would eat them to get their moisture. Many desert plants have waxy leaves to keep water from escaping.

WE CAMELS ARE PERFECTLY ADAPTED TO LIFE IN THE DESERT. WE DON'T STORE EXTRA WATER IN OUR BODIES, BUT WHEN WE FIND IT WE CAN DRINK UP TO 30 GALLONS OF IT! IN OUR HUMPS, WE STORE FAT THAT OUR BODIES USE FOR ENERGY.

I'M A TAWNY EAGLE.

I'M A JERBOA! JERBOAS LIVE IN DESERT AREAS, ALONG WITH OTHER SMALL RODENTS, SUCH AS MICE AND GERBILS. WE EAT SEEDS AND SMALL PLANTS.

I'M A SAND LIZARD.

I'M A DESERT LARK.

I'M A SAND SKINK.

I'M A YUCCA MOTH.

I'M A DESERT BUG.

I'M A YUCCA PLANT.

I'M A COBRA. DON'T TELL THE MONGOOSE THAT I'M HERE!

WE SIDEWINDERS LEAVE PARALLEL J-SHAPED PATHS IN THE SAND.

I'M A NAKED MOLE RAT. I'M ALMOST BLIND AND LIVE IN UNDERGROUND TUNNELS WITH OTHER MOLE RATS.

PRICKLY SPINES PROTECT WATER-RICH CACTUS PLANTS FROM BEING EATEN BY DESERT ANIMALS.

I'M A HORNED VIPER.

I'M A FENNEC FOX.

I'M A ROADRUNNER. LIKE MOST DESERT MEAT-EATERS, I GET MOISTURE FROM THE ANIMALS I EAT. PLANT-EATING DESERT ANIMALS GET MOISTURE FROM THEIR FOOD, TOO.

I'M A COMICUS CRICKET.

I ALSO EAT COBRAS. HAVE YOU SEEN ANY?

I'M A MONGOOSE. I HUNT FOR BEES, SPIDERS, AND SCORPIONS, AS WELL AS MICE AND OTHER SMALL MAMMALS.

I'M A STENOCARA BEETLE.

I'M A SPOTTED SAND GROUSE.

I'M A SAGUARO CACTUS. MY VERY LONG ROOTS SPREAD OUT, HELPING ME COLLECT WATER FROM A WIDE AREA.

Dinosaurs

(see also ANIMAL KINGDOM ● ARCHAEOLOGY ● FOSSILS ● PREHISTORY)

DID YOU KNOW . . . ?
The word *dinosaur* means "fearfully great lizard."

Dinosaurs were reptiles that lived on Earth for more than 160 million years. They became **extinct** (died out) about 65 million years ago. (Humans have been around only about 3 million years!) There were more than 150 species of dinosaur. Some were as small as chickens; others were enormous. Dinosaur bones, teeth, and footprints tell us a lot about how they walked, their size, what they ate, and many other things.

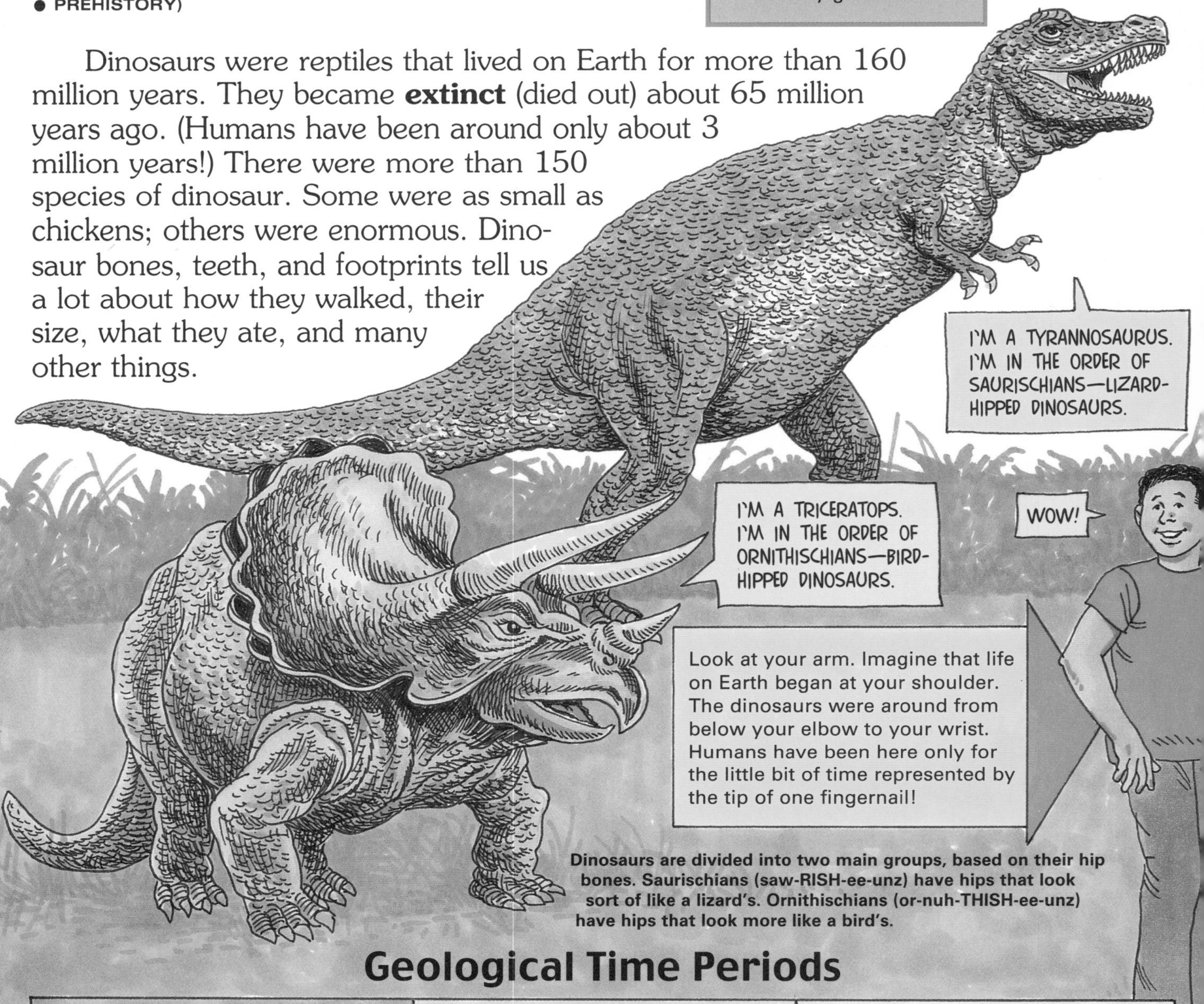

I'M A TYRANNOSAURUS. I'M IN THE ORDER OF SAURISCHIANS—LIZARD-HIPPED DINOSAURS.
I'M A TRICERATOPS. I'M IN THE ORDER OF ORNITHISCHIANS—BIRD-HIPPED DINOSAURS.
WOW!

Look at your arm. Imagine that life on Earth began at your shoulder. The dinosaurs were around from below your elbow to your wrist. Humans have been here only for the little bit of time represented by the tip of one fingernail!

Dinosaurs are divided into two main groups, based on their hip bones. Saurischians (saw-RISH-ee-unz) have hips that look sort of like a lizard's. Ornithischians (or-nuh-THISH-ee-unz) have hips that look more like a bird's.

Geological Time Periods

TRIASSIC PERIOD
(about 245 to 208 million years ago)

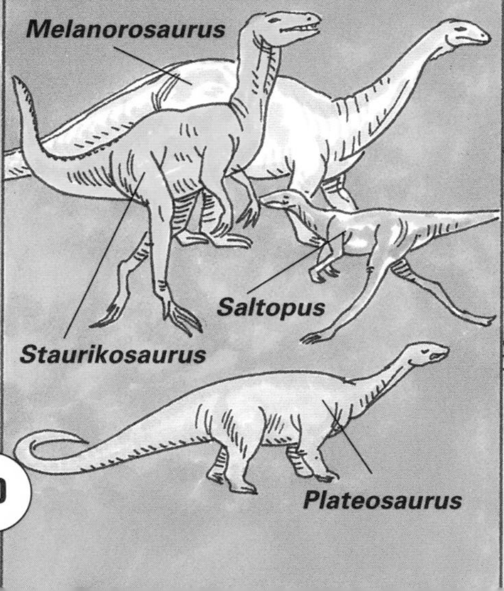

Melanorosaurus
Saltopus
Staurikosaurus
Plateosaurus

JURASSIC PERIOD
(about 208 to 145 million years ago)

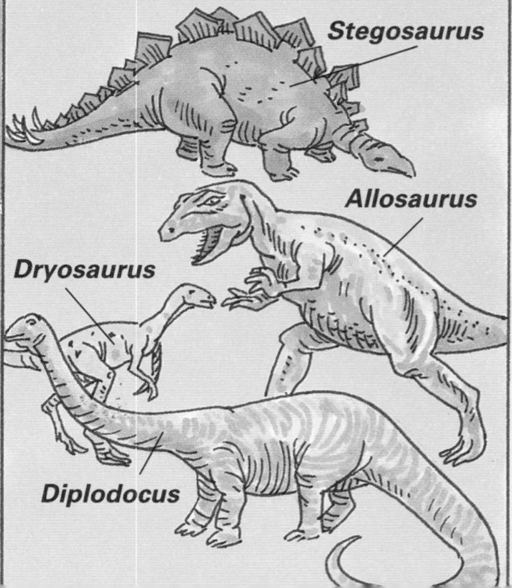

Stegosaurus
Allosaurus
Dryosaurus
Diplodocus

CRETACEOUS PERIOD
(about 145 to 65 million years ago)

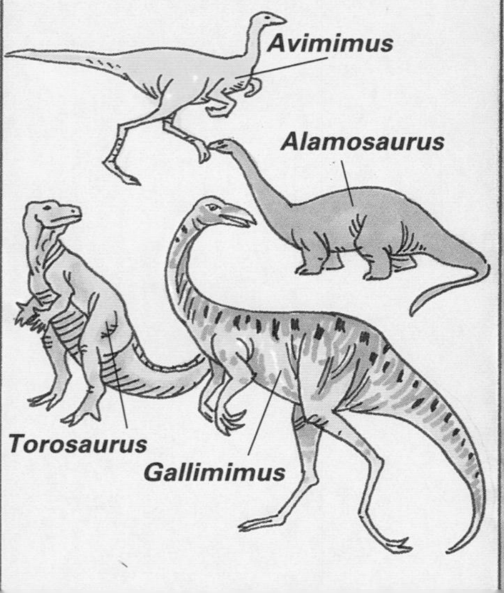

Avimimus
Alamosaurus
Torosaurus
Gallimimus

Lizard–Hipped Dinosaurs

Saurischians can be divided into two smaller groups: theropods and sauropods.

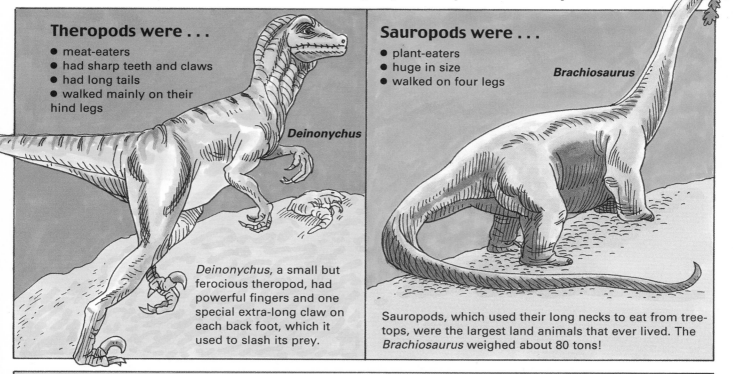

Theropods were . . .

- meat-eaters
- had sharp teeth and claws
- had long tails
- walked mainly on their hind legs

Deinonychus

Deinonychus, a small but ferocious theropod, had powerful fingers and one special extra-long claw on each back foot, which it used to slash its prey.

Sauropods were . . .

- plant-eaters
- huge in size
- walked on four legs

Brachiosaurus

Sauropods, which used their long necks to eat from tree-tops, were the largest land animals that ever lived. The *Brachiosaurus* weighed about 80 tons!

Bird–Hipped Dinosaurs

Ornithischians included several kinds of dinosaurs, all plant-eaters. They included two-legged dinosaurs, such as *Iguanodon*; dinosaurs with thick head domes, such as *Pachycephalosaurus*; and armor-plated dinosaurs, such as *Ankylosaurus*.

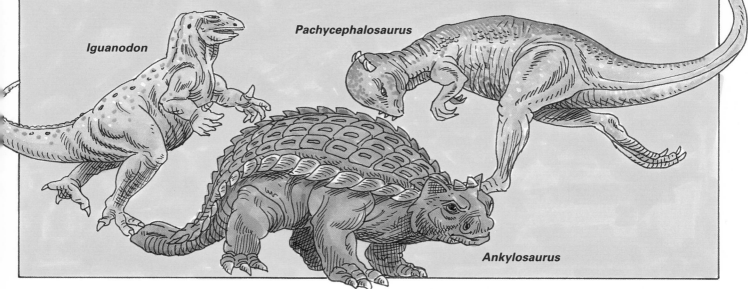

Iguanodon

Pachycephalosaurus

Ankylosaurus

How did dinosaurs become extinct? Some scientists think that they starved to death when the climate changed. Others think that a huge meteorite hit the Earth, causing worldwide damage and killing off the dinosaurs.

Dinosaur fossils have been found on every continent except Antarctica.

In 1969, almost an entire *Rioja-saurus* skeleton was discovered in Argentina. It is nearly 230 million years old.

In 1990, scientists found an entire skull of a *Tyrannosaurus rex*.

Earth

(see also AIR ● ENVIRONMENT ● GEOLOGY ● MEASUREMENTS ● MINING ● OCEANS AND
SEA LIFE ● PREHISTORY ● SUN AND SOLAR SYSTEM ● TIME ● WATER ● WEATHER ● WORLD)

Earth is the planet on which we live. Like all planets and stars, it is ball-shaped (though not perfectly round). It **orbits** (circles) the sun, along with the eight other planets in our solar system. Earth is the third planet from the sun, a giant star that is about 93 million miles away. The sun provides Earth with heat and light.

Earth formed about 4.6 billion years ago—along with the rest of the solar system—from dust clouds and hot gases.

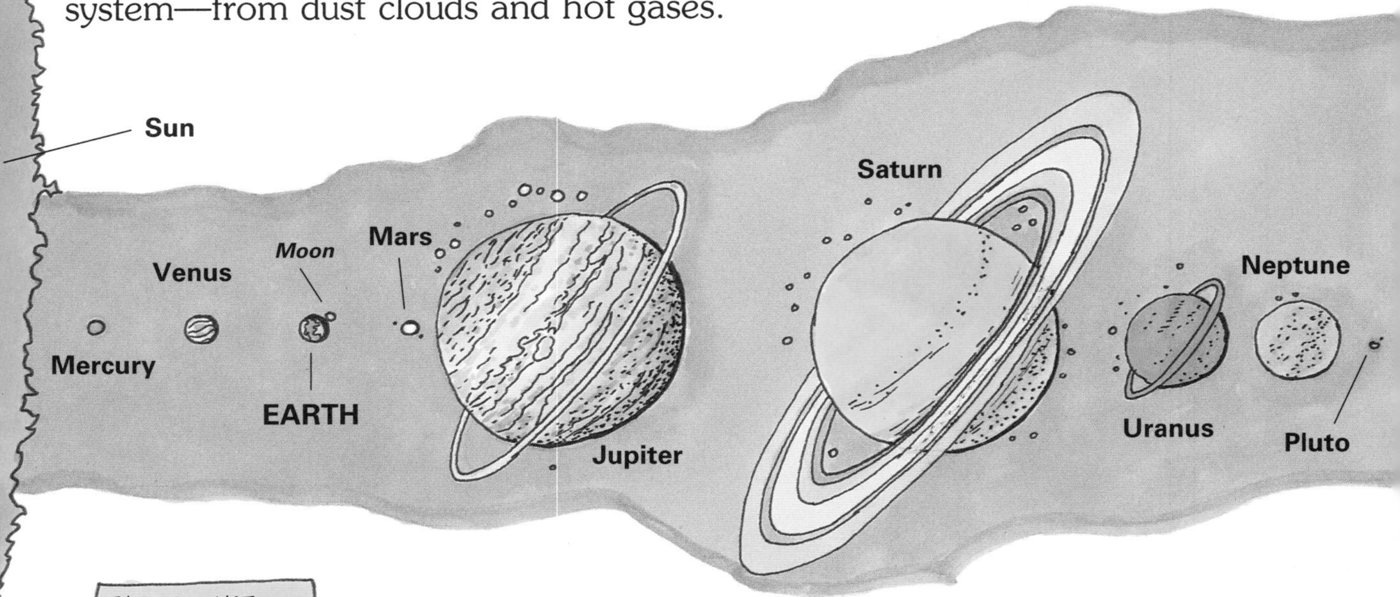

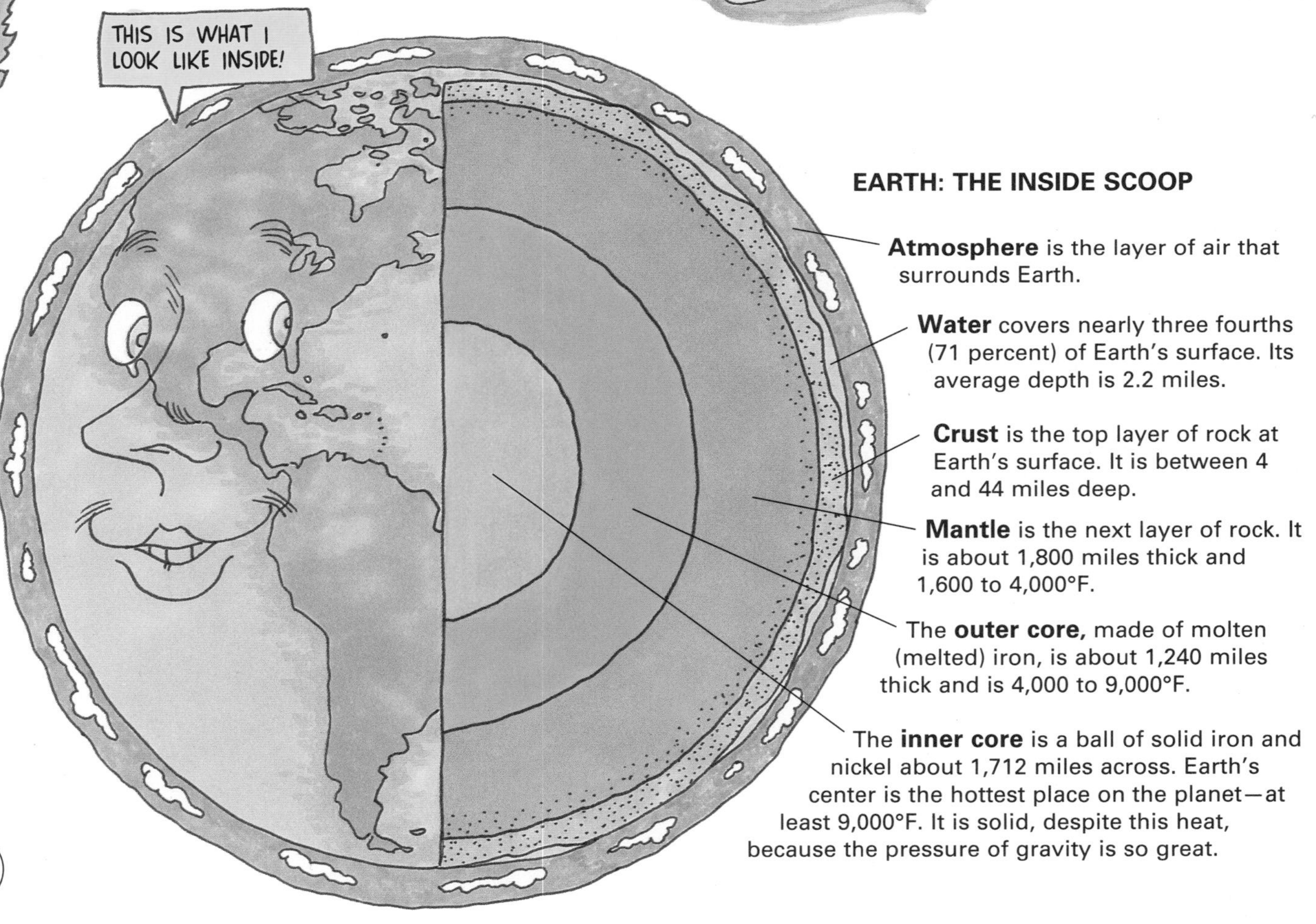

Sun

Venus

Moon

Mars

Mercury

EARTH

Jupiter

Saturn

Neptune

Uranus

Pluto

THIS IS WHAT I LOOK LIKE INSIDE!

EARTH: THE INSIDE SCOOP

Atmosphere is the layer of air that surrounds Earth.

Water covers nearly three fourths (71 percent) of Earth's surface. Its average depth is 2.2 miles.

Crust is the top layer of rock at Earth's surface. It is between 4 and 44 miles deep.

Mantle is the next layer of rock. It is about 1,800 miles thick and 1,600 to 4,000°F.

The **outer core**, made of molten (melted) iron, is about 1,240 miles thick and is 4,000 to 9,000°F.

The **inner core** is a ball of solid iron and nickel about 1,712 miles across. Earth's center is the hottest place on the planet—at least 9,000°F. It is solid, despite this heat, because the pressure of gravity is so great.

Earth's Tilt and Orbit

Direction of spin

Night

Day

Axis

Earth is constantly spinning around its axis, an imaginary line running through the core between the North and South poles. Every 24 hours (once a day), Earth makes one complete turn. As it spins, the area facing the sun has day, while the opposite side has night.

Earth also moves around the sun in an oval-shaped path—its orbit. (Depending on the time of year, Earth is closer to or farther from the sun.) One complete orbit takes 365 days (one Earth year). The planet is slightly tilted as it moves around the sun. This is what makes the seasons change. The part of Earth that is tilted toward the sun gets more light and heat, giving it spring, then summer. As its path takes it farther from the sun, it has autumn, then winter.

DID YOU KNOW . . . ?

- Earth weighs about 6 sextillion, 587 quintillion tons.
- At the surface, it measures 25,000 miles around the middle.
- It is 3,960 miles from core to surface at the equator.
- Nearly three fourths of Earth's surface is covered by water.
- Earth is the only planet that has life—at least, as far as we know now!

Earth is always changing. About 200 million years ago, there was one landmass. Over millions of years, it broke into smaller masses, now the continents.

Large sections of Earth's crust, called **tectonic plates,** float on top of the layer of molten rock. They move, but very, very slowly. From time to time, pressure builds up as they push together or slide past each other. This is what causes **earthquakes** (shock waves from plates grinding together) and **volcanoes** (molten rock boiling up from Earth's core to its surface).

North America

Atlantic Ocean

Pacific Ocean

South America

Africa

Trenches

Nazca plate
American plate

African plate

Plate movement

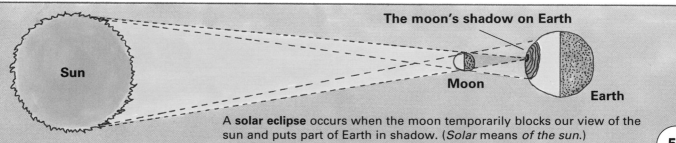

A LOOK AT ECLIPSES

Sun

The moon in Earth's shadow

Moon

Earth

A **lunar eclipse** (above) occurs when Earth moves between the moon and the sun. This temporarily casts a dark shadow across the moon, making it seem to disappear for a while. (*Lunar* means *of the moon.*)

Sun

The moon's shadow on Earth

Moon

Earth

A **solar eclipse** occurs when the moon temporarily blocks our view of the sun and puts part of Earth in shadow. (*Solar* means *of the sun.*)

53

Ecosystems

Organisms (living creatures) in all places on Earth rely on one another for survival. For example, flowers need bees to **pollinate** them (spread their seeds), and bees need flowers to provide them with food. Nearly all species are interdependent, and each one contributes to its environment. The study of the relationships between organisms and their environments is called ecology. All of the species of plants and animals living in a particular area are part of the same community. Ecologists call such a community and its environment (including air, climate, and soil) an ecosystem.

HAVE SOME NECTAR!

THANKS! I'LL SPREAD YOUR POLLEN.

Habitats

The natural home of an animal or plant is called its **habitat.** A habitat has everything that an organism needs to survive: food, water, and shelter. A habitat is a specific place, such as a freshwater riverbed or the soggy floor of a tropical rain forest. Larger, more general environments are known as **biomes.** Biomes include deserts, forests, grasslands, mountains, oceans, and tundras.

THAT'S AWFUL!

Habitats can change. This can happen naturally, or because humans have done something unnatural to bring it about.

Sometimes, a change in a habitat causes serious harm to the plants and animals that live there. When an animal's habitat is altered—by pollution, for example—the animal must **adapt** (change to fit) or find a new habitat. If it cannot do one or both of those things, it will die.

?

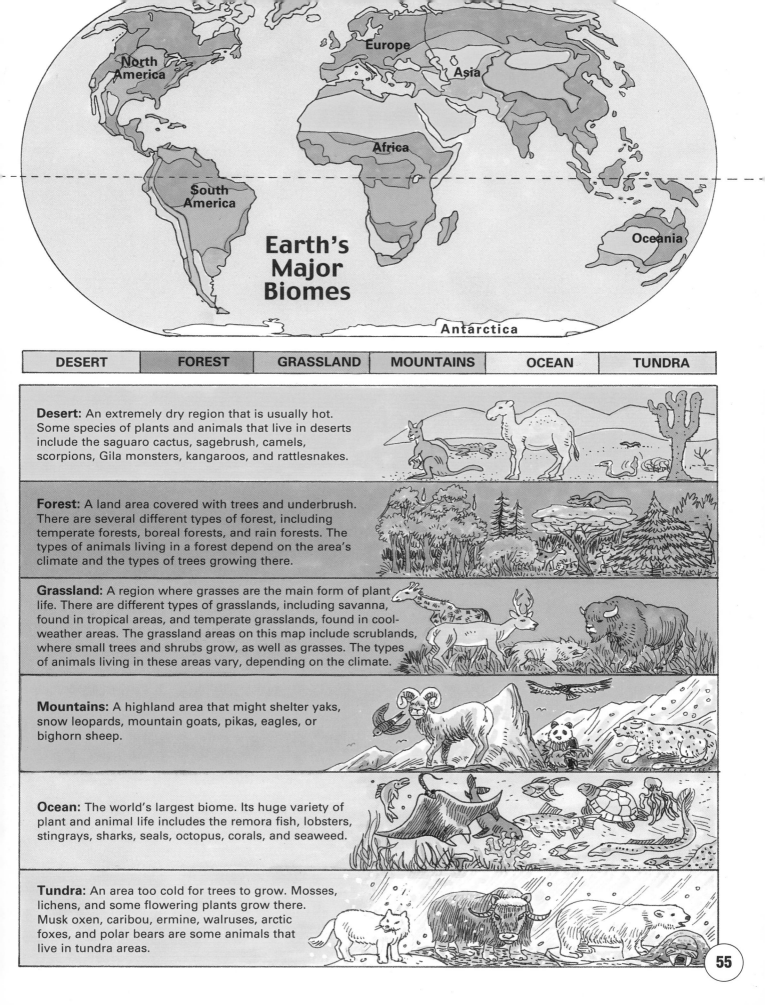

Earth's Major Biomes

| DESERT | FOREST | GRASSLAND | MOUNTAINS | OCEAN | TUNDRA |

Desert: An extremely dry region that is usually hot. Some species of plants and animals that live in deserts include the saguaro cactus, sagebrush, camels, scorpions, Gila monsters, kangaroos, and rattlesnakes.

Forest: A land area covered with trees and underbrush. There are several different types of forest, including temperate forests, boreal forests, and rain forests. The types of animals living in a forest depend on the area's climate and the types of trees growing there.

Grassland: A region where grasses are the main form of plant life. There are different types of grasslands, including savanna, found in tropical areas, and temperate grasslands, found in cool-weather areas. The grassland areas on this map include scrublands, where small trees and shrubs grow, as well as grasses. The types of animals living in these areas vary, depending on the climate.

Mountains: A highland area that might shelter yaks, snow leopards, mountain goats, pikas, eagles, or bighorn sheep.

Ocean: The world's largest biome. Its huge variety of plant and animal life includes the remora fish, lobsters, stingrays, sharks, seals, octopus, corals, and seaweed.

Tundra: An area too cold for trees to grow. Mosses, lichens, and some flowering plants grow there. Musk oxen, caribou, ermine, walruses, arctic foxes, and polar bears are some animals that live in tundra areas.

55

Energy

(see also FIRE ● FOSSILS ● GEOLOGY ● HUMAN BODY ● MACHINES ● PLANT KINGDOM ● SCIENCE AND SCIENTISTS ● WATER)

Energy is needed to make things happen; it is required for something to be moved. Humans use energy to jump, walk, or even just sit still and breathe. Machines require energy in order to work.

Most energy that we use begins as energy from the sun. Every time energy is used, it is transferred to another object or environment, and it changes to a different form. Energy produced in the sun's hot core arrives at Earth's surface as sunlight and heat. The sun heats the atmosphere, and sunlight gives energy to plants, helping them grow. When animals—including humans—eat the plants (or other animals that eat plants), they get some of that energy. Without that energy, they would die.

| Kinetic energy | Potential energy | Kinetic energy | Potential energy |

When an object moves, it has **kinetic energy.** (*Kinetic* means "active" or "in motion.") But energy can also be stored. Stored energy is called **potential energy.** (*Potential* means "possible" or "capable of becoming.")

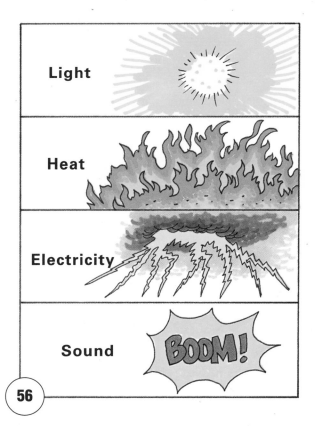

Light

Heat

Electricity

Sound

Types of Energy

Energy takes many forms. Light, heat, electricity, and sound are all different forms of energy. Most of the energy people use to heat buildings or run machines comes from coal, oil, or gas. These are called fossil fuels, because they are made from the remains of animals and plants that died long ago. Fossil fuels contain energy from the sun, stored in what is left of living things that once absorbed it. When burned, fossil fuels release that energy, providing light and heat. People use other types of energy, too, such as electricity made by wind, water, or **solar** (of the sun) power.

Electricity

Electricity is a form of energy. (A lightning bolt is electricity in the air.) When you turn on a lamp, toaster, or other appliance, electricity is changed into light, heat, or movement. Many modern conveniences are powered by electricity.

SOLAR ENERGY
Solar collectors trap sunlight to **generate** (make) power. Solar cells turn the sun's energy into electricity. In places that get sunshine most of the year, solar panels are a cheaper, cleaner alternative to other power sources.

I'M HOME!

THEY ALL HELP ME TO LIGHT UP!

HYDROELECTRIC ENERGY
Hydroelectricity is electricity made using the energy of falling water. (*Hydro* means "water.") Water let loose from a dam spins turbines connected to a generator, and this produces electricity. About nine percent of the electricity in the U.S. comes from hydroelectric sources.

THIS IS FUN!

WIND ENERGY
In places that are windy year-round, huge wind **turbines** (windmills) can be used to generate electricity— enough for a small town.

LOOKING AT THIS MAKES ME DIZZY.

NUCLEAR ENERGY
Nuclear-power plants generate energy by splitting the atoms of uranium, a type of metal. This splitting, called fission, releases heat energy that splits other atoms. This chain reaction produces a great amount of energy that can be turned into electrical power.

Environment

(see also AIR ● CLOTHING ● DESERTS ● EARTH ● ECOSYSTEMS ● FORESTS ● OCEANS AND SEA LIFE ● POLAR REGIONS ● RAIN FORESTS ● TREES ● WATER ● WEATHER ● ZOOS)

HUMANS HUNT ME FOR MY IVORY TUSKS.

Environment is a word that refers to the various conditions in a certain place that affect the growth and development of life there. Such conditions include the climate, type of soil or water, and plants and animals, all of which affect any **organisms** (living things) in that area. Human beings can hurt an environment—for instance, a lake, forest, or desert—by polluting or otherwise abusing natural resources, and by being careless about how they live. Many types of animals and plants have become **extinct** (died out) or are in danger of extinction because people have hunted them, moved into areas where they live, or changed the environment to such a degree that plants and animals can no longer survive in those areas.

Global Warming

Earth is surrounded by its atmosphere—layers of gases that protect it from extreme heat or cold. In recent years, more and more of the sun's heat has become trapped in Earth's atmosphere. This is known as the greenhouse effect. It is caused mainly by carbon dioxide (CO_2), which is produced when humans burn coal, oil, or gasoline. The CO_2 gets into the air, where it makes a sort of shield that holds the heat in—similar to the way a greenhouse's glass holds in heat. The problem gets worse when large areas of forest are cut down for timber or to clear land for farming. Live trees absorb CO_2 and give off oxygen, which most living things need in order to survive.

I'M A DODO. I'VE BEEN EXTINCT SINCE 1680.

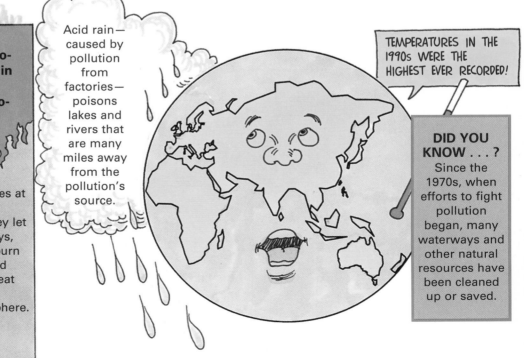

Pollution from chemicals known as CFCs (chlorofluorocarbons) helps create holes in the ozone layer, a part of Earth's atmosphere that protects us from the sun's harmful ultraviolet rays.

Holes in ozone layer

CFC-caused holes at the poles worry scientists: They let in UV rays, which burn skin and may heat Earth's atmosphere.

Acid rain—caused by pollution from factories—poisons lakes and rivers that are many miles away from the pollution's source.

TEMPERATURES IN THE 1990s WERE THE HIGHEST EVER RECORDED!

DID YOU KNOW . . . ? Since the 1970s, when efforts to fight pollution began, many waterways and other natural resources have been cleaned up or saved.

How Can You Help to Protect the Environment?

Save plastic, glass, paper, and cardboard—then recycle them.

METAL

Recycle

GLASS

Recycle

PLASTIC

Recycle

PAPER

Recycle

COMICS

You can also . . .

Use recycled products.

Walk, bike, or take public transportation (such as buses) . . .

. . . **to reduce pollution from cars.**

Using nonpolluting forms of energy—such as solar (of the sun), wind, or tidal power—can help save natural resources. Rooftop solar panels absorb the sun's energy and convert it for use inside the home.

I'M A POLLUTION-FREE SOURCE OF ENERGY!

Solar panels

National parks, preserves, and conservation groups have been established to protect plant and animal habitats and to save endangered species.

Europe

(see also WORLD)

ICELAND HAS THE MOST HOT SPRINGS IN THE WORLD!

THIS WAS THE HOME OF THE VIKINGS 1,000 YEARS AGO.

Europe is the world's second-smallest continent. It extends from the Mediterranean Sea in the South to the Arctic Ocean in the North, and westward from the Ural Mountains. Europe has 44 independent countries, vast forests, long rivers, and very high mountains, including the Alps and the Pyrenees. Its land is especially rich and contains many stores of minerals. The north is thickly forested, with broad, flat plains. The south is hilly, warm, and dry.

Europe's history and culture make it a popular area for tourists. Visitors from around the world go there to see the art, architecture, and historic monuments in Paris, Rome, London, Madrid, Vienna, and other major cities.

People

About 508 million people live in Europe. They speak many languages, including English, French, German, Greek, Italian, Portuguese, and Spanish. Europeans practice many religions, including Buddhism, Christianity, Hinduism, Islam, and Judaism. Most of the European population live in cities or small towns. Some of the most populated cities are Moscow, Paris, and London.

Industry and Natural Resources

Europe's different climates and landscapes allow a wide variety of industries. Fishing is important in countries on the coast, such as Portugal, Italy, and Greece. Farming is also important. France and Germany are world leaders in wheat and corn production. Spain, Italy, and France produce some of the world's finest wines and olives. Rotterdam in the Netherlands is one of the world's busiest ports.

Norwegian Sea

URAL MTS.
(dividing line between
Europe and Asia)

White Sea

EUROPE

RUSSIA

FINLAND

NORWAY   SWEDEN

Helsinki

Lake Ladoga

Oslo

☆ Tallinn
ESTONIA

Stockholm

Volga River

☆ Moscow

LATVIA

Copenhagen

☆ Riga

DENMARK

LITHUANIA

Baltic Sea

Vilnius ☆

RUSSIA

☆ Minsk

Russia spans two continents.
The western part is in
Europe, the eastern (and
larger) part is in Asia.

The Volga's
2,194-mile length
makes it Europe's
longest river.

POLAND

Berlin

BELARUS

GERMANY

Warsaw ☆

Vistula River

☆ Kiev

Volga River

Elbe River

Prague ☆

MOLDOVA

UKRAINE

Vaduz

CZECH
REPUBLIC

SLOVAKIA   Bratislava

Mount Elbrus
(18,510 ft) is
Europe's
highest point.

*Caspian
Sea*

Vienna ☆

☆ Budapest

Chisinau
☆

AUSTRIA

SLOVENIA   Zagreb ☆

HUNGARY

Alps

ROMANIA

CAUCASUS MTS.

SAN
MARINO

CROATIA

Ljubljana

Belgrade ☆

Bucharest
☆

*Black
Sea*

San Marino

Sarajevo ☆

VATICAN
CITY

Skopje ☆

☆ Sofia

YUGOSLAVIA
(SERBIA &
MONTENEGRO)

Rome

☆
MACEDONIA

BULGARIA

T

U

R   K   E   Y

BOSNIA AND
HERZEGOVINA

ITALY

Tirana

ALBANIA

MT. ETNA

GREECE

*Aegean
Sea*

About three percent of Turkey's land
area is in Europe. The rest is in Asia.

*Ionian
Sea*

Athens

*SICILY
(Italy)*

*CRETE
(Greece)*

MALTA — Valletta

Explorers and Exploration

(see also INVENTORS AND INVENTIONS ● NAVIGATION ● POLAR REGIONS ● RENAISSANCE ● SCIENCE AND SCIENTISTS ● SPACE EXPLORATION ● TRANSPORTATION)

Long before there were maps, ancient peoples were curious about the unknown world around them. Many early explorers were interested in science or adventure. Others wanted to conquer foreign lands and get rich through trade.

We learned a great deal from those early explorers, but there is still plenty to explore—including the deepest parts of Earth's oceans and outer space.

Early Adventurers

Some early explorers include the Phoenicians, who traveled across the Mediterranean Sea 3,000 years ago. Phoenician and Greek sailors were the first to sail far from their Mediterranean shores, and the first to sail at night, navigating by the stars. Egyptians probably first crossed the Mediterranean Sea in 2600 B.C. Around 138 B.C., Zhang Quian, a Chinese adventurer, explored Central Asia.

The Age of Discovery

The 15th century marked a new era for exploration, thanks to improvements in ship-building and navigation. Prince Henry the Navigator of Portugal supported explorers and navigational experts, and organized expeditions to seek a sea route to eastern Asia. Many European ships sailed south, exploring Africa's west coast. Christopher Columbus sailed west and came upon North America.

Conquerors and the Conquered

Often, lands that the early European explorers believed they had "discovered" and claimed for their countries were already inhabited by other peoples. In the Americas, many cultures were destroyed by the conquering invaders. Many lives, both European and Native American, were lost in battle, but many more native peoples were killed by diseases brought by the explorers—germs that the bodies of the Native Americans had no defenses against.

From the 9th to the 11th century, Vikings from Scandinavia explored and raided northern Europe and the British Isles. Crossing the Atlantic Ocean in their sturdy and swift boats, they became the first Europeans to set foot on North America.

Some Important Dates in Exploration

138 B.C.
Zhang Quian (Chinese) explores central Asia.

About A.D. 1000
Leif Ericsson (Viking) explores an area that he calls Vinland—probably on Canada's east coast or New England.

1271-1295
Marco Polo (Italian) travels through central Asia, China, and India.

1304-1368 (or 1369)
Ibn Battuta (Arab, from Tangier) explores Africa, the Arabian Peninsula, the Black Sea area, India, Indonesia, and China.

1497-1499
Vasco da Gama (Portuguese) is the first European to reach India by sea. He sails around the Cape of Good Hope, the southern tip of Africa.

1492-1504
Christopher Columbus (Italian, backed by Spain) makes four trips to the Americas.

1510-1513
Vasco Núñez de Balboa (Spanish) crosses the Isthmus of Panama. In 1513, he reaches the Pacific Ocean and claims it and all its shores for Spain.

1500s
Hernán Cortés (1519-1521) explores and conquers Mexico; Francisco Pizarro (1524-1541) explores and conquers Peru. Both men are backed by Spain.

1519-1521
Ferdinand Magellan (Portuguese, backed by Spain) leads the first expedition to sail around the world. (He does not complete the journey because he is killed in the Philippines in 1521.)

1539-1542
Hernando de Soto (Spanish) explores the southeast U.S. (He probably was the first European to see the Mississippi River.)

1768-1779
James Cook (British) sails the Pacific Ocean, exploring Antarctica and Hawaii.

1804-1806
Meriwether Lewis and William Clark (American) explore the North American West, traveling north from St. Louis, then west to the Pacific Ocean and back.

1857-1858
Richard Burton and John Speke (British) explore Africa, seeking the source of the Nile River. Henry Stanley (British) finds it at Lake Victoria in 1876.

1909
Robert Peary (American) and his team are the first people to reach the North Pole.

1911
Roald Amundsen (Norwegian) discovers the South Pole.

1961
Yuri A. Gagarin (Russian) is the first person to orbit Earth.

1969
Neil Armstrong (American) is the first person to walk on the moon.

I'M SACAGAWEA, A SHOSHONE WOMAN. I SERVED AS A GUIDE AND TRANSLATOR TO LEWIS AND CLARK, AND HELPED THEM LEARN FROM INDIANS THEY MET ALONG THE WAY.

I'M TENZING NORGAY, A SHERPA. ON MAY 29, 1953, I GUIDED SIR EDMUND HILLARY (NEW ZEALAND) TO THE TOP OF MOUNT EVEREST. WE WERE THE FIRST PEOPLE TO EVER REACH THAT PEAK. (I MADE MORE EXPEDITIONS INTO THE HIMALAYA MOUNTAINS THAN ANYONE ELSE!)

Farming

(see also FOOD AND NUTRITION ● INVENTORS AND INVENTIONS ● PLANT KINGDOM ● TIME)

All around the world, farmers grow crops and raise animals. This occupation is called agriculture. Farmers plant and harvest grains, vegetables, fruits, and other plants. They also breed and raise certain animals.

The first farmers were people who lived in the Middle East around 9000 B.C. They used their hands and simple tools to farm the land. Over time, people have developed plows, machines, fertilizers, and pesticides to make farming simpler, more efficient, and more productive.

Although only one tenth of Earth's land area is suitable for growing crops, about half of the world's population supports itself by farming.

Key Crops

People around the world use wheat, rice, and corn to satisfy their basic food and nutrition needs.

● **Wheat** is a grain that is grown in large fields in many parts of the world. It is usually ground into flour, which is used to make breads, pasta, and many other foods.

● **Rice,** another grain, is the most important crop in Asia. It is grown in flooded fields called paddies.

● **Corn** (also called maize) is raised all over the world. Some types are used for human consumption, others as feed for livestock.

Other important crops worldwide include barley, coffee, cotton, oats, potatoes, and soybeans.

> **DID YOU KNOW . . . ?**
>
> In the 18th and 19th centuries, many new inventions—including the combustion engine, the steam engine, and pesticides—revolutionized the way people farmed the land. As a result, fewer people could farm a much larger area of land while producing bigger crop yields.

Crop Cycle

Spring: Plowing the soil and planting seeds.

Summer: Spraying fertilizer (and sometimes pesticides) on crops.

YUMMY!

CORN FLAKES

Autumn: Harvesting, then storing or shipping crops.

Any time: Eating them!

Animals

Animals are often a key part of farm production. Some farmers raise cattle, pigs, sheep, goats, or chickens—animals that provide us with such food products as milk, meat, and eggs. Other animals raised by farmers provide material for clothing, such as wool, leather, and fur.

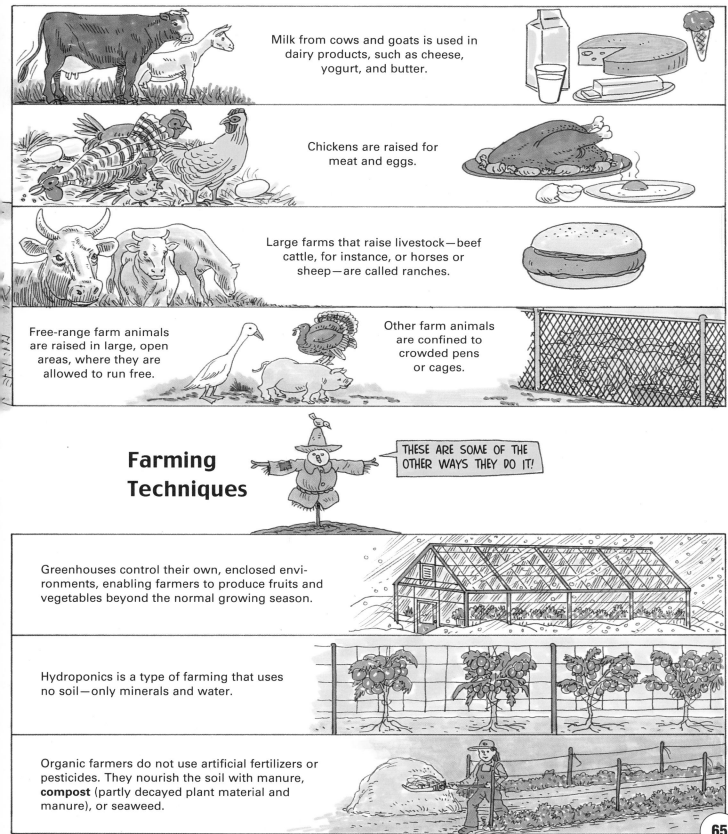

Milk from cows and goats is used in dairy products, such as cheese, yogurt, and butter.

Chickens are raised for meat and eggs.

Large farms that raise livestock—beef cattle, for instance, or horses or sheep—are called ranches.

Free-range farm animals are raised in large, open areas, where they are allowed to run free.

Other farm animals are confined to crowded pens or cages.

Farming Techniques

THESE ARE SOME OF THE OTHER WAYS THEY DO IT!

Greenhouses control their own, enclosed environments, enabling farmers to produce fruits and vegetables beyond the normal growing season.

Hydroponics is a type of farming that uses no soil—only minerals and water.

Organic farmers do not use artificial fertilizers or pesticides. They nourish the soil with manure, **compost** (partly decayed plant material and manure), or seaweed.

Festivals

(see also HOLIDAYS ● NORTH AMERICA ● RELIGIONS ● SOCIETY AND CULTURE ● SOUTH AMERICA)

Throughout the world, there are certain times of the year when people of the same culture take part in joyous festivals. Many such festivals or feasts honor historical events or religious beliefs. Others mark the changing of the seasons, often by giving thanks for a harvest. Many festivals involve the exchange of gifts, the wearing of elaborate costumes, or the eating of special foods.

Chinese New Year

In China, the new year is celebrated in late January or in February. Chinese people living all around the world have parades where they set off firecrackers and dress in dragon costumes or other festive outfits.

WE'RE HAVING A PARTY!

Party Time!

In some countries with a large Roman Catholic population, such as Brazil, people celebrate Carnival just before Lent. Lent is the 40-day period before Easter when Catholics give up certain foods or other treats. During Carnival, they eat foods they will avoid during Lent. In France, Italy, Spain, Mexico, and parts of South America, Carnival is celebrated with huge parties and parades.

EL DIA DE LOS MUERTOS

On November 1, Mexicans celebrate the Day of the Dead. This is a time to respect the dead while celebrating life. People honor dead friends and family members by decorating their graves and building little altars. Children wear costumes, paint their faces, and eat candies called sugar skulls inscribed with people's names.

Some Other Festivals

For thousands of years, all around the world, people have celebrated many things, including family, harvests, and the changing of the seasons.

In India, people celebrate Diwali, a festival of light. They light candles and lamps to mark the coming of winter and the start of a new Hindu year.

In Fregeneda, Spain, the Fiesta del Almendro celebrates the blossoming of almond trees by crossing the River Duero in boats.

In Ghana, in October, some peoples celebrate Odwira. This festival honors the goodness of the gods, the blessings of family and friends, and faith in life after death.

In the U.S. and Canada, people offer thanks for their well-being or prosperity by sitting down to a feast each autumn, on Thanksgiving Day.

Fire

(see also ENERGY • MINING • SAFETY)

Fire is the heat and light created when things burn. Burning (also called combustion) occurs when oxygen combines with a **combustible** (burnable) substance, such as wood or kerosene, in a chemical reaction that produces a flame. For a fire to start, three things must be present: heat, fuel, and oxygen.

Fire Starters

Cave dwellers probably learned about fire by observing nature—blazing hot lava, for instance, or bolts of lightning. They probably started fires by striking flints (a type of rock) together to create a spark. Some ancient peoples twirled a hard, pointed stick between their hands while pressing its point into a piece of softer wood, causing enough friction to start a fire.

Spontaneous combustion means that something has burst into flames by itself. This can happen when heat is produced by chemical reactions, such as within a pile of oily rags. If heat builds up and oxygen is present, fire can start on its own.

Ancient peoples (including Greeks, Romans, and the Inca) sometimes used lenses to focus the sun's rays to start fires. This concentrated the heat in one place, starting a small flame.

Danger

Every year, fires take lives and damage homes and other property. Fires can spread quickly and easily. If a cigarette on the ground is not stamped out, it can ignite materials around it, erupting into a flame. Burning fragments can be carried by wind, causing other fires. Even the heat from flames can set surrounding materials on fire.

Fighting the Flames

Forest fires are very difficult to control. Special planes fly over them, dumping water or chemicals on the fire.	Specially trained firefighters called smoke jumpers leap out of planes into raging forest fires to fight the flames.	When firefighters are alerted to a blaze, they speed to the site. First, they rescue people trapped in buildings. Then they use ladders, hoses, and other equipment to put out the fire. They wear special clothing and carry oxygen tanks as protection.	Since fires need oxygen to burn, they can be put out by taking oxygen away. Throwing sand on a campfire or tossing a blanket over a small fire can smother the flames.

SMOKEY THE BEAR WOULD BE PROUD OF ME.

67

Flags

(see also COMMUNICATION ● GOVERNMENT ● HOLIDAYS ● SOCIETY AND CULTURE)

Since early times, flags have been used to send messages or as symbols of loyalty. The first flags were used to identify troops at war. Soldiers looked for their flag to locate their leader. Roman troops carried a square piece of cloth on their spears during battle.

Each of the world's independent countries has its own flag, which is flown atop government buildings, at embassies throughout the world, and at many homes. These and other national flags express pride, loyalty, hope, or victory. Flags are also used as symbols of states or regions, as well as of countless clubs and organizations, such as the Boy Scouts and Girl Scouts, the Red Cross, and the United Nations.

Important Symbols

National flags often use symbols with special meaning for a country's people. For instance, many European flags have a cross in them. Here are some such symbols:

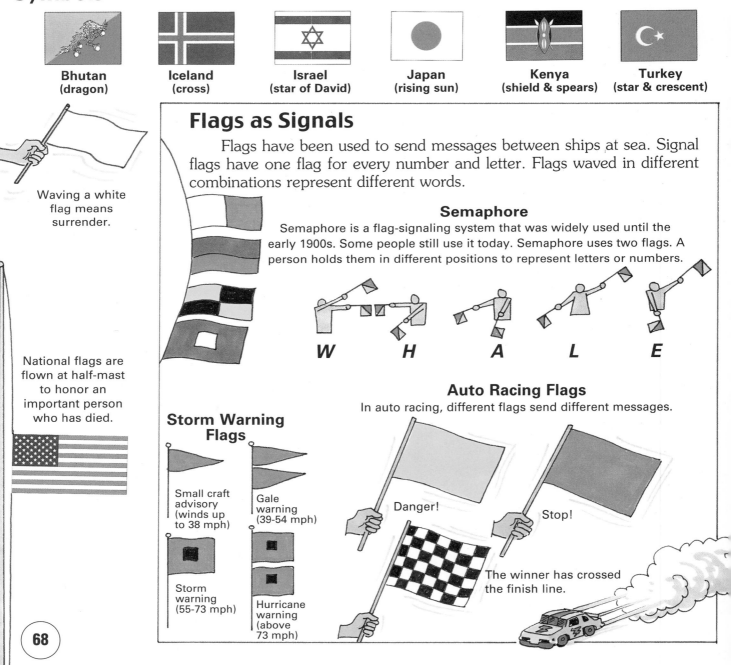

Bhutan (dragon)

Iceland (cross)

Israel (star of David)

Japan (rising sun)

Kenya (shield & spears)

Turkey (star & crescent)

Waving a white flag means surrender.

National flags are flown at half-mast to honor an important person who has died.

Flags as Signals

Flags have been used to send messages between ships at sea. Signal flags have one flag for *every* number and letter. Flags waved in different combinations represent different words.

Semaphore

Semaphore is a flag-signaling system that was widely used until the early 1900s. Some people still use it today. Semaphore uses two flags. A person holds them in different positions to represent letters or numbers.

W H A L E

Auto Racing Flags

In auto racing, different flags send different messages.

Danger!

Stop!

The winner has crossed the finish line.

Storm Warning Flags

Small craft advisory (winds up to 38 mph)

Gale warning (39-54 mph)

Storm warning (55-73 mph)

Hurricane warning (above 73 mph)

68

National Flags of the World's Independent Countries*

Afghanistan | Albania | Algeria | Andorra | Angola | Antigua & Barbuda | Argentina | Armenia | Australia | Austria | Azerbaijan

Bahamas | Bahrain | Bangladesh | Barbados | Belarus | Belgium | Belize | Benin | Bolivia | Bosnia & Herzegovina | Botswana

Brazil | Brunei | Bulgaria | Burkina Faso | Burundi | Cambodia | Cameroon | Canada | Cape Verde | Central African Republic | Chad

Chile | China | Colombia | Comoros | Congo | Congo Republic | Costa Rica | Côte d'Ivoire | Croatia | Cuba | Cyprus

Czech Republic | Denmark | Djibouti | Dominica | Dominican Republic | Ecuador | Egypt | El Salvador | Equitorial Guinea | Eritrea | Estonia

Ethiopia | Fiji | Finland | France | Gabon | Gambia | Georgia | Germany | Ghana | Greece | Grenada

Guatemala | Guinea | Guinea-Bissau | Guyana | Haiti | Honduras | Hungary | India | Indonesia | Iran | Iraq

Ireland | Italy | Jamaica | Jordan | Kazakhstan | Kiribati | Korea, North | Korea, South | Kuwait | Kyrgyzstan | Laos

Latvia | Lebanon | Lesotho | Liberia | Libya | Liechtenstein | Lithuania | Luxembourg | Macedonia | Madagascar | Malawi

Malaysia | Maldives | Mali | Malta | Marshall Islands | Mauritania | Mauritius | Mexico | Micronesia | Moldova | Monaco

Mongolia | Morocco | Mozambique | Myanmar (Burma) | Namibia | Nauru | Nepal | Netherlands | New Zealand | Nicaragua | Niger

Nigeria | Norway | Oman | Pakistan | Palau | Panama | Papua New Guinea | Paraguay | Peru | Philippines | Poland

Portugal | Qatar | Romania | Russia | Rwanda | St. Kitts & Nevis | St. Lucia | St. Vincent & the Grenadines | Samoa | San Marino | São Tomé & Principe

Saudi Arabia | Senegal | Serbia & Montenegro | Seychelles | Sierra Leone | Singapore | Slovakia | Slovenia | Solomon Islands | Somalia | South Africa

Spain | Sri Lanka | Sudan | Suriname | Swaziland | Sweden | Switzerland | Syria | Taiwan | Tajikistan | Tanzania

Thailand | Togo | Tonga | Trinidad & Tobago | Tunisia | Turkmenistan | Tuvalu | Uganda | Ukraine | United Arab Emirates | United Kingdom

United States | Uruguay | Uzbekistan | Vanuatu | Vatican City | Venezuela | Vietnam | Yemen | Zambia | Zimbabwe

*Also see the six national flags in the "Important Symbols" section on the opposite page.

69

Flight

(see also AIR ● ANIMAL KINGDOM ● INVENTORS AND INVENTIONS ● MACHINES ● TRANSPORTATION)

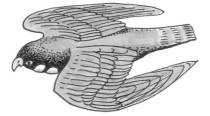

The **peregrine falcon** is the world's fastest bird. It can move as fast as 200 miles an hour as it dives for prey.

Most insects have two pairs of wings (flies have only one pair), but not all can fly. The **butterfly** is just one of the many insect species that fly.

Painted lady butterfly

The **hummingbird,** with its rapidly beating wings, moves like a tiny helicopter.

Bats are the only mammals that fly. They have large, leathery wings.

There are two basic kinds of flight: what some animals do naturally, and what humans do, using machines. (Human flight is usually called *aviation*.)

Animal Flight

Birds, insects, and bats are the only animals that really fly. A bird flies mainly by moving its wings up and down, using strong chest muscles. This pushes air down, lifting the bird up and forward. Different birds have different styles in the air. Some birds bounce, saving energy by gliding. Many small birds flap their wings constantly.

A Short History of Human Flight

1783: The Montgolfier brothers (France) build the first manned balloon. It is flown by Pilâtre de Rozier and the Marquis d'Arlandes.

1890s: Otto Lilienthal (Germany) flies and controls a hang glider.

1903: The Wright brothers (U.S.) make the first successful flight in a heavier-than-air machine.

1927: Charles Lindbergh (U.S.) makes the first solo flight across the Atlantic Ocean (from the U.S. to France).

1932: Amelia Earhart (U.S.) flies across the Atlantic Ocean from Newfoundland to Ireland.

1947: Chuck Yeager (U.S.) is the first to fly faster than the speed of sound.

1970: The largest passenger-carrying plane—the Boeing 747 jumbo jet—is launched. (It can carry up to 416 passengers, plus crew.)

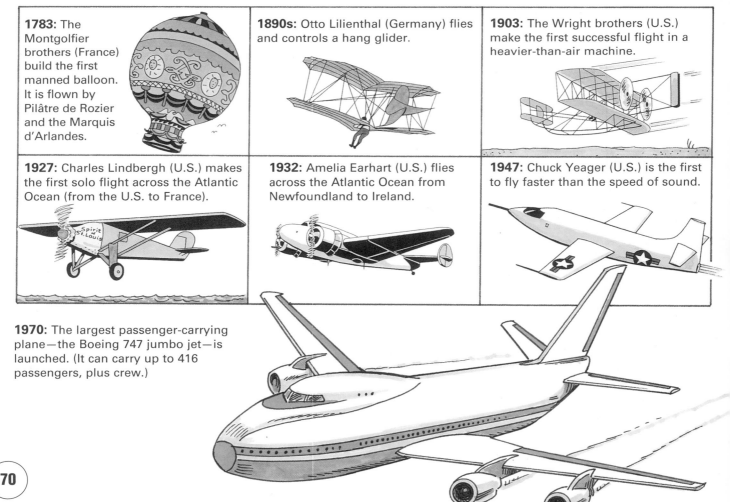

How an Airplane Works

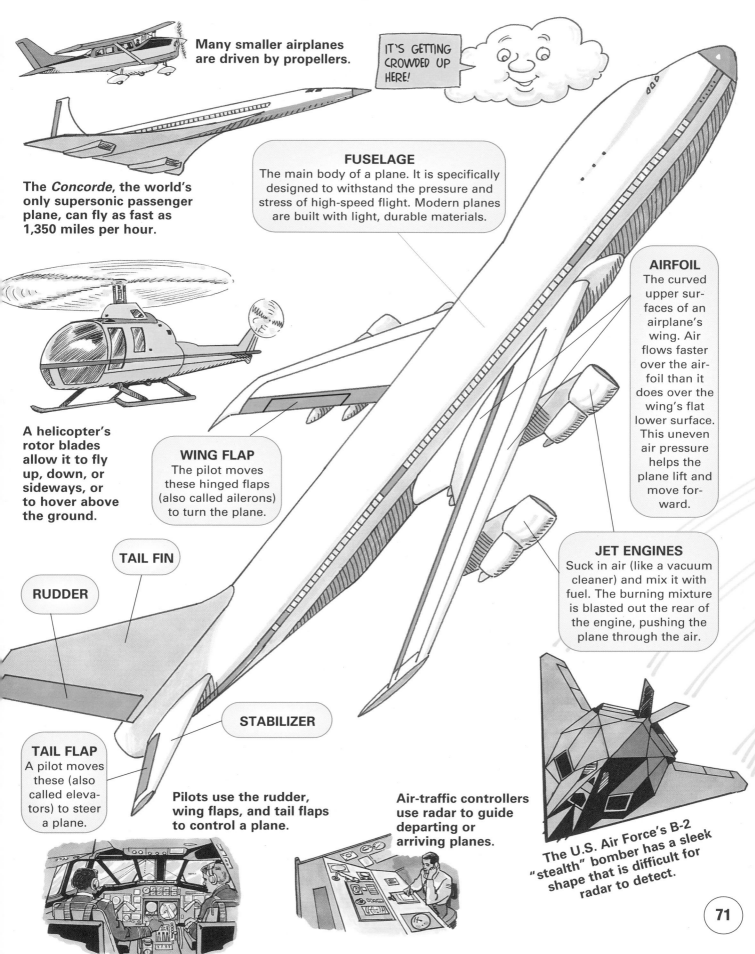

Many smaller airplanes are driven by propellers.

IT'S GETTING CROWDED UP HERE!

The *Concorde*, the world's only supersonic passenger plane, can fly as fast as 1,350 miles per hour.

FUSELAGE
The main body of a plane. It is specifically designed to withstand the pressure and stress of high-speed flight. Modern planes are built with light, durable materials.

AIRFOIL
The curved upper surfaces of an airplane's wing. Air flows faster over the airfoil than it does over the wing's flat lower surface. This uneven air pressure helps the plane lift and move forward.

A helicopter's rotor blades allow it to fly up, down, or sideways, or to hover above the ground.

WING FLAP
The pilot moves these hinged flaps (also called ailerons) to turn the plane.

JET ENGINES
Suck in air (like a vacuum cleaner) and mix it with fuel. The burning mixture is blasted out the rear of the engine, pushing the plane through the air.

TAIL FIN

RUDDER

STABILIZER

TAIL FLAP
A pilot moves these (also called elevators) to steer a plane.

Pilots use the rudder, wing flaps, and tail flaps to control a plane.

Air-traffic controllers use radar to guide departing or arriving planes.

The U.S. Air Force's B-2 "stealth" bomber has a sleek shape that is difficult for radar to detect.

71

Folk Tales and Fairy Tales

(see also LITERATURE AND WRITERS ● MYTHOLOGY ● SOCIETY AND CULTURE)

AESOP'S FABLES

Aesop, a slave of ancient Greece, is known for his fables. His characters were animals that behaved like humans, good and bad. Each Aesop's fable teaches a moral. In one, a hare is so confident he can beat a tortoise in a race that he stops along the way to take a nap. By the time he wakes up, the slow-but-steady tortoise has won the race.

Every society has developed its own unwritten literature. Folk literature is one of the oldest forms of this. It is stories that have been passed down from one generation to another by word of mouth. Folk literature includes fairy tales as well as folk tales. These stories were told, not written, so we don't know their original authors.

Most folk tales try to explain the mysteries of nature and of how Earth began. Others feature a main character who uses a special talent or quality to overcome a problem. Folk tales often teach a **moral** (lesson).

Fairy tales are traditional stories involving magic and fantasy. Strange creatures—such as dragons, spirits, fairies, elves, and goblins—have special powers. Often, the main characters are innocent maidens and knights in shining armor whose adventures end "happily ever after."

One of the first fairy tales to become popular in Europe was an Arabian story called "One Thousand and One Nights."

Among the many folk tales that explain the natural world is a Navajo story about an old woman who lived at the top of a high mountain. When the moon was full, she divided it into stars, which she then scattered across the sky.

Mother Goose Rhymes

Mother Goose tales are rhyming stories that have been around for a long time. They were first written down in 1697, by a French writer named Charles Perrault.

Who was Mother Goose? The English say that she was an old woman who told stories while selling flowers. The French say that she was Queen Bertha. Mother Goose rhymes, which are among the most well-known children's tales, include "Three Blind Mice," "Jack and Jill," "Baa, Baa, Black Sheep," "Little Miss Muffet," and "The House That Jack Built."

Trickster Tales

Some Native American and African folk tales feature tricksters. In Native American stories, the trickster is often a coyote; in West Africa, he is often a spider. The main character in trickster tales uses his cleverness and sense of humor to outsmart other creatures.

The Brothers Grimm

Many old tales were first written down in the early 1800s by two German brothers, Jakob and Wilhelm Grimm. They gathered tales from people who had heard them all their lives. Grimms' fairy tales include "Goldilocks and the Three Bears," "Hansel and Gretel," "Jack and the Beanstalk," "Little Red Riding Hood," and "Three Little Pigs." In "Cinderella"—first written by Charles Perrault but made famous by the Grimms—a fairy godmother helps a young woman escape from her cruel stepmother and stepsisters, and win the heart of a charming prince.

Food and Nutrition

(see also FARMING ● HEALTH AND FITNESS ● HUMAN BODY ● MEDICINE)

Food is any substance that provides nourishment to a living thing. The food that humans eat comes from plants and animals. By eating food, we supply our bodies with the energy to grow and be strong. Food gives the body what it needs to work properly.

Water, proteins, carbohydrates, fats, vitamins, and minerals are the main kinds of nutrients. We need them, plus fiber, to remain healthy. People who don't eat the right kinds of foods, or eat too few of them, are malnourished. They can get sick or even die. Eating too much of something—such as carbohydrates and sugar—can also be harmful.

What Is Your Diet?

A diet is what a person eats and drinks regularly. People's diets vary all around the world, depending on the climate and what plants and animals are available, as well as cultural preferences and religious beliefs. A well-rounded diet (no matter where you live) includes:

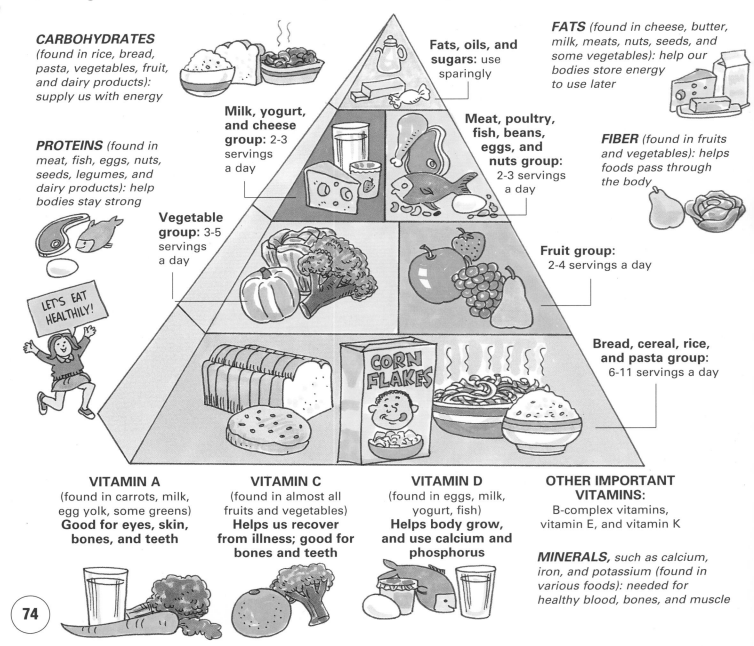

CARBOHYDRATES *(found in rice, bread, pasta, vegetables, fruit, and dairy products): supply us with energy*

PROTEINS *(found in meat, fish, eggs, nuts, seeds, legumes, and dairy products): help bodies stay strong*

LET'S EAT HEALTHILY!

Fats, oils, and sugars: use sparingly

Milk, yogurt, and cheese group: 2-3 servings a day

Meat, poultry, fish, beans, eggs, and nuts group: 2-3 servings a day

Vegetable group: 3-5 servings a day

FATS *(found in cheese, butter, milk, meats, nuts, seeds, and some vegetables): help our bodies store energy to use later*

FIBER *(found in fruits and vegetables): helps foods pass through the body*

Fruit group: 2-4 servings a day

CORN FLAKES

Bread, cereal, rice, and pasta group: 6-11 servings a day

VITAMIN A
(found in carrots, milk, egg yolk, some greens)
Good for eyes, skin, bones, and teeth

VITAMIN C
(found in almost all fruits and vegetables)
Helps us recover from illness; good for bones and teeth

VITAMIN D
(found in eggs, milk, yogurt, fish)
Helps body grow, and use calcium and phosphorus

OTHER IMPORTANT VITAMINS:
B-complex vitamins, vitamin E, and vitamin K

MINERALS, *such as calcium, iron, and potassium (found in various foods): needed for healthy blood, bones, and muscle*

74

DID YOU KNOW ...?

MOO!

MOO WHO?

Dairy Products

Dairy cows produce milk, which can be made into butter, cheese, ice cream, yogurt, and other products. (The same can be done with the milk of other animals, such as goats.)

Meat Products

Beef and veal come from cattle raised for their meat. Pork, ham, sausage, and bacon come from farm-raised pigs. Other meats include chicken and lamb.

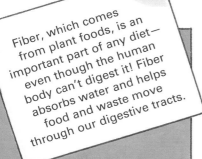

Fiber, which comes from plant foods, is an important part of any diet—even though the human body can't digest it! Fiber absorbs water and helps food and waste move through our digestive tracts.

Food Processing

Some foods are often eaten in their original state—fruits and vegetables, for instance. Others, such as meats and grains, are usually processed before they are eaten. Processing kills germs, helps prevent food from rotting, and makes some foods easier to digest.

Foods are processed in different ways. Some are frozen, smoked, dried, or salted. Others are heated, then sealed in airtight containers to kill bacteria (germs that can cause illness).

Food processing has its drawbacks. While killing germs and making food last longer, it also destroys important nutrients that are in fresh food naturally. Health-food stores, natural-food restaurants, and organic farming have grown in popularity as people have looked for ways to avoid the drawbacks of processed foods.

Vitamins and minerals are added to many foods to make them more nutritious. Preservatives—chemicals that help food stay fresh longer—are also added.

Eating too many fats (or too much food of any kind) can be bad for the heart.

Fish contains oils that are very good for the heart.

Forests

(see also AIR ● ASIAN WILDLIFE ● ECOSYSTEMS ● ENVIRONMENT ● NORTH AMERICAN WILDLIFE ● PLANT KINGDOM ● RAIN FORESTS ● SOUTH AMERICAN WILDLIFE ● TREES ● WATER)

Forests are land areas covered with trees. The trees provide forest animals with food, homes, and shelter from predators. Forests provide humans with timber, medicines, syrup, rubber, spices, gums, and fruits.

About one third of Earth's land area is covered with forest. Every year, however, huge forest areas are cleared for timber or to create grazing land. This destruction threatens Earth's environment by adding to global warming and destroying the natural habitat of many species.

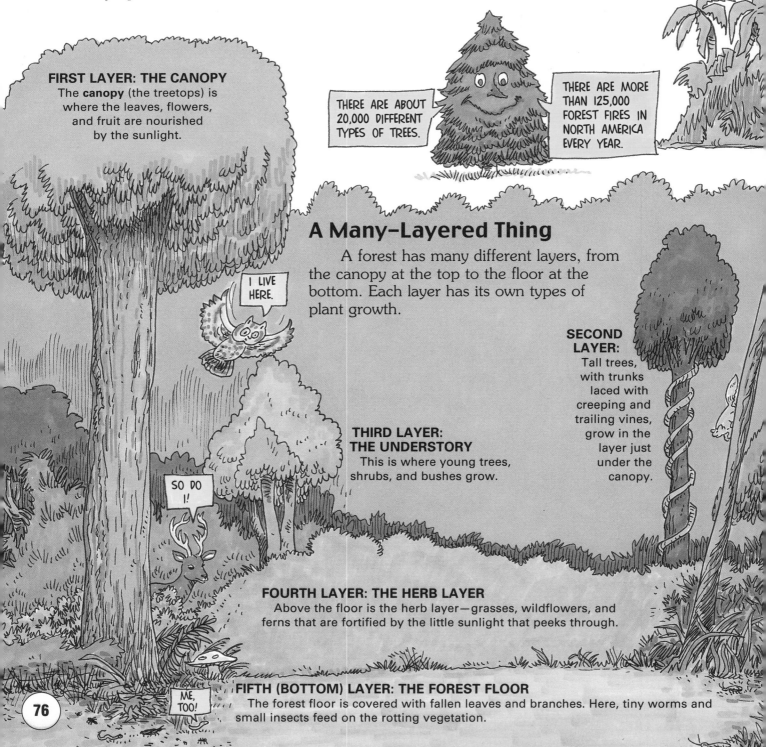

FIRST LAYER: THE CANOPY
The **canopy** (the treetops) is where the leaves, flowers, and fruit are nourished by the sunlight.

THERE ARE ABOUT 20,000 DIFFERENT TYPES OF TREES.

THERE ARE MORE THAN 125,000 FOREST FIRES IN NORTH AMERICA EVERY YEAR.

A Many-Layered Thing

A forest has many different layers, from the canopy at the top to the floor at the bottom. Each layer has its own types of plant growth.

I LIVE HERE.

SECOND LAYER:
Tall trees, with trunks laced with creeping and trailing vines, grow in the layer just under the canopy.

THIRD LAYER: THE UNDERSTORY
This is where young trees, shrubs, and bushes grow.

SO DO I!

FOURTH LAYER: THE HERB LAYER
Above the floor is the herb layer—grasses, wildflowers, and ferns that are fortified by the little sunlight that peeks through.

FIFTH (BOTTOM) LAYER: THE FOREST FLOOR
The forest floor is covered with fallen leaves and branches. Here, tiny worms and small insects feed on the rotting vegetation.

ME, TOO!

Forest Types

Coniferous forests

This type of forest usually grows in cold areas. *Coniferous* means that the trees growing there produce cones with seeds. (Pines, spruce, and firs are examples of conifers.) These trees are evergreens: They do not shed their leaves (needles) in winter. Large coniferous forests stretch across Siberia, Canada, and parts of Europe and the United States.

Deciduous forests

This type of forest usually grows in milder areas. Deciduous trees are trees that shed their leaves in the autumn and grow new ones in the spring. (Oaks, elms, beeches, and maples are examples of deciduous trees.) Deciduous forests are found in eastern North America, parts of Europe, and China.

Mangrove forests

Mangrove forests are swamp forests found near tropical coasts, where rivers meet the sea. Mangrove trees have a special adaptation that filters out the salt in the ocean water, which would otherwise harm the trees.

In mangrove forests, the soil is so water-logged and dense that it's hard for underground tree roots to get enough oxygen. That is why many roots grow above the soil, where they can absorb the oxygen they need in order to grow.

Rain forests

Rain forests thrive where there is abundant rain. Trees grow in dense clusters, and compete for sunlight. There are temperate rain forests, such as those in the northwestern U.S., and tropical rain forests, such as those in Central and South America, Africa, Asia, and Oceania.

Fossils

(see also ARCHAEOLOGY ● DINOSAURS ● ENERGY ● ENVIRONMENT
● GEOLOGY ● MINING ● PREHISTORY)

Fossils are the remains of long-dead plants and animals that have been preserved. A fossil might be the remains of a tiny one-celled plant, a small part of an animal (a bone, tooth, or shell, for example), or a nearly complete skeleton of a huge dinosaur. Studying fossils can tell us a lot about what life on Earth was like millions of years ago.

Long ago, some plants and animals—dead or alive—got buried under layers of sand and mud on land, under the sea, or at the bottom of a lake or river. As the sand and mud turned to rock, the remains were preserved and protected. Much later, some areas once covered by water became dry land. As the rock was uncovered or worn away, the fossils rose close enough to the surface to be found.

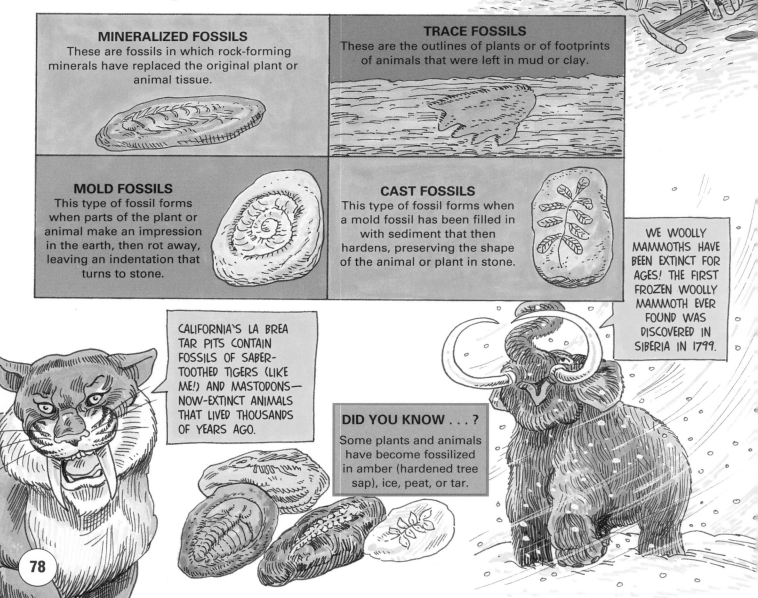

MINERALIZED FOSSILS
These are fossils in which rock-forming minerals have replaced the original plant or animal tissue.

TRACE FOSSILS
These are the outlines of plants or of footprints of animals that were left in mud or clay.

MOLD FOSSILS
This type of fossil forms when parts of the plant or animal make an impression in the earth, then rot away, leaving an indentation that turns to stone.

CAST FOSSILS
This type of fossil forms when a mold fossil has been filled in with sediment that then hardens, preserving the shape of the animal or plant in stone.

WE WOOLLY MAMMOTHS HAVE BEEN EXTINCT FOR AGES! THE FIRST FROZEN WOOLLY MAMMOTH EVER FOUND WAS DISCOVERED IN SIBERIA IN 1799.

CALIFORNIA'S LA BREA TAR PITS CONTAIN FOSSILS OF SABER-TOOTHED TIGERS (LIKE ME!) AND MASTODONS—NOW-EXTINCT ANIMALS THAT LIVED THOUSANDS OF YEARS AGO.

DID YOU KNOW . . . ?
Some plants and animals have become fossilized in amber (hardened tree sap), ice, peat, or tar.

Games provide fun, excitement, and challenges. Some games have been around since very early times and have variations all over the world. Some games are played alone; others are a contest between two or more players. Most games have specific rules that are followed. Some games require special equipment, while others require only a good imagination. Games help us improve memory, sharpen visual skills, or stay physically fit.

Games
(see also COMPUTERS ● SPORTS)

Board Games

One of the oldest game boards found was probably for a race game played in Sumer (now Iraq) about 4,500 years ago.

Egyptians began playing checkers around 1600 B.C. Each piece represented a soldier.

Card Games

Most card games use a 52-card deck with four suits: diamonds, hearts, spades, and clubs.

Electronic Games

The first video games were played in arcades or on home TV sets, using a joystick or the keyboard.

They still can be played that way, but hand-held electronic games are growing in popularity.

Group Games

In **blind man's buff,** one person—called It—is blindfolded. The other players tease and pat It, who has to catch hold of someone and guess who he or she is. If the guess is correct, that person becomes the next It.

Double dutch is a rope-jumping game. Two players swing two overlapping ropes while other players—one or several at a time—leap in and jump rope. Jumpers often try to keep pace with rhyming chants or songs. Some double-dutch players perform tricky dance steps while jumping.

In **musical chairs,** players walk around a circle of chairs while music plays. There is always one fewer chair than the number of players. The moment the music stops, everyone hurries to sit on the nearest chair. Whoever is left standing is out. One chair is taken away, and the game starts again—until only one person is left.

In a Latin American game, blindfolded players hit a hanging object called a **piñata** with sticks until it breaks—and gifts and candies spill out.

Geography

(see also ASIA ● EARTH ● ECOSYSTEMS ● ENVIRONMENT
● GEOLOGY ● NAVIGATION ● WORLD)

Geography is the study of Earth's surface, climate, and inhabitants. People known as geographers examine Earth's natural features, such as mountains, deserts, valleys, forests, and hills. Geographers study human creations on Earth, such as cities, towns, and railroads. They also study how humans are affected by their environment. Other geographers study where animals, plants, and humans live, as well as their relationships with Earth's features.

Maps

The first-known maps were drawn around 2500 B.C. They showed people from different towns how to reach one another. Today, surveyors use special instruments to precisely measure land areas. **Cartographers** (mapmakers) use those measurements to draw maps to scale. (*Scale* is a way of drawing places or things to show their sizes in relation to each other. For instance, if one country is three times larger than another, mapmakers draw it three times larger on their maps.) Aerial photographs and other modern technologies help mapmakers create accurate maps.

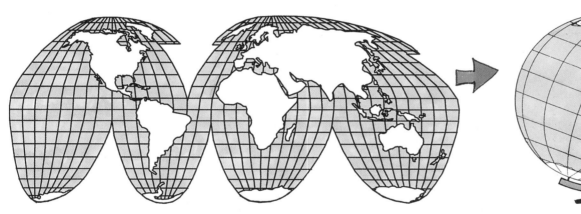

Most maps are flat. Globes are maps that are round, so they are more accurate at showing the shape and relative size of Earth's land and water areas. Relief maps have raised areas to show land elevation—hills, mountains, and valleys. Mobility maps show highways, roads, railroad tracks, and other travel pathways. Some maps give us information about population, how land is used, climate, or weather patterns.

DID YOU KNOW . . . ?

The ancient Greeks were the first people known to list different characteristics of places—such as the number of people, location of buildings, and distances from other places. Anaximander (about 611 B.C.-547 B.C.) of Greece is considered the first geographer.

A book of maps is called an atlas.

80

Some Geographical Terms

Archipelago (ar-kuh-PEL-uh-go): a large group of islands clustered together in an ocean.

Bay: a sea or lake section partially enclosed by dry land (small bays are called coves).

Beach: sandy or rocky land at the edge of a lake or ocean.

Canyon: a deep valley with rocky, steep sides. (Small canyons are called *chasms* or *ravines*.)

Glacier (GLAY-shur): a great mass of slowly moving ice.

Marsh: a spongy wetland covered with tall grasses and reeds.

Mountain: a rugged mass of rock that is much higher than the surrounding land.

Ocean ridge: a huge mountain range at the bottom of an ocean.

Ocean trench: a canyon in the ocean floor.

Valley: a gentle, rolling, low area between hills or mountains.

81

Geology

(see also EARTH ● ENERGY ● ENVIRONMENT ● FOSSILS ● GEOGRAPHY ● MATTER ● MINING ● PREHISTORY ● SCIENCE AND SCIENTISTS)

Geology is the study of Earth's formation, movement, and rocks (Earth's building blocks). Earth's crust consists of different layers of rock, formed over millions of years. Geologists study it to understand how Earth was formed, how it changes, and how humans use it. They also use their knowledge and special technologies to detect movement in the crust, which helps them predict volcanic eruptions and earthquakes.

ATMOSPHERE

CRUST: between 4 and 44 miles deep

MANTLE: about 1,800 miles thick, with a temperature of 1,600 to 4,000°F

OUTER CORE: about 1,240 miles thick, with a temperature of 4,000 to 9,000°F

INNER CORE: about 1,712 miles thick, with a temperature of about 9,000°F

DID YOU KNOW . . . ?
The deepest layers of Earth's crust are the oldest. The surface layers are the most recent.

Tectonic Plates

Earth's continents lie on top of tectonic plates—enormous slabs of Earth's crust. These plates float on a layer of hot, **molten** (melted) rock called magma. Magma moves slowly, and the plates move with it. Sometimes, the plates collide, slide past one another, or pull apart—movement that is known as continental drift. When plates drift into one another, it causes so much pressure that Earth's crust shifts or splits in weak sections, called fault lines. That shifting and splitting of the Earth is what we call an earthquake.

More than 300 million years ago, all the land on Earth was a single landmass called Pangaea (pan-JEE-uh). About 180 million years ago, it split into two continents called Gondwanaland (gahn-DWAHN-uh-land) and Laurasia (lore-AY-zhuh). Then, very slowly, some parts of these two landmasses joined together while others broke apart. This created the continents as we know them today.

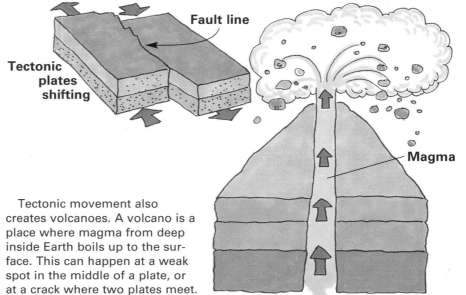
Fault line
Tectonic plates shifting
Magma

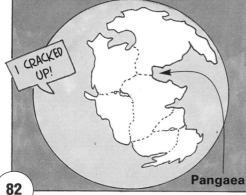
I CRACKED UP!
Pangaea

Tectonic movement also creates volcanoes. A volcano is a place where magma from deep inside Earth boils up to the surface. This can happen at a weak spot in the middle of a plate, or at a crack where two plates meet.

Over millions of years, moving tectonic plates can create mountains. Rocks at the plates' edges get squeezed together, then pushed upward as the plates crash against one another.

Earthquake Zones

There are many places on Earth where tectonic plates—also called crustal plates—meet. Earthquakes are more likely to happen in these areas, which are marked in red and yellow in the picture below. One of the most active earthquake zones, known as the Ring of Fire, lines eastern Asia.

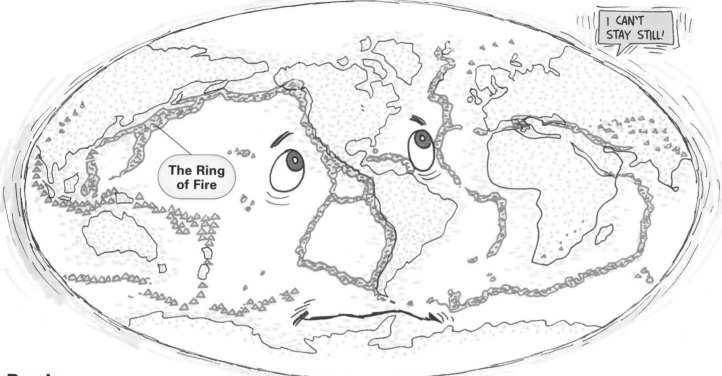

Rocks

Rocks are the solid substances that make up Earth's crust. Rocks are made of minerals. There are three main types of rock:

Igneous rock	Sedimentary rock	Metamorphic rock
Formed when **lava** (molten rock from deep inside Earth) rises to the surface and cools quickly there, or cools slowly inside Earth's crust. Basalt, granite, and pumice are examples of igneous rock.	Formed when skeletons, sand, and clay are squeezed together and slowly exposed to water, wind, and ice over a long period of time. Chalk, clay, and sandstone are examples of sedimentary rock.	Formed when intense heat and pressure inside Earth's crust cause changes in igneous and sedimentary rocks. Gneiss, marble, and slate are examples of metamorphic rock.

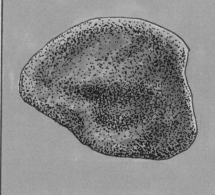

DID YOU KNOW . . . ?
Crystals are minerals that form a set of smooth surfaces called faces. Besides being used in jewelry, many crystals are collected, studied, and used in industry.

Governments

(see also FLAGS ● LAWS ● PRESIDENTS, U.S. ● SOCIETY AND CULTURE ● UNITED NATIONS ● UNITED STATES HISTORY)

Government is the system by which a community, state, or country is ruled. There are many different types of national governments, and each reflects its country's history and culture. Government leaders usually decide how money raised by taxes should be used for education, defense, welfare, health, and other types of services.

There are two basic types of government: representative and autocratic. In representative government, such as a democracy, citizens vote for the people or political parties they want to lead them. In an autocratic government, such as a dictatorship, people do not get to choose their leaders, and one person or group has absolute power.

Democratic Government

Many nations have democratic governments, which means rule by the people. People vote in elections to choose which parties or leaders should run the country. Democratic governments usually follow rules and guidelines set down in the country's constitution, a document that spells out how the government should be organized and run.

WHOEVER RECEIVES THE MOST VOTES IS THE WINNER.

VOTE

Some constitutions also spell out which rights of the people—such as freedom of speech, religion, and the press—need special protection.

Some countries—Liberia, Bolivia, and the U.S., for instance—have a **presidential-legislative democracy:** a president and a legislature (law-making body) share power. The U.S. government has three main branches: the **executive branch** (president and his advisers), which carries out the law; the **legislature** (Congress), which makes the law; and the **judiciary** (Supreme Court and lower courts), which enforces the law. This system ensures that one group or person doesn't have too much power.

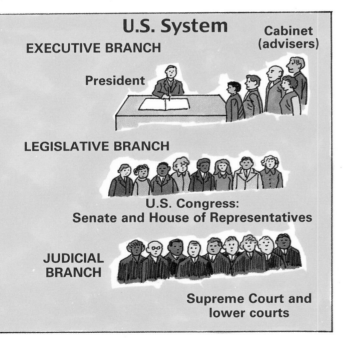

U.S. System

EXECUTIVE BRANCH

Cabinet (advisers)

President

LEGISLATIVE BRANCH

U.S. Congress: Senate and House of Representatives

JUDICIAL BRANCH

Supreme Court and lower courts

Other countries have **parliamentary** governments—Britain, Canada, Samoa, and Bangladesh, for example. People vote to choose the party that will serve in **parliament** (a law-making body), which usually has an upper and lower house. The leader of the party becomes the prime minister (sometimes called premier), who makes the major decisions in running the government.

Parliamentary System

Prime minister

Legislature or Parliament

The highest court

Communist Government

Communism is a system of government now practiced mainly in China and Cuba. In a communist system, one party—the Communist Party—controls the country's government and economy. The people have few of the rights that people in democratic countries take for granted: They are not allowed to criticize the government, practice of religion is often restricted or banned, and the government controls newspapers, radio, and television.

Communists believe that the good of the society is more important than individual rights. They believe that this system makes everyone equal—in theory, no one is really rich and no one is really poor.

Anarchy

Anarchists believe that all government is unnecessary, and that all forms of government take away the individual's liberty.

Totalitarian Government

Totalitarian governments regulate all aspects of society: family, church, arts, and business. Their leaders demand total loyalty and crush any opposition. Some totalitarian governments are run by the military.

Monarchy

A monarchy is a type of government in which an emperor, king, or queen holds power for life. There are few monarchs with real power today; most are in Asia.

Dictatorship

A dictator is a ruler who has unlimited power, unchecked by law or other leaders. Adolf Hitler (below) was dictator of Germany from 1933 until Germany lost World War II in 1945.

Health and Fitness

(see also FOOD AND NUTRITION ● HUMAN BODY ● MEDICINE ● SAFETY)

When a person is in good health, both body and mind are working properly. You can stay healthy by eating a good diet, exercising, keeping clean, sleeping well, and going to the doctor for regular checkups. A healthy diet is one that gives your body energy that helps it grow as it should, and nutrients that enable it to heal correctly. Exercise ensures that your body stays strong and fit. Good **hygiene** (cleanliness) helps protect you from germs that cause sickness. Sleeping well is necessary—your body and brain need the rest. Doctors make sure that your heart, blood, and everything else work well.

Running . . .   Roller skating . . .   Skiing . . .   Swimming . . .   Ice skating . . .

**. . . are all good for your muscles and heart.
So are . . .**

Jumping rope . . .   Bike riding . . .   Hiking . . .   Calisthenics . . .   Team sports . . .

Gardening . . .   Gymnastics . . .   Dancing . . .   Walking.

Don't be a . . .

couch potato!

**EXERCISE FOR
GOOD HEALTH!**

Hygiene

It is very important to keep both body and clothing clean. Washing with soap and water every day keeps skin clean, so that germs from dirt, other people, and animals don't spread. We also need to make sure that we change our clothes when they are dirty. Finally, don't forget to brush your teeth! This will prevent you from getting **cavities** (tiny holes) in your teeth—and having to make lots of trips to the dentist.

Handy Health and Hygiene Hints

Teeth have a very hard coating, called enamel, that keeps them strong. But too much sugar in your diet will eat away the enamel, so try drinking fewer soft drinks and eating less candy and other sweet stuff. (Brush your teeth well after every meal and snack!)

If you fall and scrape your skin, be sure that the wound is cleaned, then covered with a bandage. This will help it heal correctly.

Fruits, vegetables, and grains help build healthy bodies. Sugars and fats do not. So try to make sure that your diet has a healthy balance—more good stuff than bad stuff.

Most children need to sleep about 12 hours a day; adults need about 8 hours daily.

Most infectious diseases are spread through the air or by touch. Cover your mouth when you cough or sneeze, and always have a handkerchief or tissue handy.

Drinking too much alcohol can damage people's livers. Smoking causes heart and lung disease—in people close to smokers, as well in as the smokers themselves.

The flu is caused by a virus. If you catch it, getting plenty of rest and drinking lots of fluids (especially water!) will help you get better.

Holidays

(see also FESTIVALS ● FLAGS ● MONUMENTS ● RELIGIONS
● SOCIETY AND CULTURE ● UNITED STATES HISTORY)

Holidays are days set aside for special religious or public observance. (The word *holiday* comes from the words *holy day*.)

Many countries have national holidays. On those days, most schools and offices are closed. Some holidays are solemn observances during which people pray, **fast** (do not eat), or meditate. Other holidays are joyous occasions that are celebrated with dancing, special meals, parties, or parades. Observing holidays can help people feel more generous toward each other, and more united.

Some Religious Holidays

People in ancient Greece celebrated the Feast of Pots: They left food out for spirits that were thought to have entered the earthly world.

Christians celebrate the birth of Jesus on December 25.

On Yom Kippur, the tenth day of the Jewish new year, Jews show regret for their sins.

During the holy month of Ramadan, Muslims fast and meditate.

Christians light candles during Christmas. Jews light candles during Hanukkah, the Festival of Lights.

Patriotic Holidays

Most countries have holidays that mark important events in their histories, such as their independence day or a great leader's birthday. For instance, the people of ancient Greece celebrated important battle victories, such as the anniversary of their victory at Marathon in 490 B.C. Today, Italy celebrates Liberation Day in April, Egypt celebrates National Liberation Day in October, and Panama celebrates the anniversary of its separation from Colombia in early November.

Most national and regional governments set aside public holidays, during which banks, schools, and government buildings are closed. In the U.S., for instance, Memorial Day (the last Monday in May) honors Americans who died in foreign wars, and July 4 marks independence from Britain in 1776. Martin Luther King Jr., an important leader in the U.S. civil-rights movement, is honored on the third Monday in January. Canadians celebrate the formation of their union on Canada Day, July 1.

Some Other Holidays

All over the world, people celebrate their national holidays by displaying flags.

On Ch'usok, Koreans leave gifts and food on the graves of their ancestors.

On All Souls' Day in Poland, people set extra dinner settings for the ghosts of their ancestors, who are believed to come back to visit on that day.

Many African Americans celebrate Kwanzaa from December 26 through January 1. This American holiday is based on African traditions.

On St. Valentine's Day (February 14), many people around the world give cards, flowers, or other gifts to loved ones.

Most countries and cultures have a holiday to give thanks for something important to them. In the U.S., the fourth Thursday in November is Thanksgiving—a time for feasting with family and friends. Canadians observe Thanksgiving in October.

St. Patrick, patron saint of Ireland, is honored on March 17.

Human Body

(see also AIR ● ENERGY ● FOOD AND NUTRITION ● HEALTH AND FITNESS ● MEDICINE)

Every part of the human body is made up of many different **cells** (the basic units of life). Cells that do the same type of job are grouped together, forming tissue, and groups of tissue form organs. Organs, the most important parts of the human body, include the brain, kidneys, heart, and liver. The organs work with each other as systems that control all the bodily functions that keep us alive and well.

Artery

Vein

Human blood has different types of cells. Red blood cells contain hemoglobin, which carries oxygen. White blood cells fight infection. Platelets, the smallest blood cells, help blood to clot.

All together, the human body's arteries, veins, and capillaries are thousands of miles long!

Circulatory System

Blood from the body (blue) enters the right side of the heart, where it receives oxygen. Then it flows into the left side of the heart to be pumped back through the body.

Blood to heart   **Aorta**   **Left lung**

Right lung

Blood to heart

THAT DOESN'T LOOK LIKE ME!

There are 206 bones in the human body . . .

. . . and about 650 muscles.

Cerebrum

Brain

The brain controls all the body's activities, sending and receiving signals through the nervous system.
Cerebrum: Center of the five senses, thought, and creativity
Cerebellum: Controls signals to and from the muscles
Medulla: Controls breathing, blood pressure, basic survival

Medulla

Cerebellum   **Spinal cord**

The Skeletal and Muscular Systems

The skeleton is the framework inside the body, made of bones, that supports and protects the soft inner organs. Attached to this framework are hundreds of muscles—strong, elastic tissue—that control every movement the body makes. Signals from the brain—carried by the nervous system—tell each muscle what to do and when.

DID YOU KNOW . . . ?
Your skin is an organ! It protects the body from infection.

Respiratory System

When we breathe, we take oxygen into our lungs, then breathe out carbon dioxide. The lungs are where blood from the heart lets off carbon dioxide and picks up oxygen.

Breathing passages

Larynx

Windpipe

Oxygen in

Right lung

Left lung

Heart

Diaphragm

A person takes about 23,000 breaths each day.

Digestive System

The digestive system breaks food down into nutrients that pass through the walls of the intestines into the bloodstream. After the nutrients have been absorbed, the remains of the food leave the body as waste.

Mouth

Esophagus

Liver

Stomach

Coils of small intestine

Large intestine

Rectum

Appendix

The Five Senses

Smell: Gas molecules from an object reach the olfactory (smelling) cells in the nose.

Taste: Taste buds on the tip of the tongue detect sweetness and saltiness, those on the sides detect sourness, and buds on the back detect bitterness. Nerves connect taste buds on the tongue with the brain.

Salty   Sour   Bitter

Sweet

Hearing: Sounds enter the outer ear and go through the ear canal to the eardrum, making it vibrate. Those vibrations travel to tiny muscles in the middle ear, making them vibrate. The signals reach the inner ear's fluid-filled cochlea, which sends them to the brain.

Ear canal

Nerve to brain

Inner ear (cochlea)

Eardrum

Middle ear

Touch: Nerves under the skin respond to cold, heat, pressure, and other conditions, then send impulses to the brain. (Our fingertips are supersensitive—they have more nerves than any other body part.)

Speech

Sight

Hearing

Eye movements

Speech

Touch

Smell

RIGHT HALF OF CEREBRUM

Sight: Light bouncing off an object goes into the eye. Nerves inside the retina, in the back of the eye, send signals to the brain, which interprets what you see.

Retina

Nerve to brain

Eye

Lens

Light rays from object

Object

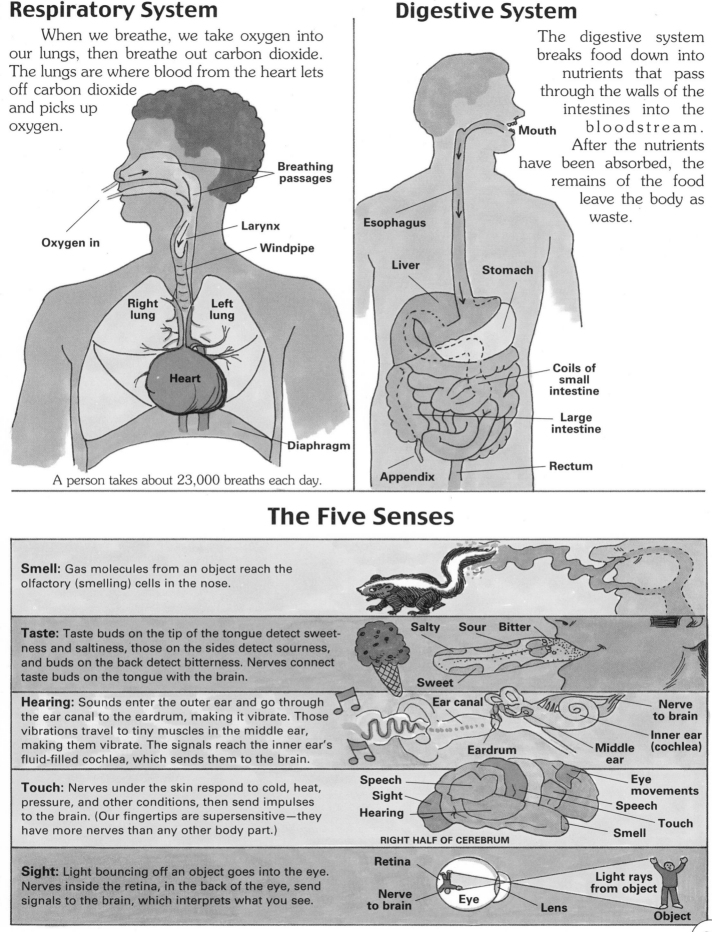

Inventors and Inventions

(see also COMPUTERS ● EXPLORERS AND EXPLORATION ● FARMING ● FLIGHT ● MACHINES ● MOVIES AND TELEVISION ● NAVIGATION ● RENAISSANCE ● SCIENCE AND SCIENTISTS ● SPACE EXPLORATION ● TECHNOLOGY ● TIME ● TRANSPORTATION)

An *inventor* is someone who has an idea for a new machine or thinks of a new way of doing something. Inventors in early civilizations in Asia, Africa, India, and the Middle East learned how to make new tools that helped improve people's lives.

Fire (date unknown)

Wheel (3500 B.C.)

Plow (4000 B.C.)

Water pump (date unknown)

Archimedes' screw (date unknown)

Paper (by A.D. 100)

Chinese Inventions

The Chinese invented paper about A.D. 100. They introduced gunpowder to the world in A.D. 1000, and began using clay blocks to print characters (letters and words) in A.D. 1045. As Europeans began exploring and trading with more of the world, they learned a great deal from their contact with China and the Middle East. The wheelbarrow and the ship's rudder are just two of the many helpful inventions that Europeans borrowed from the East.

about 1250: Roger Bacon (English) is one of the the first scientists to use a magnifying glass.

1285: Alessandro de Spina (Italian) invents eyeglasses.

1400s: Leonardo da Vinci (Italian) sketches ideas for flying machines hundreds of years before the first airplane or helicopter, as well as designs for a tank and a parachute.

1608: Hans Lippershey (Dutch) invents the telescope.

Industrial Revolution

For most of human history, machines have run on wind, water, animal, or human power. In 1690, Denis Papin (France) came up with an idea for an engine powered by steam. In 1765, James Watt refined the steam-powered engine—and his invention revolutionized the world. Steam-powered machines, with their newly developed cast-iron parts, worked quickly and efficiently, speeding production in industry. Steam-powered boats and trains carried people and products to faraway places more quickly than had been possible before.

Important inventions of the Industrial Revolution include . . .

James Watt's steam engine (1765)

James Watt

Elias Howe's sewing machine (1846)

Eli Whitney's cotton gin (1793)

James Hargreaves's spinning jenny (1765)

Information Age

1826:
Joseph Niépce (France) takes the first photograph.

1876:
Alexander Graham Bell (U.S.) invents the telephone.

1877-1894:
Thomas Edison (U.S.) invents the light bulb, the phonograph, and the high-speed movie camera.

1885:
Karl Benz (Germany) builds the first automobile.

1895:
Guglielmo Marconi (Italy) sends the first radio signal.

1947:
John Bardeen, Walter Brattain, and William Shockley (U.S.) invent the transistor, paving the way for computers and the Information Age.

HEY, READER! SMILE!

HI, TONY!

GO-GO-GO!

LET'S GO TO THE MOVIES.

ZOOM, ZOOM!

THANKS, GUYS!

Law

(see also GOVERNMENTS ● SOCIETY AND CULTURE ● UNITED NATIONS ● UNITED STATES HISTORY)

Laws are rules that help people live together. Some laws **prohibit** (ban) actions; other laws require them. Laws are written by the government leaders on a national, state, or local level. Police departments, the courts, and law officials make sure that laws are obeyed and punish offenders. Laws help give order to communities and nations. Some laws are meant to protect the rights of the individual.

Natural law:
The idea, recognized since ancient times, that nature follows general rules of justice and behavior—therefore, all people should follow them, too.

Religious law:
Law that has been based on religious codes or set according to them. One of the most famous codes of law is religious: the Ten Commandments. In the Bible, God tells Moses these rules of behavior to pass on to his people. Other types of religious law include Judaic law, based on the Torah, and Islamic law, based on the Koran.

Early Codes of Law

The Code of Hammurabi
Hammurabi ruled the Babylonian Empire from about 1792 to 1750 B.C. He drew up one of the earliest written codes of law. His laws were engraved on pillars, for everyone to see and be guided by. Each crime was given a specific penalty.

Draconian Law
In Athens, Greece, about 621 B.C., a leader named Draco (DRAY-koh) established a written code of laws that called for severe punishments if broken—including the death penalty, even for minor offenses. (The word *draconian* has come to mean "harsh" or "cruel.")

Roman Code of Law
Emperor Justinian I of the Byzantine Empire completed a written code of Roman law in A.D. 535. Roman law was the model for most of the legal systems that are used in continental Europe today.

The Magna Carta
Signed by King John of England in 1215, the Magna Carta was an agreement between the king and his nobles. That historic document required the king to promise not to abuse his power. This was the first time that kings were subjected to law.

Judge

Witness

Courts and Trials

In many democracies, laws are written and passed by a legislature, and enforced by courts and police. People accused of crimes go to trial in a court of law. The U.S. system of justice is based on the idea that everyone is innocent until proven guilty. A prosecuting lawyer tries to prove that the defendant is guilty, while a defense lawyer opposes the arguments to protect the accused. A judge or jury considers both sets of arguments, then declares that person guilty or not guilty of the charges.

Jury of 12 (some have 6)

Defense attorney

Prosecuting attorneys

Defendant

In 450 B.C., the Romans established a court system in which judges decided whether a person had broken the law.

When a person is found guilty, the judge or jury decides what the **penalty** (punishment) will be. The guilty person may have to serve time in jail, pay a fine, or perform community service.

There are two main types of law: criminal and civil.

Criminal law protects citizens from people who commit serious offenses, such as robbery and murder.

Civil law deals with noncriminal disputes between people. It also ensures that business deals, such as buying a home, are handled fairly.

95

Literature and Writers

(see also ART AND ARTISTS ● COMMUNICATION ● DANCE ● FOLK TALES AND FAIRY TALES ● MOVIES AND TELEVISION ● MUSIC ● MYTHOLOGY ● RENAISSANCE ● THEATER ● WOMEN, FAMOUS)

Literature is the art of writing. Authors have used different forms of writing to describe their experiences—either imaginary or real. Literature can be fun, relaxing, and pleasurable. It can also teach us about the world.

Fiction

Fiction is writing that comes from an author's imagination. Sometimes the characters in fiction, and the things that happen to them, are based on real life, but most of what happens in works of fiction has been made up by the author. There are different kinds of works of fiction, including short stories, novels, plays, and poetry. A **short story** is a short piece of writing with a simple plot. A **novel** is a long story whose plot usually describes dramatic events in the lives of its characters. A **play,** or drama, is a story that is told through conversations between actors. Plays are written to be acted on a stage in front of an audience. *(See THEATER, pp. 162-163.)*

Poetry can be either fiction or nonfiction. In poetry, the writer tries to arouse the emotions of the reader. Poets often arrange their words using meter—a certain pattern and rhythm, as in music. Some poets also use rhyme, playing with words that have similar sounds.

Nonfiction

Nonfiction is writing that uses facts to examine or discuss real-life people, events, or concerns. There are various types of nonfiction, including essays, biographies and autobiographies, and histories. An **essay** is a piece of writing, usually brief, in which an author describes his or her point of view on a topic. An **autobiography** is the story of a person's life written by that person; a **biography** is the story of a person's life written by someone else. A **history** describes or explores events of the past.

Some Early Works of Literature

The Book of the Dead is a collection of writings from ancient Egypt that is considered one of the world's first works of literature. The earliest-known pieces were written on rolls of papyrus about 1580 to 1350 B.C. Buried with the mummies of the dead, these writings described spells and gave other tips to help the dead in their journey into the underworld.

The Bhagavad-Gita (BAHG-uh-vahd-GEET-uh) (India, 1st-2nd century A.D.) is a dramatic poem that explains some basic principles of India's Hindu religion. In the story, Lord Krishna, a god, gives advice to Prince Arjuna, who is preparing to go into battle.

Beowulf is the oldest **epic poem** (long verse) in English. Its manuscript is from A.D. 1000, but it was probably written in A.D. 700-750. It tells two stories about a hero named Beowulf. In the first story, he battles a monster named Grendel and Grendel's mother. In the second, he fights a dragon.

DID YOU KNOW . . . ?

One of the greatest honors that a writer can receive is the Nobel Prize for Literature, first awarded in 1901. The winners for the last two decades of the 20th century were:

1980: Czeslaw Milosz (Poland/U.S.)	1986: Wole Soyinka (Nigeria)	1993: Toni Morrison (U.S.)
1981: Elias Canetti (Bulgaria/U.K.)	1987: Joseph Brodsky (U.S.S.R/U.S.)	1994: Kenzaburo Oe (Japan)
1982: Gabriel García Márquez (Colombia)	1988: Naguib Mahfouz (Egypt)	1995: Seamus Heaney (Ireland)
1983: William Golding (U.K.)	1989: Camilo José Cela (Spain)	1996: Wislawa Szymborska (Poland)
1984: Jaroslav Seifert (Czechoslovakia)	1990: Octavio Paz (Mexico)	1997: Dario Fo (Italy)
1985: Claude Simon (France)	1991: Nadine Gordimer (South Africa)	1998: José Saramago (Portugal)
	1992: Derek Walcott (Trinidad)	1999: Günter Grass (Germany)

Some Famous Writers and Works of Literature

Homer
(Greece, about 9th-8th century B.C.)
His epic poems, the *Iliad* and the *Odyssey*, are counted among the greatest works of world literature.

Plutarch
(Greece, about A.D. 46-120
This biographer's most famous book, *Parallel Lives*, studies famous figures of ancient Greece and Rome.

Murasaki Shikibu
(Japan, about A.D. 978-1031)
Her book, *The Tale of Genji*, is considered one of the world's first novels. It tells the adventures of Genji, son of an emperor.

Dante Aligheri
(Italy, 1265-1321)
Poet who wrote *The Inferno*, one of the most famous epic (long) poems. It describes Dante's imaginary journey through Hell.

Geoffrey Chaucer
(England, about 1342-1400)
Author of *The Canterbury Tales*, stories of a band of travelers going to a famous cathedral. It shows us how people lived in the Middle Ages.

Montaigne
(France, 1533-1592)
His essays, which examined the people, ideas, and beliefs of his day, inspired and influenced many French and English writers.

Miguel de Cervantes
(Spain, 1547-1616)
Author of *Don Quixote*, considered the first great modern novel. It tells the story of an old dreamer who believes himself to be a daring knight.

Jane Austen
(England, 1775-1817)
Her novels—including *Emma* and *Pride and Prejudice*—use humor to point out the strengths and weaknesses of human nature.

Hans Christian Andersen
(Denmark, 1805-1875)
His fairy tales, known around the world, include "The Princess and the Pea," "The Ugly Duckling," and "The Emperor's New Clothes."

Edgar Allan Poe
(U.S., 1809-1849)
This poet and short-story writer is known as the first master of American Gothic (spooky) tales and as the originator of detective stories.

Charles Dickens
(England, 1812-1870)
This novelist's harsh childhood influenced his hugely famous books, which include *Oliver Twist*, *David Copperfield*, and *A Christmas Carol*.

Fyodor M. Dostoyevsky
(Russia, 1821-1881)
His dark, richly human novels—*Crime and Punishment*, *The Idiot*, and others—influenced generations of writers.

Lewis Carroll (Charles Lutwidge Dodgson) *(England, 1832-1898)*
This mathematician won fame for his children's books, *Alice's Adventures in Wonderland* and *Through the Looking-Glass*.

Mark Twain (Samuel Langhorne Clemens) *(U.S., 1835-1910)*
This humorist's piercing examinations of American culture include *Adventures of Huckleberry Finn* and *The Adventures of Tom Sawyer*.

Guy de Maupassant
(France, 1850-1893)
This short-story writer is considered to be one of the best writers of short fiction.

Lillian Hellman
(U.S., 1905-1984)
A noted playwright and screenwriter, she also won fame as a memoirist, for her books about her own life.

Ralph Ellison
(U.S., 1914-1994)
His novel *Invisible Man*, about the problems of a black man in white America, is one of the most respected works of 20th-century literature.

Gabriel García Márquez
(Colombia, 1928-   )
This Nobel Prize-winning novelist, known for a style called magical realism, is also widely honored as a short-story writer and journalist.

Anne Frank
(Germany, 1929-1945)
While hiding from Nazis, this Jewish teen wrote the world's most famous diary, published after her death.

Judy Blume
(U.S., 1938-   )
Her books are among the most well-known and widely translated young-adult literature of modern times.

Machines

(see also COMMUNICATION ● COMPUTERS ● ENERGY ● FLIGHT ● INVENTORS AND INVENTIONS ● TECHNOLOGY ● TRANSPORTATION)

Passenger helicopter

Model A Ford (1903)

Machines make difficult tasks easier by adjusting a force. A machine can be a simple device, such as a screw or a lever. But it can also be complex—a plane or bulldozer, for example. All machines need energy to work. Simple machines are powered by movement, with a force called an effort. Other machines, such as engines, are powered by other types of energy.

Giant earth-moving machine

Machines: Six Basic Types

There are six types of basic, simple machines: the lever, the screw, the wedge, the inclined plane, the pulley, and the wheel and axle. Simple machines are often used as parts of complex machines.

The Lever

Levers make it easier to move heavy loads. When you use a lever, a small effort goes a long way. A lever is a bar that needs a **fulcrum** (a pivot; the point of support or balance). When you push down on the part of the bar away from the fulcrum, the other end is raised. A small effort at one end moves a big load through a shorter distance at the other.

OPENING A STUCK WINDOW

Effort

Lever

Fulcrum

The Screw

A screw is a set of grooves around a shaft. When a screw is turned, the grooves move the entire screw around and down with greater force than the effort put into turning it.

Effort

Effort

Screw

Lift

The Wedge

A wedge makes it easier to split something apart. When a wedge is struck (or a wedge-shaped tool, such as an axe, is used) its shape increases the force of the blow. (The force of the blow—the effort—is multiplied by the length of the wedge. The longer and wider the wedge, the greater the splitting force.)

Effort

Wedge

The Inclined Plane

Less force is needed to push a load up a ramp or slope than to lift it straight up.

UGH!

Effort

Inclined plane

The Pulley

A pulley is a wheel or set of wheels that a rope or chain passes around to lift a heavy load. A pulley changes the direction of a force, so a person pulling down on a rope can lift a weight at the other end.

Effort

Pulley

Lift

The Wheel and Axle

When a wheel and axle turn together, the effort put into turning the wheel is transferred to the axle and magnified by it. The axle can lift a heavier weight than the wheel alone could lift.

Wheel *Effort*

Axle

I'M THIRSTY!

Using the Basics

Many of the tools we use every day are based on one or more of the six basic types of machines.

Effort

Levers *Fulcrum*

Effort

Lever

A pair of scissors is a lever-based tool: The bolt serves as a fulcrum. When the blades pivot around it, the effort of moving the handles is transferred to the blades, giving them more cutting power.

Screw + Inclined Plane

This machine uses both to pump water up a hill.

Wheel and Axle

The bicycle is an example of a wheel-and-axle machine. The effort the cycler puts into pedaling turns the wheels, which spin on axles that magnify the effort, giving power to go up hills or ride faster and farther.

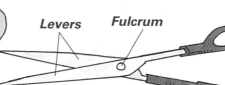

Effort

Matter

(see also AIR ● EARTH ● GEOLOGY ● MINING ● SCIENCE AND SCIENTISTS ● WATER)

WE ARE ALL IN IT TOGETHER.

Matter is every substance in the universe. It is anything that takes up space, and everything that exists is made of matter. Matter can be solid (like rock or wood), liquid (like water or oil), or gas (like air).

Matter can change from one state to another. For instance, rock is in liquid form (called magma) deep below Earth's surface.

Magma that flows out of a volcano is called lava. As it cools, it becomes solid rock.

Atoms

All matter is made of tiny particles called **atoms.** The core of each atom, which is called the **nucleus,** contains protons and neutrons. **Protons** carry a positive electric charge. **Neutrons** have no electric charge, but help hold the nucleus together. Negatively charged particles called **electrons** spin around the nucleus. The negative charge of the electrons and the positive charge of the proton hold the atom together.

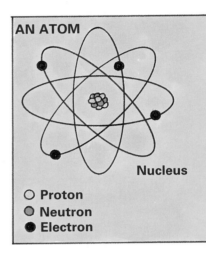

AN ATOM

Nucleus

○ Proton
◉ Neutron
● Electron

Elements

A substance made of atoms that all have the same number of protons is called an **element.** (For instance, iron, oxygen, hydrogen, calcium, and aluminum are all elements.) Each element has its own distinct qualities.

Molecules and Compounds

Atoms join together, forming **molecules.** When different kinds of atoms form molecules, it is called a **compound.** Water is an example of a compound: Each molecule of water is made of two hydrogen atoms joined with one oxygen atom. That is why the compound symbol for water is H_2O.

Oxygen atom

Hydrogen atoms

IT'S RAINING!

Iron

Solid iron being heated

Liquid

Solids

A solid is a substance that is somewhat rigid and has a definite size and shape. A solid's molecules are held tightly together by strong bonds. When a solid is heated, those bonds break up and the molecules spread out, turning the solid into a liquid.

Liquids

The molecules in liquids have enough space between each other to move about. That is why liquids flow and can change shape to fit whatever space they occupy. When a liquid is heated, its molecules move faster and faster, breaking up and moving farther apart, becoming a gas.

Gases

The molecules in gases are very far apart, and they move quickly. A gas cannot be seen, but it spreads out to fill all the space available to it. If a gas is cooled, its molecules slow down and clump closer together, becoming a liquid—or, if cold enough, a solid.

The Different States of Matter

Water is solid (ice) when its temperature is below 32° F.

OUCH! IT'S ALSO HARD!

Water is liquid when its temperature is between 32° and 212° F.

I'M MELTING.

Water turns to a gas (water vapor) when its temperature is higher than 212° F.

ARE YOU STILL THERE?

Measurements

(see also EARTH ● SCIENCE AND SCIENTISTS ● SPACE EXPLORATION ● TIME)

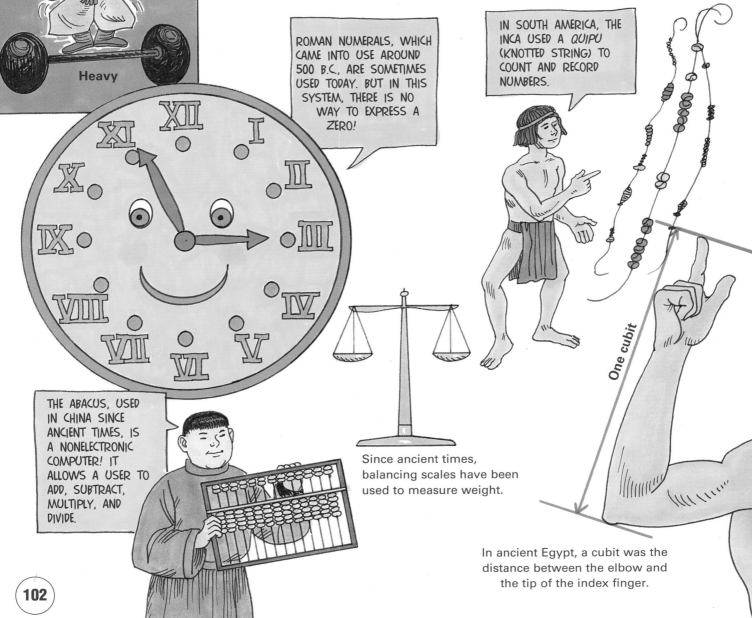

Wide
Tall
Hot
Cold
Heavy

To determine how wide, tall, hot, cold, or heavy something is, you need to measure it. Accurate measurements are needed in science and in such everyday activities as cooking. There are different types of instruments for measuring. In olden days, people used objects or their hands and feet to measure how long something was. Now a variety of different instruments is used in measuring length, width, volume, mass, and temperature.

Keeping count of things has always been important, too. People first used their fingers and toes, but eventually the Babylonians started to count using tally sticks—sticks with notches in them. In 200 B.C., Hindus used a system of counting based on ten. That system, the Hindu-Arabic system, was taken to Europe in the 10th century. It is the most popular numeric system used today.

ROMAN NUMERALS, WHICH CAME INTO USE AROUND 500 B.C., ARE SOMETIMES USED TODAY. BUT IN THIS SYSTEM, THERE IS NO WAY TO EXPRESS A ZERO!

IN SOUTH AMERICA, THE INCA USED A *QUIPU* (KNOTTED STRING) TO COUNT AND RECORD NUMBERS.

THE ABACUS, USED IN CHINA SINCE ANCIENT TIMES, IS A NONELECTRONIC COMPUTER! IT ALLOWS A USER TO ADD, SUBTRACT, MULTIPLY, AND DIVIDE.

Since ancient times, balancing scales have been used to measure weight.

One cubit

In ancient Egypt, a cubit was the distance between the elbow and the tip of the index finger.

102

The Metric and U.S. Customary Systems

Most of the world uses the metric system of measurement. The metric system, also known as the international system, was first used in France in 1795. This system uses meters to measure length, and grams to measure weight. Most countries and scientists use this system. The U.S., however, uses the U.S. customary system. It is based on the system used by the ancient Romans, and on the imperial system once used in Great Britain. The U.S. customary system uses feet and inches to measure length, and pounds and ounces to measure weight. (In the Roman system, one mile was 1,000 paces. In the U.S. customary system, one mile is 5,280 feet.)

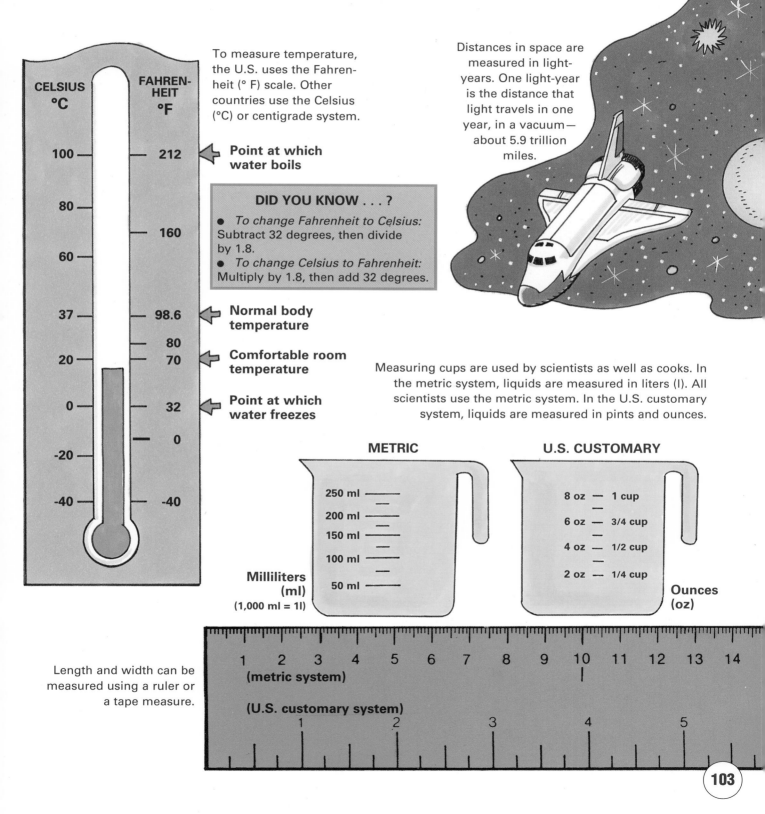

CELSIUS °C — FAHRENHEIT °F

To measure temperature, the U.S. uses the Fahrenheit (° F) scale. Other countries use the Celsius (°C) or centigrade system.

100 — 212 ◁ **Point at which water boils**

DID YOU KNOW . . . ?

● *To change Fahrenheit to Celsius:* Subtract 32 degrees, then divide by 1.8.
● *To change Celsius to Fahrenheit:* Multiply by 1.8, then add 32 degrees.

80 — 160

60 —

37 — 98.6 ◁ **Normal body temperature**

80
20 — 70 ◁ **Comfortable room temperature**

0 — 32 ◁ **Point at which water freezes**

0

-20 —

-40 — -40

Distances in space are measured in light-years. One light-year is the distance that light travels in one year, in a vacuum— about 5.9 trillion miles.

Measuring cups are used by scientists as well as cooks. In the metric system, liquids are measured in liters (l). All scientists use the metric system. In the U.S. customary system, liquids are measured in pints and ounces.

METRIC

250 ml
200 ml
150 ml
100 ml
50 ml

Milliliters (ml)
(1,000 ml = 1l)

U.S. CUSTOMARY

8 oz — 1 cup
6 oz — 3/4 cup
4 oz — 1/2 cup
2 oz — 1/4 cup

Ounces (oz)

Length and width can be measured using a ruler or a tape measure.

1 2 3 4 5 6 7 8 9 10 11 12 13 14
(metric system)

(U.S. customary system)
1 2 3 4 5

103

Medicine

(see also FOOD AND NUTRITION ● HEALTH AND FITNESS ● HUMAN BODY ● SCIENCE AND SCIENTISTS ● TECHNOLOGY)

In ancient times, many people thought that illness was a sign that the gods were punishing them. To cure the sick, some peoples sacrificed animals to please the gods; others practiced magic. In Greece during the 5th century B.C., a man named Hippocrates (hi-PAH-cruh-teez) determined that illnesses had causes that could be explained through nature. Hippocrates is considered the father of medicine—the science in which the body and mind are cared for, and in which diseases are prevented, diagnosed, and treated.

True scientific medicine began in the 1600s, when Anton van Leeuwenhoek discovered bacteria—tiny organisms that can cause illness. Since then, we have learned more about the human body. Research, especially during the 20th century, led to many life-saving discoveries. At the start of the 19th century, the average life expectancy was 37 years. By the end of the 20th century, it was 75 years!

Hippocrates

Great Events in Medicine

1796:
Edward Jenner (England) gives the first vaccination to prevent disease—in this case, smallpox. Smallpox, which once killed millions of people worldwide, now exists only in labs.

OUCH! BUT THE LITTLE PINCH IS WORTH IT.

1842:
First use of anesthesia: Crawford Long (U.S.), a surgeon, uses ether to kill pain when removing a patient's tumor.

I DIDN'T FEEL A THING!

1865:
Joseph Lister (England) begins the practice among doctors of washing their hands and sterilizing their instruments before surgery, and using antiseptics to kill bacteria.

NO BUGS CAN LIVE HERE!

1942:
Selman Waksman (U.S.) discovers the first antibiotic, used to fight tuberculosis. Today, antibiotics cure many once-fatal diseases.

WE'VE GOT THE BUGS ON THE RUN NOW.

1954:
The first successful organ transplant (of a kidney) is performed.

Heart
Stomach
Liver
Kidneys

1967:
Dr. Christiaan Barnard (South Africa) performs the first successful transplant of a human heart.

Keeping People Healthy

In addition to fighting disease, family doctors and community health programs work to keep people healthy. They emphasize regular checkups, immunizations (such as shots to prevent the flu), healthy living habits (including a sensible diet), and screening people who are at risk for certain illnesses (such as cancer).

In recent years, many people have turned to holistic medicine—a form of medicine based on the idea that the body and mind work together, so the whole person must be treated, rather than just a diseased part of the body. Ancient healing arts from Asia—such as acupuncture, the use of very thin needles to stimulate nerves—are also gaining acceptance in the West. So are treatments that use herbs and other plants.

GANGWAY! I'M ON AN EMERGENCY CALL.

EMS

Using laser surgery to improve eyesight is one of the many recent advances in medicine.

Some ancient methods of healing have been adopted by modern Western medicine. Acupuncture—applying very fine needles to certain body points—is one such practice.

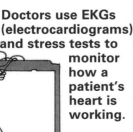

Doctors use EKGs (electrocardiograms) and stress tests to monitor how a patient's heart is working.

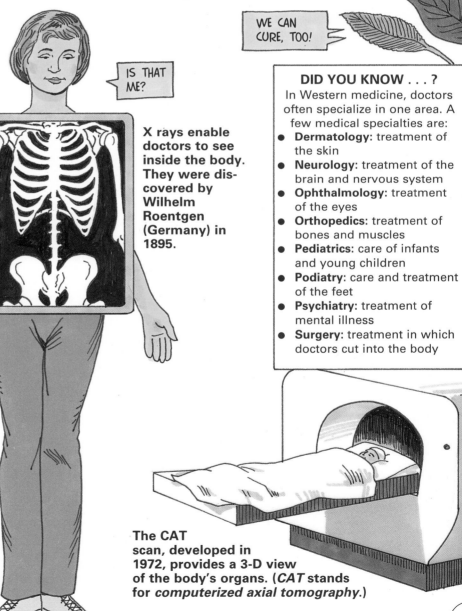

IS THAT ME?

X rays enable doctors to see inside the body. They were discovered by Wilhelm Roentgen (Germany) in 1895.

WE CAN CURE, TOO!

DID YOU KNOW . . . ?

In Western medicine, doctors often specialize in one area. A few medical specialties are:

- **Dermatology:** treatment of the skin
- **Neurology:** treatment of the brain and nervous system
- **Ophthalmology:** treatment of the eyes
- **Orthopedics:** treatment of bones and muscles
- **Pediatrics:** care of infants and young children
- **Podiatry:** care and treatment of the feet
- **Psychiatry:** treatment of mental illness
- **Surgery:** treatment in which doctors cut into the body

The CAT scan, developed in 1972, provides a 3-D view of the body's organs. (*CAT* stands for *computerized axial tomography*.)

Mining

(see also EARTH ● FOSSILS ● GEOLOGY ● MATTER)

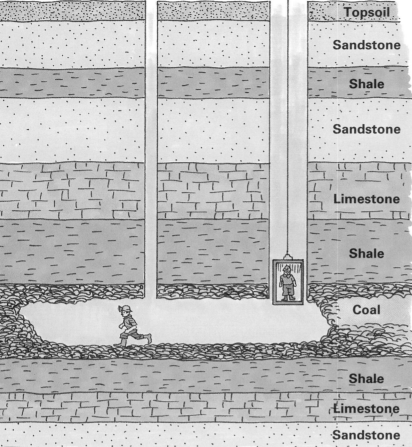

Topsoil

Sandstone

Shale

Sandstone

Limestone

Shale

Coal

Shale

Limestone

Sandstone

Miners are people who dig deep into the earth to remove resources, which we use in various ways. Mining provides us with many of the minerals (nonliving materials that make up Earth's crust) that we use every day, including iron, salt, silver, gold, copper, gemstones, and gravel (used in making concrete).

Coal is another resource that is mined. Coal is a fossil fuel, formed over thousands of years, that comes from the remains of once-living things. We burn coal as a source of heat and energy.

Miners must cut through multiple layers of earth and stone before they reach the mineral they want. The diagram at left is an example of a coal mine.

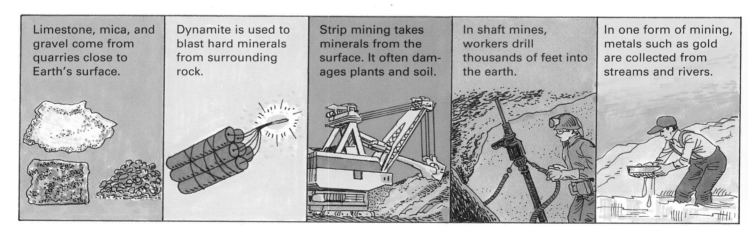

Limestone, mica, and gravel come from quarries close to Earth's surface.

Dynamite is used to blast hard minerals from surrounding rock.

Strip mining takes minerals from the surface. It often damages plants and soil.

In shaft mines, workers drill thousands of feet into the earth.

In one form of mining, metals such as gold are collected from streams and rivers.

Metals

Some metals, such as gold and copper, are found in a pure state—that is, not mixed with other elements. But most metals are found within rocks and minerals. A mineral mass that contains a large amount of a certain metal is called *ore*. Through various methods, metals can be **extracted** (taken out) from their ores and then used.

Diamonds, which can cut into very hard surfaces, are used in tools.

After being mined, diamonds, rubies, and sapphires are often cut, polished, and used for jewelry.

Money is anything that is used to pay for goods or services. Before people started using money, they bartered (traded) an object or a service for whatever they needed. Gold and silver were the most common early forms of money, but other items—such as cloth, feathers, stones, shells, and beads—have also been used as money. Today, money comes in many forms: coins, paper bills, checks, and credit cards. Different countries use different systems of money, or currency.

Money
(see also SOCIETY AND CULTURE)

I RECEIVE MY ALLOWANCE IN MONEY—AS LITTLE AS IT IS.

ASK FOR A RAISE.

Coins and Bills

Coins were probably first made around 600 B.C. in Lydia, in what is now Turkey. These coins were lumps of gold and silver stamped with a design. The use of coins soon spread into Europe. Paper money was first used in China, during the 11th century. Although the paper bills had no value themselves, they could be exchanged for gold when deposited in a bank. Most of Europe had adopted this system by the 1600s. The U.S. Mint produces all U.S. currency. It also prints and coins the currency of other nations.

Left: European Eurodollars
Above: U.S. dollar coin

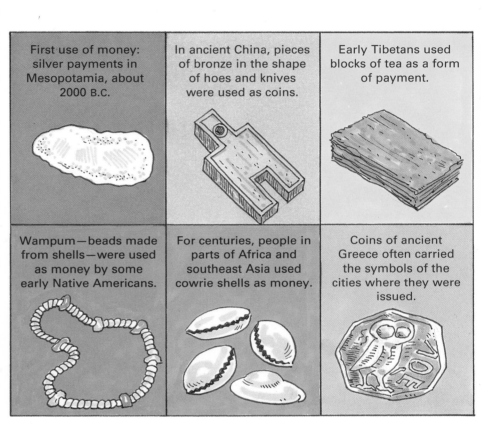

First use of money: silver payments in Mesopotamia, about 2000 B.C.

In ancient China, pieces of bronze in the shape of hoes and knives were used as coins.

Early Tibetans used blocks of tea as a form of payment.

Wampum—beads made from shells—were used as money by some early Native Americans.

For centuries, people in parts of Africa and southeast Asia used cowrie shells as money.

Coins of ancient Greece often carried the symbols of the cities where they were issued.

Some Types of Currency From Around the World

Money name*	Country**
deutsche mark	Germany
dinar	Algeria, Iraq, Kuwait; others
dollar	Australia, Belize, Fiji, Liberia, U.S.; others
franc	Belgium, Benin, France, Switzerland; others
lira	Italy, Turkey
peseta	Spain
peso	Dominican Republic, Mexico, Philippines; others
pound	Egypt, Ireland, Sudan, United Kingdom; others
ruble	Russia
rupee	India, Mauritius, Pakistan, Seychelles; others
shekel	Israel
yen	Japan
yuan	China
zloty	Poland

*A unit of money may have the same name in more than one country, but the bills and coins look different and have different values. For instance, an Australian dollar is not the same as a U.S. dollar.

**Many countries that are part of the European Community (EC) are switching to a new unit of currency called the euro.

Monuments

(see also ARCHITECTURE ● HOLIDAYS)

A monument is a landmark—natural or made by humans—that is of special historic or scenic interest. (The word *monument* comes from a Latin word meaning "to remind.") Some natural wonders are designated as monuments because they are rare or interesting, such as Devils Tower, in Wyoming. Others are designated as monuments to honor someone, such as the Muir Woods in northern California, a forest of giant redwood trees named for John Muir, the conservationist who worked to conserve them. Monuments are protected against change or harm.

Devils Tower (Wyoming): This natural rock tower, 865 feet high, was named the first U.S. national monument in 1906.

A giant redwood can live more than 2,000 years.

Mount Rushmore (South Dakota): The faces of four U.S. presidents, 50-70 feet tall, were carved into a mountainside by sculptor Gutzon Borglum.

Some monuments are created to honor people or events. These monuments may be buildings, pillars, tombs, sculptures, or statues. Governments often build monuments to honor important people or events in that country's history. For instance, Canada's Cabot Tower was built in 1898-1900 to honor the Diamond Jubilee (75th anniversary) of Britain's Queen Victoria as well as explorer John Cabot.

Cabot Tower, Signal Hill (St. John's, Canada): Marconi received the first transatlantic radio signal on this hill in 1901.

Lincoln Memorial (Washington, D.C.): The vast, open-air hall contains a huge marble statue of the 16th U.S. president.

Some Famous Monuments of the World

The Parthenon
The Parthenon, a marble temple, was built nearly 2,500 years ago to honor the goddess Athena. This famous ruin stands on the Acropolis, a high point of land in the city of Athens, Greece.

Easter Island statues
These huge faces, carved from stone, stand on Easter Island, in the South Pacific Ocean west of Chile. Some of the statues are as tall as 65 feet and stand on 10-foot high platforms. No one knows what the huge faces symbolize or how they got there.

The Eiffel Tower
This iron-framework tower, 984 feet tall (and topped by a 67-foot antenna), has become a national symbol of France. It was designed by engineer Alexandre Gustave Eiffel and built for the Paris Exposition of 1889. The Eiffel Tower was the first structure of its time to be built with steel beams, which led to the construction of skyscrapers.

The Great Pyramid
This structure is a huge tomb that was built at Giza, Egypt, for the pharaoh Khufu (also known as Cheops) about 2600 B.C. It is the only one of the Seven Wonders of the Ancient World that still exists today.

The Great Sphinx
This is an immense stone sculpture that was built at Giza, Egypt. A sphinx is a mythical beast with a human head and a lion's body.

The Great Wall of China
This wall, which is close to 4,160 miles long, was built more than 2,000 years ago to protect China's borders from enemies. It is the only man-made structure that can be seen from space.

The Taj Mahal
This huge, white-marble mausoleum (tomb), with gardens and pools, was built in 17th-century India by Shah Jahan, for his wife, Arjumand Banu Begam (also known as Mumtaz Mahal). It took 20,000 workers 22 years to build.

Movies and Television

(see also ANIMATION ● ART AND ARTISTS ● COMMUNICATION ● DANCE ● INVENTIONS AND INVENTORS ● MUSIC ● TECHNOLOGY ● THEATER)

Moving images have been part of our culture since cameras were invented in the 1800s. Through movies and television, we watch stories unfold, follow the lives of people real and fictional, and learn about every topic under the sun.

A movie is a . . . long strip of . . . thousands of still . . . pictures called frames . . . projected one after . . . the other. This . . . is done so fast (about . . . 24 frames per . . . second) that the picture . . . seems to be moving! (That is where . . . the term *movies* . . . came from!)

FILMING OF THE MOVIE *MAYBLOSSOM* (1917)

Overhead lights

Spotlight

Props

Camera

Scenery

Lighting technician

Director

Camera operator

Producer

Grip (stagehand)

Actors

Gaffer (lighting electrician)

Key Developments in Movie History

1894: Thomas Edison introduces the kinetoscope. It shows brief films that can be seen by only one person at a time.

1895: Auguste and Louis Lumière are the first to project moving pictures to an audience.

MOVING PICTURE SHOWING TODAY!

1903: *The Great Train Robbery*, the first movie to tell an original story, is released.

1911: The first film studio opens in the little town of Hollywood, California. (Till then, the film industry was in New York and New Jersey.)

THE NESTOR COMPANY

THIS IS THE FIRST MOTION PICTURE STUDIO IN HOLLYWOOD! I WANT TO AUDITION FOR A PART AND BECOME A BIG STAR.

1927: *The Jazz Singer* is the first full-length "talkie," or sound film. Earlier films were silent.

I HOPE SHE DOESN'T SIT IN FRONT OF ME!

Television

TV cameras use lenses to pick up the light and color of an image. Each image falls onto light-sensitive tubes and is turned into electrical signals. The signals are then transmitted (sent) as radio waves—either UHF (ultrahigh frequency) or VHF (very high frequency) radio waves—or by underground cables. Signals may also be transmitted by a satellite orbiting Earth, which beams the signal to a receiving dish or antenna. When a TV set receives the signals, it changes them back into images, which appear on the screen.

A TELEVISION BROADCAST

1926:
Inventor John Logie Baird (England) demonstrates the first true television.

1940s:
U.S. families begin buying TV sets. (They are big wooden boxes with small screens.)

1951:
President Harry S. Truman gives a televised speech—the first transcontinental TV broadcast.

1970s:
Videocassette recorders (VCRs) become popular for taping TV programs and watching movies on tape.

111

Mummies

(see also ANCIENT CIVILIZATIONS ● ARCHAEOLOGY)

A mummy is a corpse, or dead body, that has been dried out and precisely treated so it will not decay. Sometimes, mummification occurs naturally, such as in peat bogs or in ice. In some ancient societies, however, it was done on purpose.

The people of ancient Egypt believed that the dead moved on to another world. They preserved bodies to help the dead live forever in the next world. At first, they mummified bodies by burying them in the hot, dry desert sand. But later, they learned ways of **embalming** (specially treating a body) so the bodies would last a very long time. Quite a few mummies of ancient Egypt survive today—mostly in museums.

John Torrington's mummy
British sailor (found near South Pole)

Man
2,000 years old
(found in Denmark)

Woman
(found in Chile)

Tollund Man
2,000 years old
(found in Denmark)

DID YOU KNOW . . . ?

Naturally mummified bodies of people who died long ago have been found in peat bogs, glaciers, and on snowy mountaintops.

Embalming

Embalm means to treat a dead body so that it will not decay. The ancient Egyptians had various ways of embalming bodies, but all contained the same basic steps. First, all internal organs—except the heart—were removed. The lungs, stomach, and intestines were removed through a slit in the side of the body, and the brain was pulled out through a hole in the skull (sometimes, through the nostrils!). These organs were wrapped in strips of cloth and put into jars with special chemicals, which prevented decay, for several weeks.

The inside of the corpse was stuffed with aromatic herbs, powders, and other materials to dry it out. The body was soaked in chemicals for several weeks. It was then cleaned and wrapped in strips of preservative-soaked cloth. Finally, the head was covered with a mask, and another shroud covered the whole body. The body was placed in a coffin, and the coffin was placed in a tomb.

Internal organs (except the heart) were placed in herb-filled vases called canopic jars.

Burial

All Egyptians were mummified. However, the richer the person, the more elaborate the preservation and burial. **Pharaohs** (kings) were thought to become gods after they died, so they were buried with riches, gems, and treasure.

Amulets (charms) were often tucked between layers of linen that covered the bodies of wealthy people.

After being wrapped, a mummy was placed in one or more coffins. The rich were placed in three different coffins, one inside the other, then into a sarcophagus (sar-KOFF-uh-gus). The sarcophagus—a large stone coffin—was often decorated in gold and painted with gods, goddesses, and hieroglyphics.

To keep fortune hunters from raiding the treasure-filled tombs of the pharaohs, Egyptians began to bury their kings in hidden chambers in tombs at a secret location called the Valley of the Kings.

A pharaoh was buried with statues of himself, as well as jewelry, gold, and other treasures. The walls were painted with scenes of everyday life. The tomb was like a home for the mummy.

King Tut

In 1922, Howard Carter, a British archaeologist, found and opened the long-hidden tomb of Tutankhamen, boy-king of ancient Egypt. Among the many treasures found in the tomb was the mummy of Tut, the pharaoh who died in 1323 B.C., at age 17. The mummy lay inside the smallest of three coffins—each one sitting inside a slightly larger one. All three coffins had been placed inside a stone sarcophagus. The mummy's face was covered with a mask of solid gold, and its neck and chest were draped in a collar made of glass beads, semiprecious stones, bund flowers.

113

Music

(see also ART AND ARTISTS ● DANCE ● MOVIES AND TELEVISION ● RENAISSANCE ● SOCIETY AND CULTURE ● THEATER)

Music is the art of arranging sounds in a pattern in time. Music probably started as chanting by prehistoric people. People originally sang and played musical instruments to honor gods, and music remains a part of most religious ceremonies. Music also is a popular form of art or entertainment. Although traditional and other forms of music vary from culture to culture, there also are many striking similarities.

Making Music

A **composer** (someone who writes music) uses four main "tools" to make music: **pitch** (how high or low the sound is), **volume** (how loud or soft the sound is), **rhythm** (the timing of the sound), and **tone** (the quality of the sound).

Each musical **note** is the particular sound created when air—in a voice or an instrument—is vibrated. A **scale** is a series of notes—usually seven—that increases in pitch in a step-by-step pattern. When musical notes are played in a certain order at a particular pitch and rhythm, it creates **melody**—a pattern that we find memorable, especially when singing the words to a favorite song. **Harmony** is produced when two or more notes of a different pitch are played at the same time.

Types of Musical Instruments

WOODWINDS
Blowing into a woodwind instrument—a flute, clarinet, or saxophone, for example—vibrates air within a tube, making sound. Musicians play notes by using their fingers or keypads to cover and uncover specific holes in that tube.

BRASS
Blowing into the mouthpiece of a brass instrument—such as a trumpet, tuba, or trombone—makes sound. Musicians control the sound with their lips, which make different vibrations, and by squeezing valves or moving slides, which affect the way air flows through the instrument's tube.

Music Around the World

People make music in every country and every culture around the world. No matter where you go, there are great similarities in music, as well as fascinating differences.

AFRICA
- Tamani (talking drum)
- Mbira (thumb piano)
- Kora

SOUTH AMERICA
- Bandoneon
- Charango
- Samponas

CELTIC EUROPE
- Uilleann (Irish bagpipes)
- Bagpipes (Scottish)

ABORIGINAL AUSTRALIA
- Didgeridoos (of various styles)
- Didgeridoos with different bends make different sounds.

ASIA
- Samisen (Japan)
- Sitar (India)

I LOVE ALL KINDS OF MUSIC!

DID YOU KNOW . . . ? The word *music* comes from *mousikos*, a Greek word meaning "of the Muses." The Muses were nine sister goddesses whom the ancient Greeks believed responsible for inspiring creativity in all the arts and sciences.

STRINGS

String instruments create different sounds when a musician plucks, strokes, or strums their strings. Different widths and lengths of string make higher or deeper pitches. A bow is used to play the violin and the cello; guitar and harp strings are plucked or strummed.

PERCUSSION

Percussion instruments are struck or shaken to create rhythm as well as sound. Drums, xylophones, triangles, and other percussion instruments help other band members keep time.

PIANO

The piano uses strings as well as percussion to make musical sounds. A pianist strikes a piano's keys, which moves small, felt-covered hammers (percussion). The hammers hit tightly stretched wires (strings), producing the notes.

115

Mythology

(see also ANCIENT CIVILIZATIONS ● ANCIENT EMPIRES ● FOLK AND FAIRY TALES ● LITERATURE AND WRITERS ● RELIGIONS ● SOCIETY AND CULTURE)

DID YOU KNOW . . . ?

Many cultures have similar myths. There are many myths about wind, rain, the moon, and the sun. In Egypt, the sun god's name was Ra. In India, it was Surya, who rode a chariot across the sky. In Greece, Helios was the chariot-riding sun god.

In Celtic mythology, female goddesses were usually identified with nature.

During the Zhou dynasty of ancient China, the people worshipped T'ien (heaven) as the Supreme Being.

People have always been awed by the world and asked questions about it—wondering how it began, why seasons change, and what makes stars and the sun shine. Myths grew out of people's attempts to explain these mysteries. Mythology is a type of literature that describes and explains nature and the world. Its stories about **mortals** (regular humans) and **deities** (gods and goddesses) are a mix of realistic details and fantasy. The first myths were handed down **orally** (by word of mouth). Later, they were written down. Mythology is a type of folk literature: It tells us a great deal about how people once lived and what they believed.

Greek goddess Athena

Classical Mythology

Ancient Greeks and Romans worshipped many gods and goddesses. The city of Athens was named after the Greek goddess Athena, protector of cities and heroes. The Greeks believed that gods and goddesses lived atop Mount Olympus, led by Zeus, god of the sky, and Hera, goddess of the sky. In Roman mythology, the chief god is called Jupiter, and the chief goddess is called Juno.

Roman god Mercury

DID YOU KNOW . . . ?

Seven of the nine planets in our solar system were named for Roman deities: **Mercury** (god of trade and travelers), **Venus** (goddess of love), **Mars** (god of war), **Jupiter** (ruler of the gods), **Saturn** (god of agriculture), **Neptune** (god of the sea), and **Pluto** (god of the underworld). **Uranus** was named for the Greeks' god of the sky.

116

Wind and Weather

Quetzalcoatl (ket-SAHL-kwat-ul) was the plumed serpent and most important god of the Aztec, an ancient civilization of Mexico. The Aztec believed that Quetzalcoatl was responsible for the winds, which brought the rain and other weather.

In myths of the ancient Romans, thunder was the god Vulcan, a metalworker, pounding metal at his furnace. In Viking (Norse) myths, thunder was the god Thor, who threw his magic hammer at enemies. In myths told by the Iroquois, a Native American people, thunder came when the chief thunderbird flapped its wings; lightning flashed from its eyes.

Aztec god
Quetzalcoatl

Roman god
Vulcan

Creation Myths

Many cultures have stories that explain how the world came into being, or how the first people appeared. In a myth of ancient India, human beings and the universe were formed from the parts of one original being. In Babylonian myth, a god named Marduk divided the ocean to form earth and sky. In some Native American cultures, supernatural animals were the world's first inhabitants. In an ancient Norse myth, the first living things were a giant named Ymir and a cow named Audhumla.

Anubis was a jackal-headed god honored by the people of ancient Egypt. They believed that Anubis led the souls of dead people to judgment in the under-world.

Ymir and
Audhumla

Egyptian god Anubis

117

Native Americans

(see also NORTH AMERICA ● SOUTH AMERICA ● UNITED STATES ● UNITED STATES HISTORY ● WOMEN, FAMOUS)

People from northern Asia crossed the Bering Strait to North America 20,000 to 30,000 years ago, using a land bridge that no longer exists. They settled all over North and South America, long before people arrived from Europe, and formed civilizations that became known as Indian, or Native American. The arrival of Europeans, which began in the 15th century, almost destroyed these civilizations. European diseases ravaged native populations, who had no defenses against the new germs. Waves of European settlers forced Native Americans off their traditional homelands. Beginning in the 1780s, the U.S. government began moving them onto reservations.

Varied Ways of Life

When European settlers arrived, some tribes were living mainly as farmers, raising corn, squash, and other crops. Others lived mainly by hunting and fishing. Some tribes of the Great Plains were always on the move, following huge herds of buffalo. The type of shelter Native Americans built depended on where and how they lived. For instance, the Navajo of the Southwest lived in earth-covered homes called hogans, while the neighboring Pueblo had houses made of sun-baked adobe brick. The Iroquois of the Northeast lived in longhouses covered by tree bark, while the nomadic Sioux of the Plains lived in tipis made of buffalo hides. Many other traditions and beliefs distinguish each tribe from the others.

Native Americans Today

There are now about 2 million Native Americans living in the U.S.; about one third live on reservations. In the 1970s, many tribes again started fighting for their rights, including getting back their original land. Present-day tribes govern themselves. Some have developed successful ways of improving their economies, including running gambling casinos, developing natural resources on their lands, and opening scenic areas of their lands to tourists.

DID YOU KNOW . . . ?
When Christopher Columbus arrived in the Americas in 1492, he mistakenly believed that he had reached India, in Asia. That is why Europeans began referring to the natives as Indians.

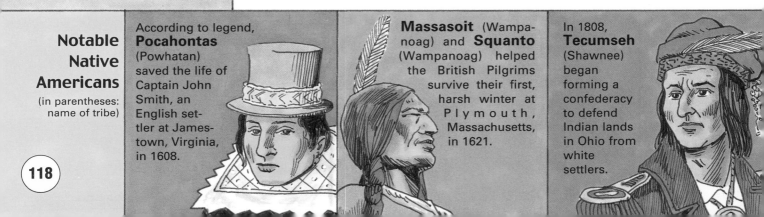

Notable Native Americans
(in parentheses: name of tribe)

According to legend, **Pocahontas** (Powhatan) saved the life of Captain John Smith, an English settler at Jamestown, Virginia, in 1608.

Massasoit (Wampanoag) and **Squanto** (Wampanoag) helped the British Pilgrims survive their first, harsh winter at Plymouth, Massachusetts, in 1621.

In 1808, **Tecumseh** (Shawnee) began forming a confederacy to defend Indian lands in Ohio from white settlers.

Some Tribes of North America

Snowshoe

GREENLAND (KALAALLIT NUNAAT) (Denmark)

In the 17th and 18th centuries, many tribes of northeastern U.S. and Canada sold animal skins and furs to Europeans.

Bering Sea

Eskimo

Koyukon

Ingalik

Aleut

Yuit

Kutchin

Eyak

Tlingit totem pole

Pacific Ocean

Tlingit

Nootka

Beaufort Sea

Hare

Tutchone

Yellowknife

Kaska

Carrier

Beaver

Caribou

Chipewyan

Baffin Bay

Inuit

Inuit

Baffinland Inuit

Labrador Sea

Labrador Inuit

Naskapi

Hudson Bay

Cree

Cree

The Chinook were skilled at fishing, as well as at the carving of totem poles and masks.

Chinook

Tlingit

Blackfeet

Nez Percé

Flathead

Crow

Shoshone

Ojibway

Winnebago

Sioux

Fox

Kickapoo

Cheyenne

Chippewa

Algonquin

Cree

Huron

Erie

Seneca

Cree

Iroquois

Mohican

Iroquois

Massachuset

Peace pipe

Kachina doll of the Hopi

Papoose carrier

Drill

Smoke signal

Hupa

Hopi

Navajo

Mohave

Papago

Apache

Yaqui

Mayo

Arapaho

Comanche

Pueblo

Illinois

Shawnee

Cherokee

Creek

Tunica

Apalachee

Pueblo adobe village

Gulf of Mexico

Iroquois lacrosse racket

Delaware

Powhatan

Atlantic Ocean

Seminole

Calusa

Blowgun

War club

Indian standard (flag)

Tepecano

Toltec

Aztec

Zapotec

Maya

Symbolic writing

Miskito

Cuna

Paddle

Birch-bark canoe

Tipi

Roundhouse

Sequoya (Cherokee) developed a written alphabet for the Cherokee language. Starting in 1828, it was used in a newspaper, the *Cherokee Phoenix*.

Sitting Bull (Hunkpapa Sioux), a spiritual leader of his people, was one of the chiefs who defeated General George Armstrong Custer's cavalry at the 1876 Battle of the Little Bighorn.

In 1877, **Chief Joseph** (Nez Percé) led his people on a trek of about 1,500 miles through Oregon, Idaho, Wyoming, and Montana to avoid life on a reservation.

Navigation

(see also EXPLORERS AND EXPLORATION ● GEOGRAPHY ● INVENTORS AND INVENTIONS ● TECHNOLOGY)

Navigation is the science of determining the location of a vessel in water, air, or space, and charting its course from one point to another.

Long ago, the first explorers had little knowledge of what existed outside their homelands. When they traveled, they had no maps, charts, or computer equipment to guide them. To find their way, they relied on *celestial navigation*, which means that they looked at the positions of the stars, the moon, and the sun. Today, thanks to the work of scientists, inventors, explorers, ocean surveyors, and technology experts, we have highly sophisticated maps, radar, computers, satellites and other electronic systems to guide us—whether we travel by land, sea, or air.

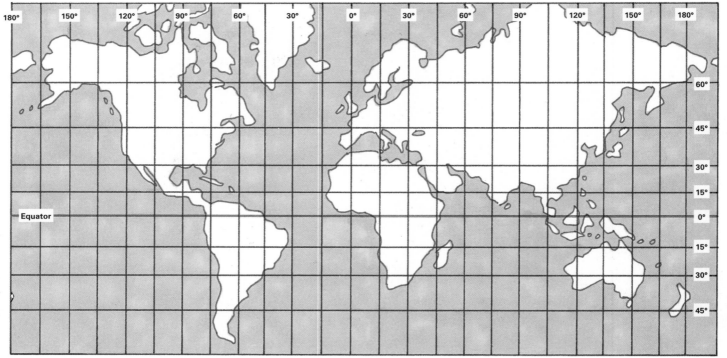

Most of the world's surface has been surveyed, so today's airplane pilots and sailors can have charts and maps for almost any place on Earth.

NOW I KNOW WHERE I AM!

Mapmakers use vertical lines called **longitude** and horizontal lines called **latitude** to pinpoint the location of a particular place.

Piloting

Piloting is a type of navigation in which sailors and pilots use landmarks—natural or man-made—to guide their vessels. This is not the most reliable form of navigation, because fogs and storms can prevent people from seeing clearly. But coastal lighthouses have helped sailors for hundreds of years. Their powerful signal beams cut through fog, helping sailors avoid obstacles such as rocks and other boats, and see their way safely to port. Buoys are also very useful. They are floating markers that show a safe course and indicate areas to avoid. Sailors and fishing-boat crews also keep track of winds, currents, storms, and tides.

Navigational Equipment

Compass
One of the earliest navigational instruments, the compass has a magnetic needle that points toward Earth's magnetic pole. This helps travelers figure out whether they are heading north, south, east, or west.

Sextant
A navigation instrument developed in the 1700s, the sextant measures the angle between the horizon and an object in the sky. This helps a navigator figure out a vessel's position.

Radios
They provide weather reports, navigational warnings, and other information. Signals received from radio transmitters help a navigator determine the position and direction of ships or aircraft.

Radar scanners
These beam out radio waves and pick up echoes that bounce off nearby obstacles, so ships or aircraft can avoid collisions.

Space satellites
These bounce radio signals from Earth back to various locations, helping aircraft and ships calculate where they are.

North America

(see also AFRICAN AMERICANS ● FESTIVALS ● NATIVE AMERICANS ● NORTH AMERICAN WILDLIFE ● RAIN FORESTS ● UNITED STATES ● UNITED STATES HISTORY ● WORLD)

North America is the world's third-largest continent. It consists of Greenland, Canada, the United States, Mexico, the region called Central America (Belize, Guatemala, Honduras, El Salvador, Nicaragua, Costa Rica, and Panama), and islands in the Caribbean Sea. The terrain of North America's 9.4 million square miles ranges from permanently frozen earth in northern Canada and Greenland to tropical rain forests in Central America. In between, there are dry prairies, hot deserts, and woodlands. North America has immense mountain ranges: the Rocky Mountains in the west, and the Appalachian Mountains in the east.

People

There are now 460 million people living in North America. English and Spanish are the languages most commonly spoken. The original North Americans—Native Americans—were people who arrived from Asia about 20,000 to 30,000 years ago.

WE ARE ALL AMERICANS!

Many other North Americans are descended from European settlers who arrived hundreds of years ago seeking religious freedom or economic opportunity.

Millions of Europeans immigrated to North America in the 19th and 20th centuries, searching for freedom and opportunity. Other North Americans come from all over the world—Asia, Africa, and Oceania, as well as South America. English is the dominant language in Canada and the U.S.; French is spoken in part of Canada. Spanish is the dominant language in Mexico and Central America, where many people have Spanish ancestors. Others are mestizo (of mixed European and Native American heritage), have Portuguese or African ancestors, or are direct descendants of the region's original (Native American) inhabitants.

DID YOU KNOW . . . ?
The name *America* honors Amerigo Vespucci (1454-1512), an Italian navigator. He made several voyages to the New World—including the 1499-1500 expedition that first "discovered" mainland North America. (Columbus's 1492 voyage reached Caribbean islands.)

NICE TO MEET YOU!

ARCTIC OCEAN

Bering Strait

Alaska (U.S.)

MT. McKINLEY (20,320 ft) Highest point in North America

Arctic Circle

CANADA HAS VAST RESERVES OF COAL, OIL, NATURAL GAS, AND TIMBER.

ROCKY MTS.

UNITED STATES

ROCKY MTS.

Missouri River

NORTH AMERICA'S LARGEST RIVER SYSTEM IS THE MISSISSIPPI-MISSOURI!

PACIFIC OCEAN

Rio Grande R.

SIERRA MADRE OCCIDENTAL

Gulf of California

MEXICO

SIERRA MADRE DEL SUR

Greenland Sea

GREENLAND (KALAALLIT NUNAAT) (Denmark)

NORTH AMERICA

Baffin Bay

Davis Strait

Hudson Bay

Labrador Sea

CANADA

Lake Superior is the world's largest freshwater lake.

APPALACHIAN MTS.

Mississippi River

BERMUDA (U.K.)

ATLANTIC OCEAN

Gulf of Mexico

BAHAMAS

Bay of Campeche

CUBA

HAITI DOMINICAN REPUBLIC

PUERTO RICO (U.S.)

ST. KITT & NEVIS

ANTIGUA & BARBUDA

JAMAICA Caribbean Sea

DOMINICA ST. LUCIA BARBADOS

ST. VINCENT & THE GRENADINES

GRENADA

TRINIDAD & TOBAGO

BELIZE

HONDURAS

NICARAGUA

Rain forest

Panama Canal

FARMING IS CENTRAL AMERICA'S MAJOR INDUSTRY.

GUATEMALA

EL SALVADOR

COSTA RICA

PANAMA

SOUTH AMERICA

MAJOR CROPS INCLUDE COFFEE, BANANAS, SUGAR, AND COTTON.

LAND USE

Canada
Farmable: 5%
Forests/woodland: 54%
Permanent pastures: 3%
Other: 38%

United States
Farmable: 19%
Forests/woodland: 30%
Permanent pastures: 25%
Other: 26%

Mexico
Farmable: 12%
Forests/woodland: 26%
Permanent pastures: 39%
Other: 23%

123

North American Wildlife

(see also ANIMAL KINGDOM ● DESERTS ● ECOSYSTEMS ● ENVIRONMENT ● FORESTS ● NORTH AMERICA ● RAIN FORESTS ● TREES ● ZOOS)

From the northern tundra of Canada to the tropical forests of Central America, North America contains a huge variety of plant and animal life. Although human settlement and pollution have caused many species to die out, conservation has enabled some endangered species to hang on and has enabled others to make a comeback. Comeback-success stories include the bald eagle, the gray wolf, and the California sea otter.

Animals of Southern Canada and Northern U.S.

Animals of Alaska, Canada, and Greenland

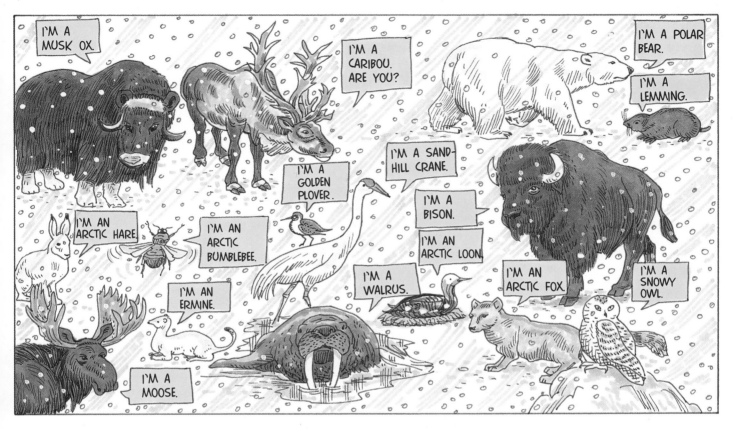

Animals of Southern U.S., Mexico, and Central America

Oceans and Sea Life

(see also ANIMAL KINGDOM ● EARTH ● ECOSYSTEMS ● ENVIRONMENT ● GEOLOGY ● WATER ● ZOOS)

Water covers 71 percent of Earth's surface. About 97 percent of the planet's water is salt water (also called seawater), contained in the oceans. The four oceans are the Arctic, Atlantic, Indian, and Pacific. (The Pacific is the largest ocean; the Arctic is the smallest.) Ocean water contains salt and many other minerals from rocks that have worn down over time. Oceans are bursting with fish, plants, and many other kinds of life.

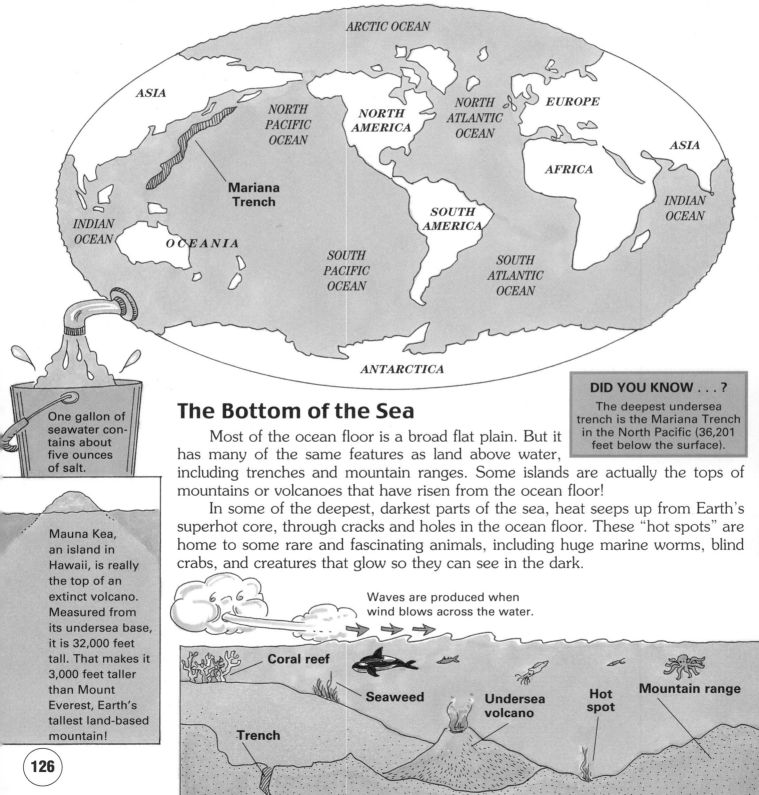

One gallon of seawater contains about five ounces of salt.

Mauna Kea, an island in Hawaii, is really the top of an extinct volcano. Measured from its undersea base, it is 32,000 feet tall. That makes it 3,000 feet taller than Mount Everest, Earth's tallest land-based mountain!

The Bottom of the Sea

Most of the ocean floor is a broad flat plain. But it has many of the same features as land above water, including trenches and mountain ranges. Some islands are actually the tops of mountains or volcanoes that have risen from the ocean floor!

In some of the deepest, darkest parts of the sea, heat seeps up from Earth's superhot core, through cracks and holes in the ocean floor. These "hot spots" are home to some rare and fascinating animals, including huge marine worms, blind crabs, and creatures that glow so they can see in the dark.

DID YOU KNOW . . . ?
The deepest undersea trench is the Mariana Trench in the North Pacific (36,201 feet below the surface).

Waves are produced when wind blows across the water.

Coral reef
Seaweed
Undersea volcano
Hot spot
Mountain range
Trench

Sea Life

The ocean is filled with some of the most fascinating wildlife in the world. Tiny plants and animals called plankton are food for tiny fish, mollusks, and corals. Larger fish eat the smaller fish.

In deep waters, whales, dolphins, squids, and octopus lurk. Sleek seals and walruses glide about in waters near their homes on shore. Most of the ocean's animals and fish can be found in shallow waters. Coral reefs, formed in shallow tropical waters, are created by sea animals that build huge skeletons that join together. Here, the most beautiful and brightly colored tropical fish are found.

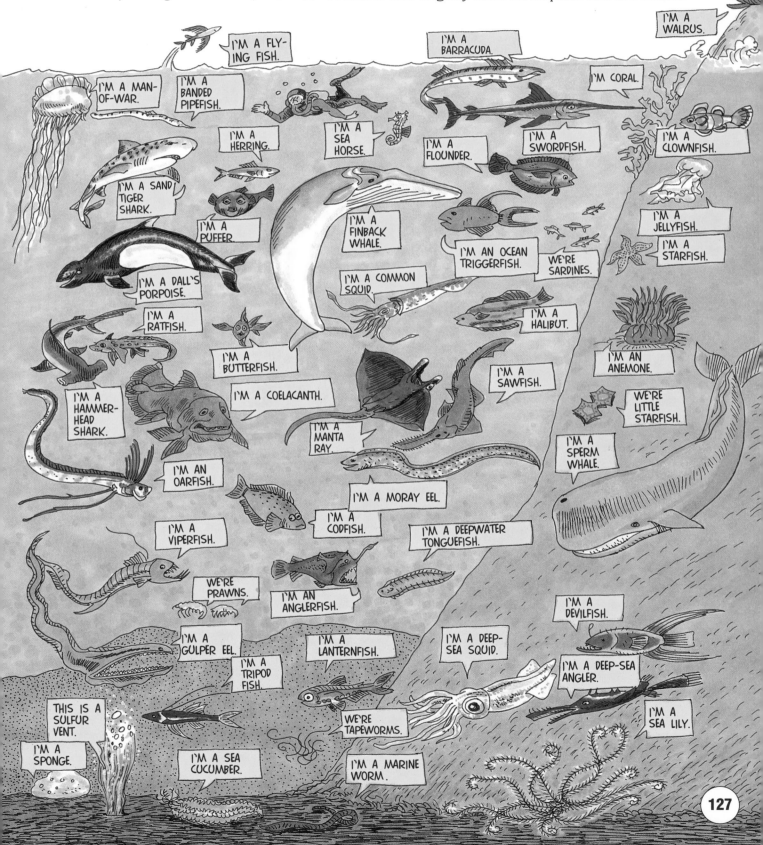

127

Olympics

(see also SPORTS
● WOMEN, FAMOUS)

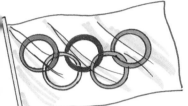

The Olympic Games are an international sports competition. Every four years, athletes from around the world compete in either the Summer or Winter Olympic Games, each taking place in a different city. About 10,000 athletes from 200 nations take part.

The first Olympic Games were held in Olympia, Greece, in 776 B.C. They were part of a festival that honored Zeus, chief of the Greek gods. The ancient games were held every four years for 1,000 years—until A.D. 393, when they were canceled by a Roman emperor. That was the end of the Olympics until a French sportsman and educator, Baron Pierre de Coubertin (1863–1937), convinced a group of leading countries to bring back the Games. In 1896, the first modern Olympic Games were held in Athens, Greece. It took several years before the games became a successful world event. The Winter Olympics were introduced in 1924, in Chamonix, France. Olympic athletes who place first in their events win a gold medal; second-place winners receive silver medals, and third-place winners receive bronze medals.

DID YOU KNOW . . . ?
The five rings on the Olympic flag represent five geographic areas: Europe, Asia, Africa, Australia, and the Americas.

A discus thrower of ancient Greece

Jesse Owens (U.S.) was a hero in 1936, winning four gold track-and-field medals in the 1936 Olympics, in Berlin.

Muhammad Ali (U.S.), then called Cassius Clay, won a 1960 Olympic gold in boxing as a light-heavyweight. In 1996, he returned to the Olympics, to light the Olympic flame at the opening ceremony.

The amazing Paavo Nurmi (Finland), known as the Flying Finn, won both the 5,000- and 10,000-meter track events, in 1924 in Paris.

Olympic Ceremonies

Four weeks before each Olympics start, the Olympic flame is lit in Greece, then carried—by many different athletes—from there to the host country. On opening day, the last athlete runs into the stadium and lights a huge torch. This flame, a symbol of "keeping alive the flame of the revived Olympic spirit," burns until closing day. Opening-day ceremonies also include a "parade of nations," in which the Olympic athletes of all participating countries march. The parade is led by Greece, the founding nation, and ends with the athletes of the host country. During opening day, the Olympic flag is raised, and doves are released as a sign of peace.

Norwegian figure skater Sonja Henie was the queen of the ice in the 1928, 1932, and 1936 Winter Games.

The Olympic marathon celebrates the legendary 25-mile run of a Greek soldier in 490 B.C. He was carrying news of victory in battle.

Mark Spitz

Carl Lewis

U.S. athletes Mark Spitz and Carl Lewis are tied for most career Olympic gold medals won. Spitz won nine for swimming, Lewis won nine for track and field.

In 1988, East German swimmer Kristin Otto became the first woman to win six medals in a single Olympics.

U.S. skier Picabo Street came back from an injury to win the giant slalom at the 1998 Olympics.

Snowboarding became an Olympic sport in the 1998 Winter Games.

129

Plant Kingdom

(see also ANIMAL KINGDOM ● ECOSYSTEMS ● ENERGY ● FARMING ● FORESTS ● OCEANS AND SEA LIFE ● PREHISTORY ● RAIN FORESTS ● TREES)

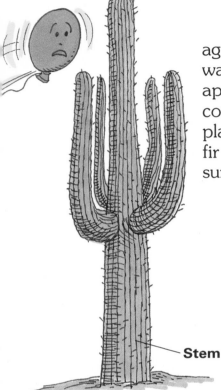

Plants were the first living things on Earth. Three billion years ago, the first plants were blue-green algae, which grew in or near water. Three or four hundred million years after blue-green algae appeared, land plants (mosses and ferns) appeared, followed by cone-bearing trees. Over millions of years, many different kinds of plants evolved, each adapted to its environment. For instance, fir trees can grow where it is cold and dark, while cactuses can survive on little water in hot, dry deserts.

Stem

The giant saguaro cactus can grow to 60 feet tall. It stores water in its stem. Another type of plant, the baobab tree, stores water in its trunk.

Ferns and mosses—among the oldest plants—have no seeds or flowers.

Photosynthesis

Plants need food to get energy. They take it from sunlight, water, and air in a process called photosynthesis. (*Photo* means *light*; *synthesis* means *combining to produce something else*.) A substance called chlorophyll in a plant's leaves helps turn sunlight into energy the plant can use. This process ends with oxygen being released into the atmosphere—oxygen that humans and other animals need in order to survive.

How It Works
  1. Roots absorb water from the soil.
  2. Stems carry the water to the leaves.
  3. Chlorophyll uses the sun's energy to combine carbon dioxide from the air with the water from the soil.
  4. This produces sugars and starches for the plant to use as food.
  5. Oxygen is released into the air.

Vines and other climbing plants grow up trees to get sunlight.

Trees, flowers, and other plants provide us with food, materials for clothing and shelter, medicine, perfume, and many other resources.

130

Reproduction

Plants reproduce in different ways. Many do so by pollination: when **pollen** (grains in the anthers) is brought together with **ova** (egg cells).

Insects help with pollination. Flowers produce sweet nectar, which attracts bees. When a bee drinks nectar, pollen sticks to its body. When it flies to another flower, it carries the pollen with it, fertilizing the next flower. Wind also carries pollen from flower to flower.

After the plant is pollinated, its ovaries grow into a seed-bearing fruit. When the fruit drops to the ground or is eaten by a bird, the seeds are taken to another place where they can grow into new plants—and the process starts all over again.

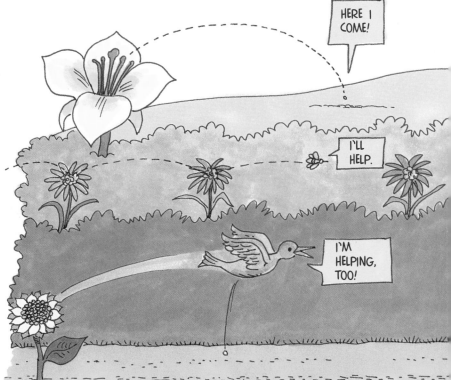

HERE I COME!

I'LL HELP.

I'M HELPING, TOO!

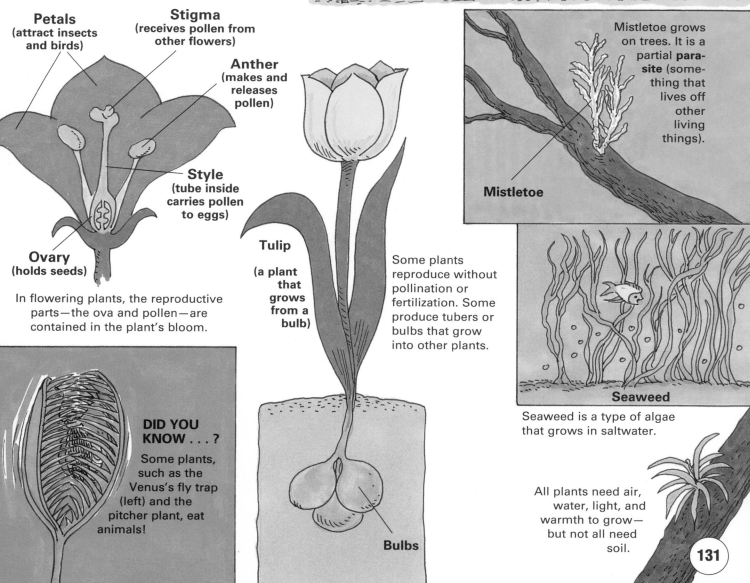

Petals (attract insects and birds)

Stigma (receives pollen from other flowers)

Anther (makes and releases pollen)

Style (tube inside carries pollen to eggs)

Ovary (holds seeds)

In flowering plants, the reproductive parts—the ova and pollen—are contained in the plant's bloom.

DID YOU KNOW . . . ?

Some plants, such as the Venus's fly trap (left) and the pitcher plant, eat animals!

Tulip

(a plant that grows from a bulb)

Some plants reproduce without pollination or fertilization. Some produce tubers or bulbs that grow into other plants.

Bulbs

Mistletoe grows on trees. It is a partial **parasite** (something that lives off other living things).

Mistletoe

Seaweed

Seaweed is a type of algae that grows in saltwater.

All plants need air, water, light, and warmth to grow—but not all need soil.

131

Polar Regions

(see also ECOSYSTEMS ● ENVIRONMENT ● EXPLORERS AND EXPLORATION ● WATER ● WORLD)

The polar regions—the areas around the North Pole and the South Pole—are the coldest regions on Earth. The north polar region is called the Arctic. The south polar region is the continent of Antarctica. In these areas, temperatures are usually well below freezing, and fierce winds blow. Because conditions are so harsh, few plants and animals can survive there—only those that have adapted to winds and bitter cold.

The Arctic

The Arctic region consists of the Arctic Ocean, the surrounding seas and islands, and the northernmost parts of Canada, Alaska, Russia, Sweden, Finland, Norway, and Greenland. The Arctic Ocean is usually covered by ice up to 98 feet thick! Most of the surrounding land is **tundra** (treeless plains). In the winter, it is always dark and cold, and the tundra is blanketed in snow. Only a few animals, such as the polar bear, thrive in winter. But in summer, reindeer, arctic hares, lemmings, and musk oxen live on the area's mosses, lichens, and low-growing shrubs. Birds such as the Arctic tern spend summers in the Arctic, but migrate south for the rest of the year.

THE NORTH POLE AND SOUTH POLE HAVE ONLY TWO SEASONS EACH. FOR ONE HALF OF THE YEAR, THE SUN NEVER RISES. FOR THE OTHER HALF OF THE YEAR, IT NEVER SETS!

I'M A POLAR BEAR.

I'M A PTARMIGAN.

ARCTIC TERN, THAT'S ME!

I'M A LONG-TAILED DUCK.

NORTHERN GANNET IS WHAT I AM.

I'M AN ARCTIC FOX.

I'M AN ARCTIC HARE.

I'M A BELUGA WHALE.

I'M AN ARCTIC OWL.

I'M A HOODED SEAL.

I'M A SEAL, TOO—A BEARDED SEAL.

I'M A NARWHAL.

I'M COLD.

Alaska
CANADA
RUSSIA
Arctic Ocean
North Pole
GREENLAND
ASIA
EUROPE

There is no solid land at the North Pole, only a floating ice pack.

On April 6, 1909, Robert Peary (U.S.), Matthew Henson (U.S.) and four Eskimos were the first people to reach the North Pole.

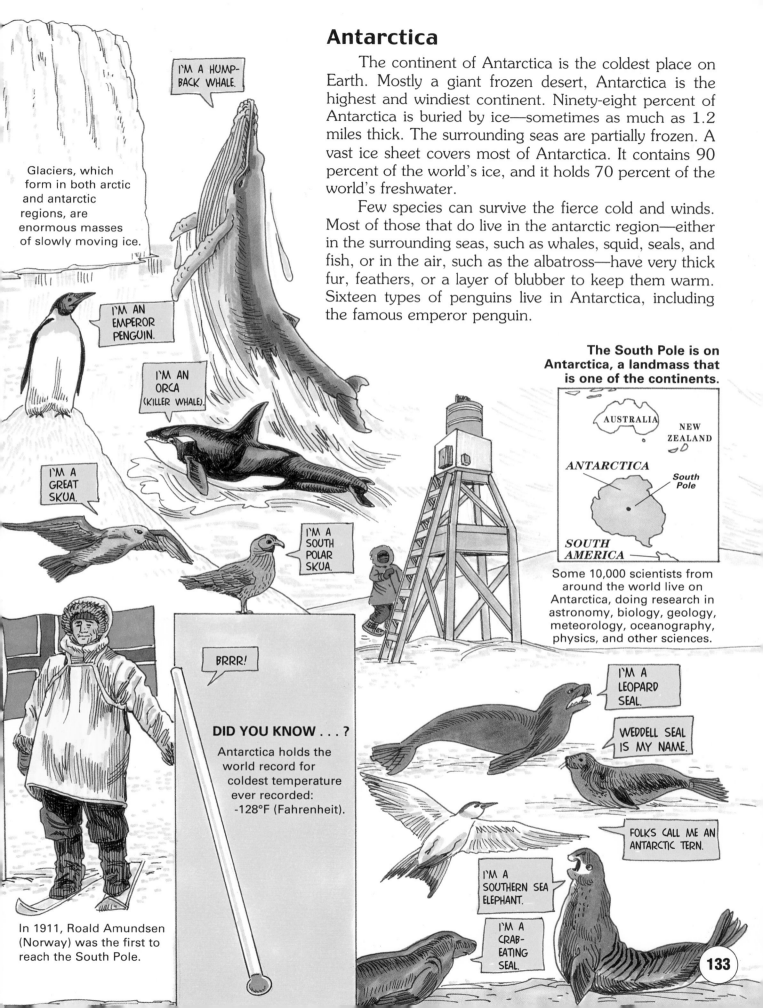

Antarctica

The continent of Antarctica is the coldest place on Earth. Mostly a giant frozen desert, Antarctica is the highest and windiest continent. Ninety-eight percent of Antarctica is buried by ice—sometimes as much as 1.2 miles thick. The surrounding seas are partially frozen. A vast ice sheet covers most of Antarctica. It contains 90 percent of the world's ice, and it holds 70 percent of the world's freshwater.

Few species can survive the fierce cold and winds. Most of those that do live in the antarctic region—either in the surrounding seas, such as whales, squid, seals, and fish, or in the air, such as the albatross—have very thick fur, feathers, or a layer of blubber to keep them warm. Sixteen types of penguins live in Antarctica, including the famous emperor penguin.

Glaciers, which form in both arctic and antarctic regions, are enormous masses of slowly moving ice.

The South Pole is on Antarctica, a landmass that is one of the continents.

Some 10,000 scientists from around the world live on Antarctica, doing research in astronomy, biology, geology, meteorology, oceanography, physics, and other sciences.

DID YOU KNOW . . . ?
Antarctica holds the world record for coldest temperature ever recorded: -128°F (Fahrenheit).

In 1911, Roald Amundsen (Norway) was the first to reach the South Pole.

Prehistory

(see also DINOSAURS ● EARTH ● FOSSILS ● GEOLOGY ● PLANT KINGDOM)

Prehistory usually means the time before 3500 B.C.—when people first started to record their lives and surroundings. To learn what Earth was like in prehistoric times, scientists study fossils and rocks. Based on these studies, scientists have divided prehistory into different **eras** (time periods), based on which life forms existed when.

When Earth formed about 4.6 billion years ago, there was no life on it. Two billion years ago, the earliest forms of life gradually developed in the warm oceans. The first organisms were similar to bacteria existing today. Eventually, blue-green algae developed and began producing oxygen. The presence of oxygen set the stage for other life forms. While life was developing, the land was shifting. More than 300 million years ago, there was one big landmass called Pangaea (pan-JEE-uh). It later split into the seven continents that exist today.

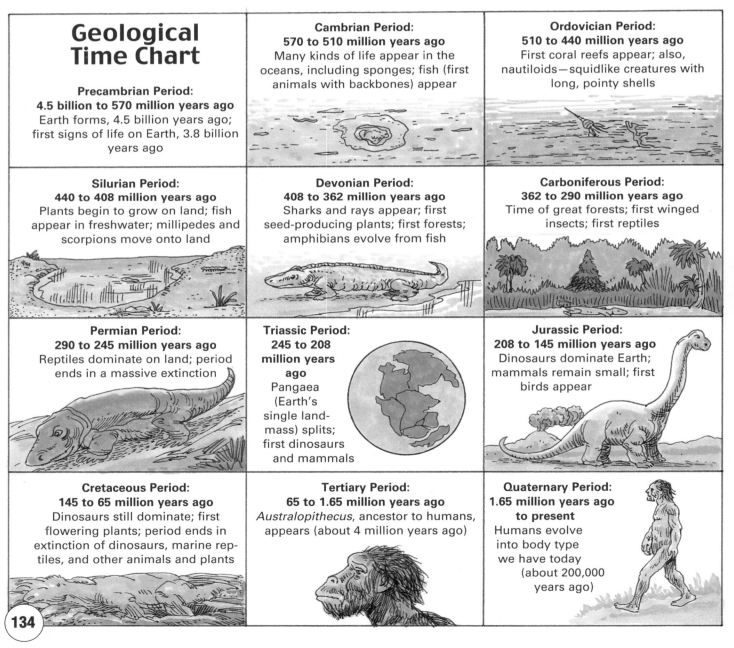

Geological Time Chart

Precambrian Period:
4.5 billion to 570 million years ago
Earth forms, 4.5 billion years ago; first signs of life on Earth, 3.8 billion years ago

Cambrian Period:
570 to 510 million years ago
Many kinds of life appear in the oceans, including sponges; fish (first animals with backbones) appear

Ordovician Period:
510 to 440 million years ago
First coral reefs appear; also, nautiloids—squidlike creatures with long, pointy shells

Silurian Period:
440 to 408 million years ago
Plants begin to grow on land; fish appear in freshwater; millipedes and scorpions move onto land

Devonian Period:
408 to 362 million years ago
Sharks and rays appear; first seed-producing plants; first forests; amphibians evolve from fish

Carboniferous Period:
362 to 290 million years ago
Time of great forests; first winged insects; first reptiles

Permian Period:
290 to 245 million years ago
Reptiles dominate on land; period ends in a massive extinction

Triassic Period:
245 to 208 million years ago
Pangaea (Earth's single land-mass) splits; first dinosaurs and mammals

Jurassic Period:
208 to 145 million years ago
Dinosaurs dominate Earth; mammals remain small; first birds appear

Cretaceous Period:
145 to 65 million years ago
Dinosaurs still dominate; first flowering plants; period ends in extinction of dinosaurs, marine reptiles, and other animals and plants

Tertiary Period:
65 to 1.65 million years ago
Australopithecus, ancestor to humans, appears (about 4 million years ago)

Quaternary Period:
1.65 million years ago to present
Humans evolve into body type we have today (about 200,000 years ago)

Some Prehistoric Life Forms

Trilobites, which lived on sea floors in the Cambrian Period, were the ancestors of modern-day crabs.

Amphibians were the first **vertebrates** (animals with backbones) to appear on land (about 350 million years ago).

Pterosaurs and some other prehistoric reptiles could fly. (They were not dinosaurs.) Birds evolved from dinosaurs, not from these creatures.

Dinosaurs dominated Earth's land areas during the Triassic, Jurassic, and Cretaceous periods.

The first flowering plants evolved during the Cretaceous Period (145 to 65 million years ago).

Woolly mammoths, woolly rhinoceroses, and saber-toothed tigers had thick fur to help them survive the ice ages.

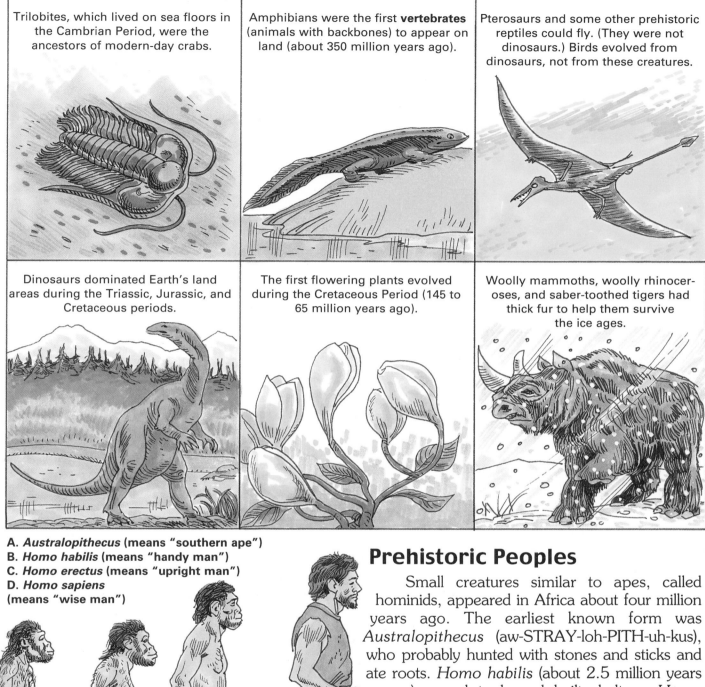

A. *Australopithecus* (means "southern ape")
B. *Homo habilis* (means "handy man")
C. *Homo erectus* (means "upright man")
D. *Homo sapiens*
(means "wise man")

A   B   C   D

Prehistoric Peoples

Small creatures similar to apes, called hominids, appeared in Africa about four million years ago. The earliest known form was *Australopithecus* (aw-STRAY-loh-PITH-uh-kus), who probably hunted with stones and sticks and ate roots. *Homo habilis* (about 2.5 million years ago) carved tools and built shelters. *Homo erectus* (about 1.75 million years ago) had a bigger brain, better tools, and probably started to use fire. Neanderthals began to appear in Europe about 130,000 years ago. Most scientists think that the first modern humans, *Homo sapiens*, spread out from Africa about 100,000 years ago, eventually replacing Neanderthals. All humans lived as wandering hunter-gatherers until about 10,000 years ago, when they began farming and living in permanent communities.

Presents, U.S.

(see also GOVERNMENTS ● UNITED STATES ● UNITED STATES HISTORY)

The president of the United States can be any natural-born citizen of the U.S. over the age of 35 who has lived in the country for at least 14 years. As the chief executive of the United States, the president plays a big part in shaping foreign policy, makes treaties with other nations, and appoints ambassadors. (All appointments must be approved by the Senate.) The president signs bills into law and can **veto** (reject) bills that are passed by Congress. The president nominates Supreme Court justices and cabinet members, serves as commander in chief of the U.S. armed forces, and is leader of his political party.

Electing a President

The president is elected to a term of four years, and cannot serve more than two terms. The president is elected by a majority vote of the Electoral College, which is made up of electors (representatives) chosen from every state. Each elector usually votes for the candidate supported by a majority of the voters in his or her state.

The U.S. Constitution outlines the succession to the office of the presidency. If the president dies, the vice president becomes president. Next in line is the speaker of the House of Representatives, then the president pro tempore of the Senate, then the secretary of state.

The only president to serve more than two terms was Franklin D. Roosevelt, in office from 1933 to 1945. He was elected four times, but he died in office, cutting his fourth term short.

Eight U.S. presidents died while in office . . .

William Henry Harrison (natural causes, 1841)

Zachary Taylor (natural causes, 1850)

Abraham Lincoln (assassination, 1865)

James Garfield (assassination, 1881)

William McKinley (assassination, 1901)

Warren G. Harding (natural causes, 1923)

Franklin D. Roosevelt (natural causes, 1945)

John F. Kennedy (assassination, 1963)

Presidents on Our Money

Abraham Lincoln: Pennies and $5 bills

Thomas Jefferson: Nickels and $2 bills

Franklin D. Roosevelt: Dimes

George Washington: Quarters and $1 bills

Andrew Jackson: $20 bills

Ulysses S. Grant: $50 bills

U.S. President Political party	Years in office	U.S. President Political party	Years in office
1. George Washington Federalist	1789-1797	22. Grover Cleveland Democratic	1885-1889
2. John Adams Federalist	1797-1801	23. Benjamin Harrison Republican	1889-1893
3. Thomas Jefferson Democratic-Republican	1801-1809	24. Grover Cleveland Democratic	1893-1897
4. James Madison Democratic-Republican	1809-1817	25. William McKinley Republican	1897-1901
5. James Monroe Democratic-Republican	1817-1825	26. Theodore Roosevelt Republican	1901-1909
6. John Quincy Adams Democratic-Republican	1825-1829	27. William Howard Taft Republican	1909-1913
7. Andrew Jackson Democratic	1829-1837	28. Woodrow Wilson Democratic	1913-1921
8. Martin Van Buren Democratic	1837-1841	29. Warren G. Harding Republican	1921-1923
9. William Henry Harrison Whig	1841	30. Calvin Coolidge Republican	1923-1929
10. John Tyler Whig	1841-1845	31. Herbert Hoover Republican	1929-1933
11. James K. Polk Democratic	1845-1849	32. Franklin D. Roosevelt Democratic	1933-1945
12. Zachary Taylor Whig	1849-1850	33. Harry S. Truman Democratic	1945-1953
13. Millard Fillmore Whig	1850-1853	34. Dwight D. Eisenhower Republican	1953-1961
14. Franklin Pierce Democratic	1853-1857	35. John F. Kennedy Democratic	1961-1963
15. James Buchanan Democratic	1857-1861	36. Lyndon B. Johnson Democratic	1963-1969
16. Abraham Lincoln Republican	1861-1865	37. Richard M. Nixon Republican	1969-1974
17. Andrew Johnson Democratic	1865-1869	38. Gerald R. Ford Republican	1974-1977
18. Ulysses S. Grant Republican	1869-1877	39. Jimmy Carter Democratic	1977-1981
19. Rutherford B. Hayes Republican	1877-1881	40. Ronald Reagan Republican	1981-1989
20. James A. Garfield Republican	1881	41. George Bush Republican	1989-1993
21. Chester Alan Arthur Republican	1881-1885	42. Bill Clinton Democratic	1993-2001
		43. _____	2001-

Rain Forests

(see also AFRICAN WILDLIFE ● ASIAN WILDLIFE ● AUSTRALIAN WILDLIFE ● ECOSYSTEMS ● ENVIRONMENT ● FORESTS ● NORTH AMERICAN WILDLIFE ● PLANT KINGDOM ● SOUTH AMERICAN WILDLIFE ● TREES)

A **rain forest** is a densely wooded area, in a hot climate near the equator, that gets at least 70 inches of rainfall per year. Rain forests have tall trees with broad leaves forming a dense, spreading **canopy** (top). Some dense forests grow in cool areas of high rainfall; they are known as temperate rain forests. However, when most people use the term *rain forest*, they are referring to tropical rain forests.

The world's largest rain forest is in the Amazon River region of South America; others grow in the tropical regions of Central America, Africa, Asia, and Oceania.

> **DID YOU KNOW . . . ?**
> One half of all the world's rain forests grow in Central and South America. The world's largest rain forest, the Amazon, covers 2.3 million square miles, from the Atlantic Ocean to the tree line of the Andes Mountains!

Very Important Places

Rain forests, especially the Amazon, are vital to the health of the planet, as well as to the people on it. They function as Earth's lungs, taking in carbon dioxide (which is poisonous to most animal life) and giving off oxygen (which animals—including humans—need to survive).

Humans rely on many things that grow in rain forests, such as coffee, chocolate, and various kinds of nuts, fruits, and hard wood. Many medicines are made from rain-forest plants or animals. (About 70 percent of all plants found useful in treating cancer grow only in rain forests!) Scientists think that many yet-undiscovered rain-forest plants could prove to be important aids for human health.

Coffee beans

Hard wood

Medicines

Teeming Wildlife

Rain forests are teeming with plant and animal life. Different animals live at different levels. Termites, centipedes, worms, and rodents live on or below the damp, dark soil. They feed on rotting leaves and animal carcasses, keeping the forest floor clear. Wasps, bees, and birds help fertilize flowers. Monkeys swing or hang by their tails from branches, while brilliantly colored birds, butterflies, and moths fly about the treetops.

I'M A CHAMELEON. I LIVE IN AFRICA'S RAIN FOREST.

I'M AN ANTEATER OF SOUTH AND CENTRAL AMERICAN RAIN FORESTS. WOULD YOU LIKE SOME ANTS?

WE'RE ANTS.

I'M AN UNCLE.

I'M A BLUE MORPHO BUTTERFLY, OF THE AMERICAS.

Endangered Areas

Rain forests are disappearing at an alarmingly rapid rate. Over the last half-century, more than one half of the world's rain forests have been chopped down for timber or to clear land for farms and homes. This drives animals from their natural habitats.

I'M A COLUGO—A FLYING LEMUR. I LIVE IN ASIA.

I'M A TREE FROG OF THE AMERICAS.

I'M A MACAW, OF SOUTH AND CENTRAL AMERICA.

I'M A BIRD OF PARADISE, OF OCEANIA.

Rain forest trees grow an average of 150 feet above the ground. A few trees reach 300 feet!

The high tangle of branches and leaves is called the canopy. It is so thick that barely any sun can pass through.

WE'RE ORCHIDS.

More than half of all known plant and animal species live in rain forests.

I'M A BUSHBABY, OF CENTRAL AFRICA.

I'M A BLUE FAIRY FLY-CATCHER, OF AFRICA.

I'M A BOA CONSTRICTOR, OF SOUTH AND CENTRAL AMERICA.

I'M A SPIDER MONKEY. I LIVE IN SOUTH AND CENTRAL AMERICA. ORANGUTAN AND I ARE ENDANGERED SPECIES.

I'M AN ORANGUTAN. I LIVE IN SOUTHEAST ASIAN RAIN FORESTS. WANT TO SWING ON SOME VINES WITH ME?

I'M A GOLD COAST TOURACO, OF AFRICA.

Equator

Major tropical rain forests (in green)

The rain forest is a noisy place, filled with sounds made by the birds, monkeys, frogs, insects, and other animals that live in its high canopy and undergrowth.

TALL RAIN FOREST TREES HAVE LONG, THICK ROOTS THAT LIE CLOSE TO THE SURFACE, TO CATCH RAINWATER THAT FALLS FROM THE BROAD LEAVES.

I'M A TIGER. I LIVE IN SOUTH-EAST ASIA.

Religions

(see also FESTIVALS ● HOLIDAYS
● MYTHOLOGY ● SOCIETY AND
CULTURE)

A religion is set of beliefs that help people understand the world around them, including life and death. Religions also usually include rules guiding how people should live. There are many different religions around the world. Some religions worship one god; others worship several. In many religions, people pray together in a church, mosque, temple, or synagogue, usually guided by a priest, minister, imam, rabbi, or other leader of worship. Most religions teach that, if followers obey the rules, they will gain some reward, such as life after death. The world's major religions include Christianity, Islam, Hinduism, Buddhism, and Judaism.

Christianity

The cross is the major symbol of Christianity. It represents the cross on which Christ died.

Followers of **Christianity** worship Jesus Christ, who preached in Palestine (parts of present-day Israel, Jordan, and Egypt) from about 4 B.C. to A.D. 30. Christians believe that Christ was the Son of God, and that after he was crucified by the Romans, he rose from the dead. Christians worship in churches, chapels, and cathedrals. Christianity has more followers than any other religion. There are about two billion Christians worldwide.

Christians receive communion—a ceremony that commemorates the death of Christ.

The Bible is the holy book of Christians.

Islam

The star and crescent is an Islamic symbol that appears on the flag of several Muslim countries.

Islam was founded by the prophet Muhammad, who preached in the Middle East around A.D. 613. The followers of his teachings, called Muslims, believe in one god, called Allah. The holy book of Islamic teachings is called the Koran. There are more than one billion Muslims worldwide.

Thousands of Muslims a year make a pilgrimage (called a *hajj*) to the holy city of Mecca, in Saudi Arabia.

Muslims are required to pray five times a day, facing Mecca.

Muslim houses of worship are called mosques. Muslims attend mosque on Fridays.

Hinduism

A sacred symbol of Hinduism is the word *Om* (shown above, in Sanskrit). It represents Hindu gods and the universe.

Hinduism developed in India around 1500 B.C. Today, it is practiced throughout most of Asia. Hindus worship many gods and believe that after death we continue to have other lives as animal or human spirits, until we reach our perfect state. There are about 800 million Hindus worldwide; most live in Asia.

Brahma   **Vishnu**   **Siva**

The three major gods of Hinduism are Brahma, the creator; Vishnu, the preserver; and Siva, the destroyer.

Buddhism

One of Buddhism's symbols is a wheel, the spokes of which represent the religion's eightfold path.

Buddhism is based on the teachings of the Buddha, who lived in Asia around 503-483 B.C. (The word *buddha* means "enlightened one.") There are about 325 million Buddhists worldwide; most live in Asia.

The Daibatsu, a huge bronze statue of the Buddha, sits in meditation at Kamakura, Japan. It was made in 1252.

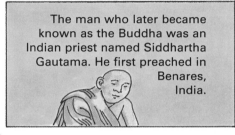

The man who later became known as the Buddha was an Indian priest named Siddhartha Gautama. He first preached in Benares, India.

Judaism

The Star of David is a widely recognized symbol of Judaism.

Judaism began more than 5,000 years ago in Palestine. Jewish teachings center on the Torah, the first five books of the Bible, and the Talmud (TAHL-mood), which contains the teachings of early rabbis. There are about 14 million Jews worldwide.

Many Jewish men wear a *tallith* (prayer shawl) while worshiping.

The Torah is kept in the ark—a special place in each **synagogue** (Jewish house of worship).

Chinese Philosophies

In this symbol, yin (darkness, cold, or wetness) and yang (light, heat, or dryness) are both necessary to life. Together, they create harmony.

Ancestor Worship
For thousands of years, many Chinese worshipped their dead ancestors. Many still do.

Confucianism
Confucius (551-479 B.C.) set forth a system of rules for how one should live life. Many Chinese have observed his teachings ever since.

Taoism
The teachings of Lao-tzu (6th century B.C.) say that following the Tao—a path of simplicity and honest living—can lead to a long and happy life.

Renaissance

(see also ARCHITECTURE ● ART AND ARTISTS ● EXPLORERS AND EXPLORATION ● INVENTIONS AND INVENTORS ● LITERATURE AND WRITERS ● MUSIC ● SCIENCE AND SCIENTISTS)

DID YOU KNOW . . . ?
The word *renaissance* means *rebirth*.

Many historians say that modern times began during the Renaissance. The Renaissance, which emerged in Italy in the 14th century, was a time of renewed interest in learning. It lasted into the 17th century. As Italian scholars copied old Roman manuscripts about the history of the world, architecture, literature, philosophy, and art, a spirit of rediscovery spread across Europe. People began to question their beliefs and explore the importance of the human being.

The Renaissance owed a great deal to the Medicis, the ruling family of Florence, Italy. They used their wealth to support many scholars, poets, painters, and architects.

Johannes Gutenberg (Germany, about 1400-1468) invented movable type, making the printing press possible. For the first time, books could be printed quickly and in great numbers, spreading knowledge faster and farther than ever before.

Universities such as Oxford and Cambridge in England and the Sorbonne in France trained students in new ways of thinking.

I NEVER HEARD OF ELVIS, AND I DIDN'T PLAY ROCK 'N' ROLL ON MY LUTE.

Polish astronomer **Nicolaus Copernicus** (1473-1543) discovered that Earth revolved around the sun—a revolutionary and controversial idea in its time. (Before then, people believed that the sun revolved around Earth, and that Earth was the center of the solar system.)

With the new availability of printed music, people began playing instruments in their homes. The most popular instrument for this was the lute (above). Before this time, most composers had concentrated on writing religious music. Renaissance composers began writing more popular music—including dance tunes.

When **Galileo Galilei** (1564-1642), an Italian artist and inventor, heard of the invention of the telescope, he built his own. He made key improvements to the telescope, making more powerful tools that he used to study the moon, stars, and Jupiter. (It was Galileo who, in 1610, discovered Jupiter's moons.)

Renaissance Art

Vanishing point

Studies of ancient Greek and Roman art greatly influenced the painting, sculpture, and architecture of the Renaissance. Painters gave their works more depth, using the technique of perspective.

Sandro Botticelli's
◄ *Birth of Venus*
(1487)

St. Peter's Basilica, Rome (1506-1626)
▼

Giotto (1266?-1337), **Botticelli** (1445-1510), **Raphael** (1483-1520), and other Renaissance artists often painted subjects from the Bible and mythology.

◆ ◆ ◆ ◆ ◆

Renaissance artists studied anatomy and the human form: **Michelangelo Buonarroti** (1475-1564) constructed lifelike sculptures of humans showing muscles, veins, and other details accurately and in correct proportion.

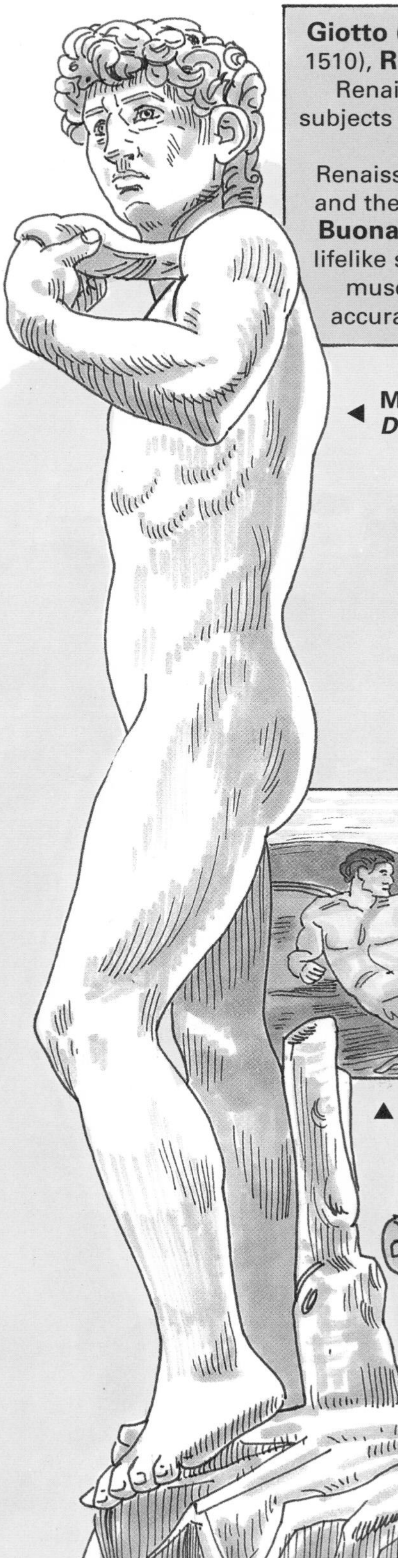

◄ Michelangelo's
David (1504)

Renaissance architects, following the classical elements of evenness and simplicity, replaced the towers of the Middle Ages with domes and columns based on Greek and Roman buildings.

La Gioconda (1503)—also known as the *Mona Lisa*—may be the most-recognized painting in the world. It was painted by **Leonardo da Vinci** (1452-1519), a skilled architect, scientist, musician, engineer, and sculptor, as well as painter.

▲ Michelangelo painted the world-famous ceiling of the Sistine Chapel, at the Vatican in Rome, Italy (1508–1512).

Many of the works of Renaissance playwright **William Shakespeare** (1564-1616) of England were first performed at the Globe Theater in London.

143

Safety

(see also FIRE ● HEALTH AND FITNESS)

The world can be a dangerous place if you don't pay attention to your safety. Always be alert and careful—it can help you avoid accidents and stay safe. Here are some tips that will help you stay safe in different places and situations:

Street Safety

Always walk where other people can see you.

Obey traffic signals and crossing guards.

If you walk at night, wear light-colored clothing so you can be seen.

Always look both ways before you cross a street.

Wear seat belts when riding in a car.

Always carry extra change or a phone card in case you need to make a call.

Never take anything—not even money, candy, or gifts—from a person you don't know.

Avoid wandering alone into unfamiliar neighborhoods or countryside.

Always go to a police officer or an adult you trust if you are lost or think that someone is following you.

Home Safety

Keep an up-to-date list of emergency telephone numbers near every phone in your home. The most important number to know is 911, a special number for emergency services.

The list should also include the telephone numbers of:

- your parents or guardians at work
- other close relatives
- trusted neighbors
- the police department

- the fire department
- emergency medical services
- your family's doctor
- a poison control center

Fire Safety

Fire is extremely dangerous. Encourage your family to take fire-safety precautions around your home.

Prevention is the best way to avoid fires! Take care when cooking, do not overload electrical outlets or use frayed or improper electrical cords, and never play with matches.

Every home should have smoke detectors—at least one on each floor of the house—and a fire extinguisher (especially in the kitchen) that everyone knows how to use.

Plan a fire-escape route with your family. Everyone should know ways to get out of the house in case of fire, and know where to meet once you are outside.

Hold fire drills to practice your fire-escape route.

Never go back into a burning building—for any reason!

Outdoor Safety

Follow these tips to keep safe while swimming, hiking, or playing outside:

Never go swimming (not even in your own pool!) by yourself.

Some animals carry diseases. Ticks, insects that feed on blood, can transfer illness from animals to people. Deer ticks carry bacteria that cause Lyme disease, a serious illness.

If you are caught in a storm, seek shelter. Lightning strikes the highest point, so if you can't find shelter, crouch low and avoid poles or trees. Avoid fallen power lines, which can give you a deadly electric shock.

Always wear a helmet when you ride a bike. Wear a helmet and wrist, elbow, and knee pads whenever you in-line skate. Learn safety laws, too!

Wear a life preserver whenever you are in any kind of boat.

STAY SAFE!

Very Important!

If an accident occurs, stay calm. Do not try to move a person who may have sprained a muscle or broken a bone. Get help right away by calling 911.

Science and Scientists

(see also ENERGY ● GEOLOGY ● INVENTORS AND INVENTIONS ● MATTER ● MEASUREMENTS ● MEDICINE ● RENAISSANCE ● SPACE EXPLORATION ● TECHNOLOGY)

Science is the study of the world and how it works. The job of a scientist is to think, solve problems, and constantly learn new things. Scientists must be good observers, using their senses and special instruments (such as microscopes and telescopes).

Scientists follow the **scientific method** to do their work. First, they make observations. Then they collect data (taking careful measurements) and record them. Then, based on that data, they come up with theories or hypotheses (hy-PAH-thuh-seez)—ideas that may explain what was observed. Finally, they carry out experiments to test their theories—and use what they find to improve or change their theories. The scientific process helps us understand diseases, weather, behavior, chemical reactions, the skies and stars—anything and everything in the universe.

Many scientists work in laboratories . . .

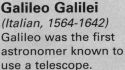

. . .others work in the field (on site).

Noted Scientists

Pythagoras
(Greek, about 580-500 B.C.)
The ideas of this philosopher and mathematician are the basis of later important theories in astronomy, geometry, and other areas of study.

Galileo Galilei
(Italian, 1564-1642)
Galileo was the first astronomer known to use a telescope.

Isaac Newton
(English, 1642-1727)
This mathematician and physicist, called "the greatest scientist of all time," discovered the law of universal gravitation: what gravity is and how it works.

Dmitri Mendeleev
(Russian, 1834-1907)
A chemist, he developed the periodic table, used by every scientist since. It classifies every element and its properties. (Each element is listed by a symbol—for instance, oxygen is *O* and silicon is *Si*.)

Charles Darwin
(English, 1809-1882)
He is known for his theory of evolution, which says that living things develop slowly over millions of years, adapting to their environments.

Astronomy is a science that studies the stars and the universe. The development of the telescope in the 17th century allowed astronomers to study galaxies, comets, planets, stars, and other far-off places in space. Today, astronomers send satellites and probes into space to observe Earth and other planets.

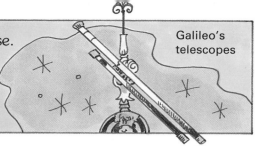
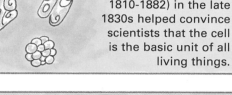

Galileo's telescopes

Biology is a science that studies living things— from tiny organisms to human beings to giant sequoia trees. There are many different types of biologists. For example, herpetologists study reptiles, ornithologists study birds, and botanists study plants.

The work of Theodor Schwann (German, 1810-1882) in the late 1830s helped convince scientists that the cell is the basic unit of all living things.

Chemistry is a science that examines how substances react with one another. Every substance in the universe is made from a group of building blocks called elements. By observing and manipulating chemical behavior, chemists can create materials that are useful. For example, chemists created plastic, which is used in cars, bags, boats, and lots of other everyday products.

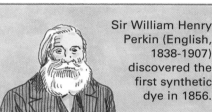

Sir William Henry Perkin (English, 1838-1907) discovered the first synthetic dye in 1856.

Physics is a science that attempts to explain the universe—from the smallest particle to enormous galaxies. Physicists study matter and energy.

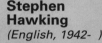

Sir Isaac Newton demonstrated that white light is made up of all colors.

Marie Curie *(Polish, 1867-1934)* With her husband, Pierre, she discovered radium in 1898. She later discovered other radioactive elements. She was the first person to win two Nobel Prizes (in physics in 1903, in chemistry in 1911).

Albert Einstein *(German, 1879-1955)* Perhaps the most influential physicist of all time, he developed ground-breaking theories about how the universe began.

Jonas Salk *(American, 1914-1995)* He developed a vaccine that was effective against polio, a disease that crippled countless people, often children.

Francis Crick *(English, 1916-),* **James Watson** *(American, 1928-),* and **Maurice Wilkins** *(Irish, 1916-)* They figured out what DNA—a key chemical found in living things— looks like and how it works.

Stephen Hawking *(English, 1942-)* This noted physicist and astronomer has probed and explained the laws that govern the universe, expanding on ideas set forth by Einstein.

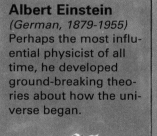

147

Society and Culture

(see also CLOTHING ● COMMUNICATION ● DANCE ● FESTIVALS ● FOLK TALES AND FAIRY TALES ● GOVERNMENTS ● HOLIDAYS ● LAW ● MONEY ● MYTHOLOGY ● RELIGIONS)

A society is a group of people who form a community. Every society has its own culture, or way of life. A society's culture includes its beliefs, customs, arts, languages, values, and how it is organized. You can find out about a society and its culture by observing what its people eat, how they dress, how they raise their children, how they honor their dead, and how they work and play. Children learn their culture as they grow up by watching their parents, teachers, and friends, and copying their behavior. They also learn their culture from stories, songs, and myths.

Rites of Passage

Many cultures have special ceremonies to mark important life changes, such as:

Birth
Most cultures hold ceremonies or give gifts to honor the birth of a child. These rites are usually done to wish the child good health and a happy life, and to strengthen the bonds between parents and child.

Coming of Age
Rites marking the shift from childhood to adulthood vary from culture to culture. They may involve instruction in life or faith, as in a Jewish Bar or Bat Mitzvah (see picture), or tests of courage or strength.

Marriage
Marriage ceremonies celebrate a change from single life to a union. Most involve feasting, dancing, and giving gifts to help the couple start their new life together, or to help parents cope with "losing" a child.

Death
Every culture marks death in some way. Most death rites involve disposing of the body (burial or cremation, for example) while allowing loved ones to celebrate the person's life, or to prepare the dead one's spirit for the afterlife.

Foods and Eating Habits

What, where, when, and how people eat may vary from culture to culture. In North America, for instance, a common breakfast is cold cereal, while in northern Europe, smoked fish is. In Asia, many people sit on mats on the floor to eat; in Europe, most people sit in chairs. Many Asians use chopsticks to eat, while most Westerners use forks, spoons, and knives.

Pizza (Italian)

Fast-food hamburger (American)

Pita bread (Greek) and shish kebab (Arab)

Sushi (Japanese)

Worldwide Eats

Many foods once eaten only by people of a particular country or culture are now regularly eaten by people of many places and cultures. The hamburger and hot dog, probably brought to the U.S. by German immigrants, became popular American foods—then popular worldwide. Other worldwide favorites include Japanese sushi, Greek pita bread, and Italian pizza.

Some types of foods are made in a variety of ways, depending on the place—dumplings, for instance. In Chinese cooking, they are won tons; in Italian cooking, they are gnocchi or ravioli; in Jewish cooking, they are kreplach; and in Polish cooking, they are pierogi.

Signs and Actions

One of the most fascinating ways that cultures vary is in the way that its people greet and say good-bye to each other.

| In the United States, it is customary for people to shake hands. | Europeans kiss one another on both cheeks. | Japanese bow when they are introduced. |

People also use distinct signs, words, or actions that may mean different things in various cultures. For example:

| In Saudi Arabia, kissing the top of a person's head is a way of apologizing. | In Chile, whistling—a way of expressing disapproval, like booing—is considered rude. | Tibetans stick out their tongues to show respect. |

DID YOU KNOW . . . ?

Proverbs are often-used sayings that suggest ways that people should behave. Many societies give similar advice using different proverbs. For example, people in many places and at different times have used similar sayings advising people to appreciate what they have, instead of always wishing for something more:
- "A bird in the hand is worth two in the bush." (modern-day U.S. and 17th-century Spain)
- "He is a fool who lets slip a bird in the hand for a bird in the bush." (ancient Greece)
- "A sparrow in the hand is better than a hawk in the air." (Iran)
- "Better one bird in the hand than ten in the wood." (modern-day Britain and Elizabethan England)

Multiculturalism

Although some societies have been associated with a single culture, many are multicultural. A multicultural society is influenced by the traditions of people from a number of distinct cultures. In France, for instance, some people speak English as well as their native language. They may enjoy U.S.-style foods, such as hamburgers, or food from another country while still eating their own traditional meals. Many people also enjoy the music of other cultures, as well as of their own.

South America

(see also FESTIVALS ● MINING ● RAIN FORESTS ● SOUTH AMERICAN WILDLIFE ● WORLD)

South America, Earth's fourth-largest continent, has a land area of 6,885,000 square miles. There are 12 independent countries on the continent—Argentina, Bolivia, Brazil, Chile, Colombia, Ecuador, Guyana, Paraguay, Peru, Suriname, Uruguay, and Venezuela—and two territories (French Guiana and Great Britain's Falkland Islands).

South America's terrain is mostly broad scrubland, grassy plains, rain forests, and deserts. The Andes mountain chain snakes down the western part of the continent.

People

Three fourths of the continent's population live in cities, such as São Paolo, Buenos Aires, Caracas, Rio de Janeiro, Lima, and Santiago. Many South Americans are moving from rural to urban areas seeking better jobs, homes, and other opportunities.

Most South Americans are descended from three groups: (1) Native Americans who arrived 20,000 to 30,000 years ago from Asia and North America; (2) European settlers who came in the 16th century and afterward; and (3) slaves brought from Africa in the 17th, 18th, and 19th centuries. Many people are **mestizos** (a mix of Indian and European ancestry) or **mulattos** (a mix of European and African ancestry).

Spanish is the major language spoken in every South American country except Brazil, where most people speak Portuguese; Guyana, where English is the official language; and Suriname, where Dutch is the official language.

Resources and Industry

Most rural South Americans live on small mountain farms and are barely able to grow enough food to feed themselves. Yet some of the world's largest farms are in Argentina and Brazil. (A few are larger than some countries!)

Ecuador, Colombia, and Brazil export some of the world's best coffee beans. Other major South American crops include wheat and sugar. Fishing is another key industry, as is mining—the Andes Mountains region is rich in copper, gold, lead, and tin. Brazil—one of the continent's few industrial countries—exports airplanes, fabrics, chemicals, and many other goods. The Amazon River Basin is rich in rare plants and herbs used in medicines.

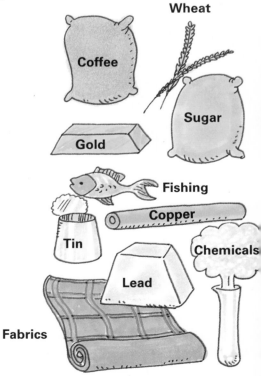

Wheat

Coffee

Sugar

Gold

Fishing

Copper

Tin

Chemicals

Lead

Fabrics

Caribbean Sea

NORTH AMERICA

VENEZUELA

Caracas

Angel Falls

Georgetown

SURINAME

Paramaribo

FRENCH GUIANA (France)

Cayenne

GUYANA

Venezuela's oil reserves make it one of the wealthiest countries on the continent.

SOUTH AMERICA

ATLANTIC OCEAN

Equator

Bogotá

COLOMBIA

Quito

ECUADOR

THIS WAY

PERU

Negro River

Amazon River

Purus River

Madeira River

Tapavos River

Xingu River

Tocantins River

BRAZIL

GALÁPAGOS ISLANDS (Ecuador) 600 miles off the coast

ANDES MOUNTAINS

Lima

THE GALÁPAGOS ISLANDS ARE HOME TO ANIMAL SPECIES FOUND NOWHERE ELSE IN THE WORLD.

BOLIVIA

La Paz

Lake Titicaca

Sucre

Brasília

THE YANOMAMÖ PEOPLE LIVE DEEP IN THE RAIN FOREST OF BRAZIL AND VENEZUELA.

BRAZIL, THE LARGEST COUNTRY IN SOUTH AMERICA, TAKES UP ABOUT HALF OF THE CONTINENT'S LAND AREA.

SUGARLOAF MOUNTAIN (1,295 ft)

LICANCÁBUR VOLCANO (19,425 ft)

ATACAMA DESERT (the driest place on Earth)

CHILE

PARAGUAY

Paraguay River

Asunción

Paraná River

The Amazon River Basin is home to . . .
● one fifth of Earth's freshwater supply
● more than one third of all the world's plant and animal species
● 30,000 plant species
● one third of all the world's tropical tree species (2,500 species of tropical trees)

PACIFIC OCEAN

ARGENTINA

MOUNT ACONCAGUA (22,834 ft)

Paraná River

URUGUAY

Montevideo

DID YOU KNOW . . . ?
The continent of South America is home to:
● the Amazon River, world's second-longest river
● the Amazon, world's largest rain forest—about 10 times the size of France, though it is shrinking (the dotted red line on the map shows its approximate area)
● Angel Falls (Venezuela), world's highest waterfall (3,212 feet)
● Lake Titicaca (Peru and Bolivia), world's highest lake (12,500 feet above sea level)
● Atacama Desert (Chile), world's driest place
● Mount Aconcagua (Argentina), highest peak in the Western Hemisphere (22,834 feet above sea level)

Santiago

Buenos Aires

Río de la Plata

Bahía Blanca

COWBOYS CALLED GAUCHOS HERD CATTLE ON THE DRY PAMPAS (GRASSLANDS) OF ARGENTINA.

THE QUECHUA INDIANS OF ECUADOR AND PERU HAVE LIVED HIGH IN THE ANDES FOR THOUSANDS OF YEARS. THEIR BODIES HAVE ADAPTED TO THE LOW-OXYGEN ATMOSPHERE.

PATAGONIA

FALKLAND ISLANDS (United Kingdom)

Straits of Magellan

CAPE HORN

South American Wildlife

(see also ANIMAL KINGDOM ● ECOSYSTEMS ● FORESTS ● RAIN FORESTS ● SOUTH AMERICA ● ZOOS)

The South American continent has a larger variety of plants than are found anywhere else in the world. There are 2,500 types of trees; many hundreds of different species of orchids grow there, too. South America's rain forest, pampas, deserts, and mountains all contain some very different and exciting animals. The Amazon River Basin has the greatest variety of animals on the planet; and some very odd, unique species can be found in such areas as the Galápagos Islands and Patagonia.

Several kinds of armadillo, all with sharp claws and hard scales, live in South America.

The Pampas

The grasslands of Argentina are called pampas. (However, pampas grass—a type of grass with fluffy, feathery tops—grows in the wild all over Argentina.) The animals that live on the pampas survive mainly on plants and grass. The viscacha—a rodent that is cousin to the guinea pig—eats plant stems and leaves, and burrows underground to hide from predators. The giant anteater uses its long tongue to break into termite nests and lap up the insects. The guanaco—a humpless cousin to the camel—also lives in the pampas. The sprightly vicuña, a wild relative of the llama, can run up to 30 miles an hour.

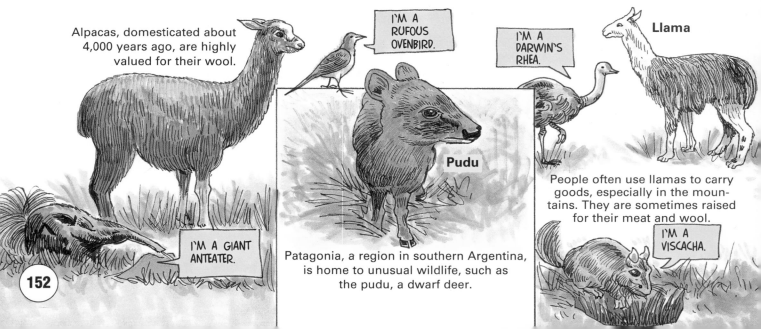

Alpacas, domesticated about 4,000 years ago, are highly valued for their wool.

I'M A RUFOUS OVENBIRD.

I'M A DARWIN'S RHEA.

Llama

People often use llamas to carry goods, especially in the mountains. They are sometimes raised for their meat and wool.

I'M A VISCACHA.

Pudu

I'M A GIANT ANTEATER.

Patagonia, a region in southern Argentina, is home to unusual wildlife, such as the pudu, a dwarf deer.

Amazon River Basin

The area in and around South America's Amazon River has the greatest variety of wildlife in the world. One of the largest wild animals of the forest is the tapir, a cousin of the rhinoceros. The peccary, a wild, piglike animal, also lives there. The slow-moving two-toed sloth lives its entire life upside down, hanging from tree branches with its powerful legs and tough claws. The manatee, an enormous water mammal of the Amazon, can weigh up to 1,000 pounds. Piranhas—flesh-eating fish—lurk in the waters, while anacondas and emerald tree boas slither about. Various types of monkeys, wild cats, squirrels, and rodents also live in this region.

Other Parts of the Continent . . .

DID YOU KNOW . . . ?
More bird species live on South America than on any other continent.

Galápagos Islands

The Galápagos Islands of Ecuador lie in the Pacific Ocean, about 600 miles from the South American mainland. Because the Galápagos are so remote, over hundreds of thousands of years the animals living there have developed very distinct adaptations. Many of the animal species are found nowhere else in the world. Some spectacular Galápagos species include the giant tortoise, the marine iguana (the only water-dwelling lizard), the Galápagos albatross, fur seals, and flamingoes.

153

Space Exploration

(see also EARTH • EXPLORERS AND EXPLORATION • INVENTORS AND INVENTIONS • MEASUREMENTS • SCIENCE AND SCIENTISTS • SUN AND SOLAR SYSTEM • TRANSPORTATION • UNIVERSE)

Sputnik I

Ever since the people of ancient Mesopotamia began observing the stars and planets, astronomers have tried to find out more about space and the universe. The invention of the telescope in the 17th century allowed astronomers to see distant objects. But the Space Age did not begin until October 4, 1957, when the Soviet Union sent *Sputnik I*—a satellite equipped with a radio transmitter—into orbit around Earth.

Rockets and Satellites

For centuries, people dreamed of exploring space, but that was impossible until we had an engine capable of reaching Earth's upper atmosphere. The first successful launch of a fueled rocket was on March 16, 1926, by physicist Robert Goddard. His rocket reached a height of 41 feet. Within a few decades, rockets were powerful enough to launch satellites into space.

Man-made satellites orbit Earth, taking pictures, collecting data, or sending signals. They usually have cameras, computers, measuring instruments, transmitters, and other special equipment on board. Satellites help scientists predict weather and relay telephone, video, or computer signals, as well as help with scientific research.

ATS I

Space Probes

Probes are unmanned spacecraft that are sent far into space to collect information and transmit it back to Earth. Probes can be sent to places where humans could not survive. Much of what we now know about the sun and the planets came from such space probes as *Pioneer*, *Mariner*, and *Voyager*.

December 7, 1966: The U.S. launches the *ATS I* weather satellite.

Rocket being launched

Mariner 2, launched in 1962, was the first successful space probe. It traveled for four months before reaching and exploring Venus.

Mariner 10, launched in 1973, photographed Venus and Mercury. The *Mars Global Surveyor* was launched in 1996 to study the climate, geology, and natural resources of Mars.

The **Hubble Space Telescope,** launched in 1990, sends images of galaxies and stars back to Earth.

People in Space: Famous Firsts

April 1961:
Soviet cosmonaut Yuri A. Gagarin becomes the first person in space.

May 1961:
Alan Shepard becomes the first American in space.

June 1963:
Soviet cosmonaut Valentina Tereshkova becomes the first woman in space.

Eagle I, the *Apollo 11* lunar module

July 20, 1969:
U.S. astronauts Neil Armstrong and Buzz Aldrin are the first people to land on the moon.

Space Shuttles

Space shuttles are reusable craft that blast off like rockets but can return to Earth and land like planes. The first space shuttle flight was in 1981. The shuttles, which can carry up to eight astronauts each, are used to launch or repair satellites. They also serve as orbiting laboratories.

International Space Station

Space Stations

A space station is an orbiting spacecraft in which astronauts live and work for a long period—months at a time. The Soviet Union launched the first space station, *Salyut I*, in 1971. It later launched six other *Salyut* stations. In 1986, the Soviet Union launched its *Mir* space station. In 1998, construction began in space on an International Space Station, scheduled to be completed by the year 2004.

155

Sports

(see also GAMES ● OLYMPICS ● WOMEN, FAMOUS)

Sports are activities and games that involve special physical skills. To most people, a sport is a hobby—something they do for fun. Many people play sports to stay healthy and in shape. For professional athletes, however, participating in a sport is their job.

Some sports are played alone; others involve teams of people. Every sport has its own rules, and many sports require a special area for play.

Spectator sports are a popular form of entertainment around the world. Fans attend games and races to cheer on their favorite team or competitor. Others listen to events on the radio or watch them on television.

Types of Sports

There are so many different types of sports, it is almost impossible to put them into categories. However, some are:

Athletics:
Sports in which people strive for physical strength, skill, and endurance. These include gymnastics, swimming, and track and field.

Team sports:
Competitions between teams of people. Cooperating with teammates is as important as knowing the rules of the game. Team sports include football, soccer, baseball, basketball, and lacrosse.

Transportation sports:
When people race for speed and skill. These include skiing, rowing, cycling, car racing, and horse racing.

Combat sports:
Started in ancient times, these sports include boxing, wrestling, and the martial arts.

Some athletes try to beat a record; others try to outperform other competitors.

The first organized baseball game was played between two "gentleman's" clubs—the New York Club and the Knickerbocker Base Ball Club, on June 19, 1846, in Hoboken, New Jersey.

From pickup games on playgrounds and city streets to organized clubs at roller rinks, the sport of roller hockey has grown with the rising popularity of in-line skates.

Some Great Modern Athletes

Jim Thorpe
Thorpe was one of the greatest all-around athletes. He won the pentathlon and the decathlon at the 1912 Olympic games; he played major-league baseball, and was an All-American football player, 1911-1912.

Mildred (Babe) Didrikson Zaharias
Considered the greatest female athlete of the century, she excelled at baseball and basketball, won two gold medals for track at the 1932 Olympics, and won 33 pro golf tournaments.

Jesse Owens
In 1936, Owens won four gold medals in track-and-field events at the Olympic Games in Berlin, Germany. This embarrassed Nazi leader Adolf Hitler, who had claimed that the Aryan (white) race was superior.

Jack Nicklaus
"The Golden Bear" was a dominant force in men's professional golf. Between 1962 and 1986, he won the British Open three times, the U.S. Open four times, the PGA Tournament five times, and the U.S. Masters six times.

Muhammad Ali
A skilled and charismatic boxer, Ali made boxing popular in the 1960s and 1970s. Once controversial for his boastful talk and his political and religious ideas, Ali is now widely respected.

Chris Evert
One of the greatest athletes, male or female, in pro tennis history. She turned pro in 1972 at age 17. By the time she retired in 1989, she had won 1,309 matches.

Wayne Gretzky
"The Great One" more than earned his nickname. He retired in 1999, after 20 years in pro hockey, with 61 National Hockey League records—including 894 goals, 1,963 assists, and 2,857 points scored.

Michael Jordan
During the 1990s, "Air" Jordan—one of the most popular and world-famous athletes of modern times—led his team to six NBA championships, set a number of NBA records, and played on two gold-medalist Olympic teams.

Mark McGwire   *and*   Sammy Sosa
These two players made baseball history in 1998, when both surpassed the long-standing record for single-season home runs. The record, set by Roger Maris in 1961, had been 61 home runs. In 1998, McGwire hit 70 home runs—the new record—and Sosa hit 66.

The sport of lacrosse was invented by Native Americans.

Soccer is played all around the world. Most countries call it football, but it is different from American football.

Basketball got its name because it was first played with a peach basket nailed to a wall.

The four strokes in competitive swimming are freestyle (the crawl), the breaststroke, the butterfly, and the backstroke.

Sun and Solar System

(see also EARTH ● SCIENCE AND SCIENTISTS
● SPACE EXPLORATION ● UNIVERSE)

It would take 1.3 million Earth-sized bodies to fill the space the sun occupies!

The sun is a star, or ball of hot gas, around which Earth **orbits** (travels in an oval pattern). The sun is the nearest star to Earth, and it gives us light and warmth. About 93 million miles from Earth, the sun has been shining for about 4.5 billion years. Its diameter is 865,400 miles—more than 100 times Earth's diameter. The temperature at the surface of the sun is about 11,000°F. The "surface" is really nothing more than gaseous atoms. It is too hot there for any liquid or solid to exist—either would burn up immediately! The sun has enough "fuel" to keep burning, hotter and hotter, until—like all stars—it eventually burns out. However, that will not happen for billions of years.

Hydrogen core
(140,000 miles in diameter)
Creates energy; the hottest part of the sun (about 36 million degrees Fahrenheit!)

Radioactive layer
(about 167,000 miles deep)

Convection layer
(about 125,000 miles deep)

Photosphere
The sun's "surface"

Atmosphere
The chromosphere (6,000 miles deep) and outer corona

Neptune: first observed in 1846. It takes 164 Earth years to make one orbit of the sun.

Saturn has 18 rings made of ice, dust, and rock. It takes 29.5 Earth years to make one orbit of the sun.

The Solar System

The sun, the nine planets and their moons, plus the asteroids, comets, and other objects that orbit the sun, make up our solar system. All of these objects, except comets, travel around the sun in a regular path, held in their orbits by the sun's gravity. Pluto has an irregular orbit: Part of its path takes it farther from the sun than any other planet; the rest of the time its path loops inside that of Uranus. *(See the picture below.)*

DID YOU KNOW . . . ?

This handy sentence will help you remember the names of the nine planets, moving from the sun out:
My very educated mother just showed us nine planets.
(*My* = **M**ercury, *V* = **V**enus, *E* = **E**arth, *M* = **M**ars, *J* = **J**upiter, *S* = **S**aturn, *U* = **U**ranus, *N* = **N**eptune, *P* = **P**luto.)

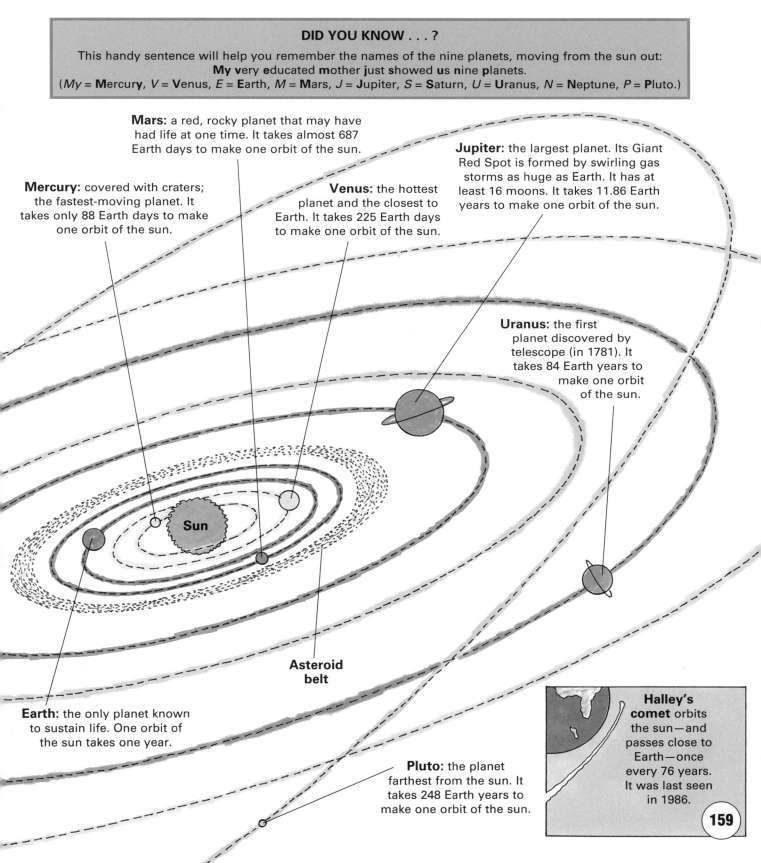

Mars: a red, rocky planet that may have had life at one time. It takes almost 687 Earth days to make one orbit of the sun.

Jupiter: the largest planet. Its Giant Red Spot is formed by swirling gas storms as huge as Earth. It has at least 16 moons. It takes 11.86 Earth years to make one orbit of the sun.

Mercury: covered with craters; the fastest-moving planet. It takes only 88 Earth days to make one orbit of the sun.

Venus: the hottest planet and the closest to Earth. It takes 225 Earth days to make one orbit of the sun.

Uranus: the first planet discovered by telescope (in 1781). It takes 84 Earth years to make one orbit of the sun.

Sun

Asteroid belt

Earth: the only planet known to sustain life. One orbit of the sun takes one year.

Pluto: the planet farthest from the sun. It takes 248 Earth years to make one orbit of the sun.

Halley's comet orbits the sun—and passes close to Earth—once every 76 years. It was last seen in 1986.

Technology

(see also ANIMATION ● ARMS AND WEAPONS ● COMMUNICATION ● COMPUTERS ● INVENTORS AND INVENTIONS ● MACHINES ● MEDICINE ● MOVIES AND TELEVISION ● NAVIGATION ● SCIENCE AND SCIENTISTS)

The word *technology* refers to how people apply knowledge and use inventions to make their lives easier. Humans have invented many tools, machines, and substances that have enabled them to solve problems, cure diseases, and save time, money, or energy. During the 19th and 20th centuries, rapid advances in technology brought great changes to almost every aspect of our lives, from communications to transportation, housing to health care, and industry to entertainment.

Today, technology is used in many different ways, including such fields as building construction, ceramics, weaving, and farming. Highly developed technologies (often called high tech) are also used in a variety of ways, including robotics, home and office computing, and medicine.

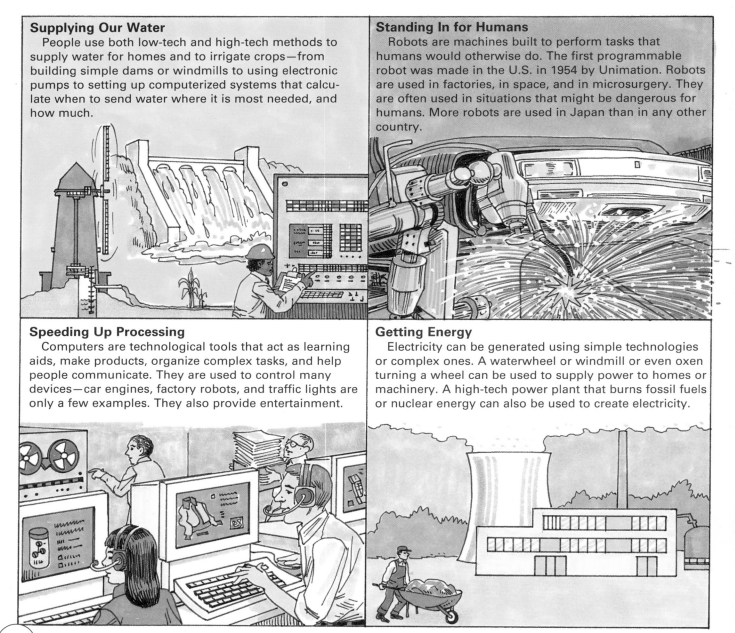

Supplying Our Water
People use both low-tech and high-tech methods to supply water for homes and to irrigate crops—from building simple dams or windmills to using electronic pumps to setting up computerized systems that calculate when to send water where it is most needed, and how much.

Standing In for Humans
Robots are machines built to perform tasks that humans would otherwise do. The first programmable robot was made in the U.S. in 1954 by Unimation. Robots are used in factories, in space, and in microsurgery. They are often used in situations that might be dangerous for humans. More robots are used in Japan than in any other country.

Speeding Up Processing
Computers are technological tools that act as learning aids, make products, organize complex tasks, and help people communicate. They are used to control many devices—car engines, factory robots, and traffic lights are only a few examples. They also provide entertainment.

Getting Energy
Electricity can be generated using simple technologies or complex ones. A waterwheel or windmill or even oxen turning a wheel can be used to supply power to homes or machinery. A high-tech power plant that burns fossil fuels or nuclear energy can also be used to create electricity.

Engineering Our Genes

Animals and plants pass certain traits from generation to generation. The science that studies this process is called genetics. Geneticists can now change genes to alter a plant or animal—a technique called genetic engineering. In one technique, a gene from the DNA of one species is inserted into another **organism** (living thing). A major breakthrough in genetic engineering occurred in 1997, when scientists were able to create a **clone** (a living being with identical genes) of a sheep named Dolly.

Keeping Us Fit

Technological know-how is improving how people get in shape and stay that way. Exercise equipment—such as treadmills, weight machines, bicycles, and in-line skates—has become more efficient as new materials and design methods are developed. Even something as simple as footwear has been improved. Today's athletic shoes, designed to suit specific activities, are high-tech compared to the simple sneakers of a decade or so ago!

Keeping Us in Touch

Communications technologies have changed the way people keep in touch. Telephone-answering machines take messages when you are away from your phone. Or, you can take the phone with you: Modern cordless phones are smaller, lighter, and more efficient than ever before.

Helping Around the Home

Technology has transformed how people cook. Dinners that once took hours to prepare can now be cooked in a microwave oven in minutes or even seconds. Modern kitchens also have refrigerators that never need defrosting (The freezers in old-time refrigerators became coated with ice that had to be chipped away from time to time.)

Investigating Crimes

Forensic doctors, biologists, and dentists help police investigate crimes. If death has been sudden, they examine the body to determine what caused that death. They may also study hair, fingerprints, teeth, blood, DNA, and even fabric samples to find important clues as to how a crime may have been committed and who was involved.

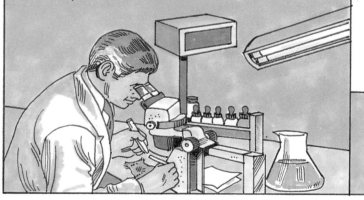

Seeing Inside

X rays are radiation—a type of energy that makes the inside of plants, animals, machines, and humans visible. The CT scanner—also called a CAT scan—is a high-tech X-ray machine that helps doctors "see" inside a patient's body. (*CAT* stands for computerized axial tomography.) It makes 3-D images of the inside of the body, which are displayed on a screen.

Medicine is not the only field taking advantage of X-ray technology. X-ray scanners are now common in most airports, where they are used to detect bombs and other illegal devices hidden in carry-on luggage or packages being shipped.

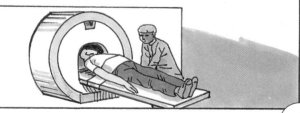

Theater

(see also ANCIENT CIVILIZATIONS ● ART AND ARTISTS ● DANCE ● LITERATURE AND WRITERS ● MOVIES AND TELEVISION ● MUSIC ● MYTHOLOGY)

Theater is a story performed by actors, usually using dialogue (speaking), and usually on a stage. It can be drama, music, comedy, dance, mime, or some combination of these. Many theatrical productions involve stage directions, sets, and costumes. A playwright writes the words to be spoken and describes the action and where it occurs. A director uses that script in guiding the actors, the set and costume designers, and the backstage crew.

Beginnings

Modern theater began in ancient Greece. A group of singers called a chorus told a story while performers acted it out. Greeks performed tragedies—serious stories based on well-known myths—to help them understand life. They also introduced comedies, making audiences laugh while teaching them about life. The first permanent theater in Athens was constructed in 450 B.C.

In ancient Greece, all the actors were men, including those playing women, girls, and boys.

The audience purchased stone tokens, which were used like tickets.

The Middle Ages

In Europe: William Shakespeare was among the actors and playwrights active in London, England, in the 1500s. In addition to being a poet, he wrote more than 37 plays, most of which were hugely popular. Today, Shakespeare's plays are performed more often than those by any other playwright in the world. His plays have been made into films, and many writers have based their poems, novels, film scripts, and plays on Shakespearean plots and characters.

In Asia: Two forms of theater developed in Japan during the Middle Ages. In Noh, a form of theater that arose in the 1200s, actors perform wearing special masks. In Kabuki, which began in the 1600s, actors wear makeup and elaborate costumes.

Japanese Noh actor wearing a traditional mask

Some Famous Playwrights of Western Literature

 **Aeschylus**
(Greek, 525-456 B.C.)
First great Greek writer of tragedy; wrote *The Seven Against Thebes*; the *Oresteia*

 **Euripides**
(Greek, 484-406 B.C.)
Wrote tragic plays that examined the evils of society, including The *Trojan Women* and *Medea*

 **William Shakespeare**
(English, 1564-1616)
Hugely influential author of *Romeo and Juliet*; *Hamlet*; *A Midsummer Night's Dream*; *Henry V*

Henrik Ibsen
(Norwegian, 1828-1906)
His portrayal of independent women (as in *A Doll's House*) shocked audiences.

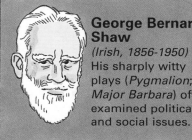 **George Bernard Shaw**
(Irish, 1856-1950)
His sharply witty plays (*Pygmalion*; *Major Barbara*) often examined political and social issues.

 **Anton Chekhov**
(Russian, 1860-1904)
His plays (*The Cherry Orchard*; *The Three Sisters*; *Uncle Vanya*) showed compassion for human weakness.

 **Eugene O'Neill**
(American, 1888-1953)
Nobel- and Pulitzer Prize-winner known for his powerful, tragic dramas (*The Iceman Cometh*; *Long Day's Journey Into Night*)

 **Bertolt Brecht**
(German, 1895-1956)
Founder of a world-famous theater company; wrote *The Threepenny Opera*

 **Thornton Wilder**
(American, 1897-1975)
Wrote of small-town America, as in *Our Town*; his characters often speak directly to the audience

 **Samuel Beckett**
(Irish, 1906-1989)
Wrote *Waiting for Godot* and other plays known for their simple staging and unusual, poetic dialogue

 **Tennessee Williams**
(American, 1911-1983)
Wrote *The Glass Menagerie* and *A Streetcar Named Desire*, which won the 1948 Pulitzer Prize

 **Arthur Miller**
(American, 1915-   )
Wrote *Death of a Salesman*, which won him the 1949 Pulitzer Prize; also known for *The Crucible*

Musical Theater

Most musicals are combinations of lively music and songs, comedy, dancing, elaborate stage sets, and bright costumes. New York City is famous for Broadway, its theater district. Some famous Broadway musicals include *Oklahoma*, *West Side Story*, *My Fair Lady*, *Camelot*, *The Sound of Music*, *Annie*, *Cats*, and *The Lion King*.

Cats, the longest-running show in Broadway history so far, was performed 7,397 times from October 1982 to June 2000.

CATS IS MY FAVORITE MUSICAL!

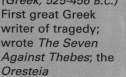

Time

(see also EARTH ●
FARMING ● INVENTORS
AND INVENTIONS
● MEASUREMENTS)

Since the beginning of humankind, people have needed to know how to tell time. Early hunters watched the sun, moon, and stars to determine when the seasons would change, so they would know when the animals they hunted would migrate. When agriculture began, farmers had to know when to plant their crops.

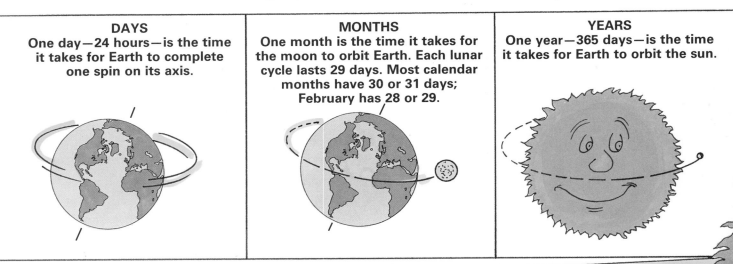

DAYS
One day—24 hours—is the time it takes for Earth to complete one spin on its axis.

MONTHS
One month is the time it takes for the moon to orbit Earth. Each lunar cycle lasts 29 days. Most calendar months have 30 or 31 days; February has 28 or 29.

YEARS
One year—365 days—is the time it takes for Earth to orbit the sun.

Days

Earth is constantly spinning, so different parts of the planet face the sun at different times of the day. In about 2400 B.C., Babylonians started dividing each day into 24 parts, called hours. We use their system today. Each new 24-hour day begins at midnight.

Hours

The U.S. uses a 12-hour system, which divides the day in half, with *a.m.* and *p.m.* distinguishing the two parts. *Ante meridiem* (a.m.) refers to the 12 hours before noon. *Post meridiem* (p.m.) refers to the 12 hours after noon. Many other countries use a 24-hour system: Instead of beginning at 1 again for the hours after 12 noon, the hours are counted up to 24—13:00, 14:00, and so on.

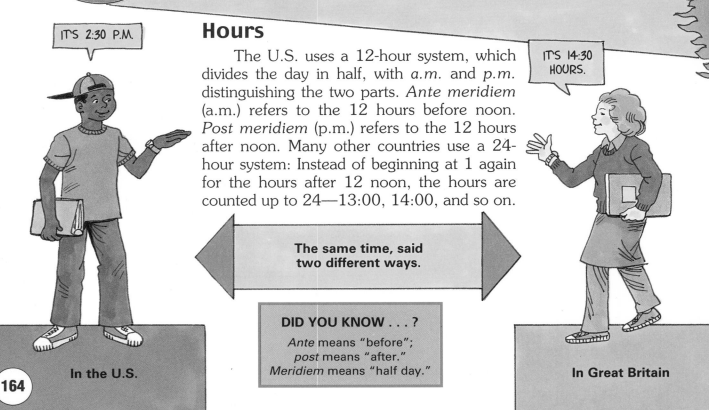

IT'S 2:30 P.M.

IT'S 14:30 HOURS.

The same time, said two different ways.

DID YOU KNOW . . . ?
Ante means "before";
post means "after."
Meridiem means "half day."

In the U.S.

In Great Britain

Time Zones

Earth is divided into 24 parts by imaginary lines called longitudes, or meridians, that run from the North Pole to the South Pole. Each part is a time zone.

Astronomers began this system in 1866, using Greenwich Mean Time (GMT) as the international standard. GMT is the time along the prime meridian, which runs through Greenwich, England. Moving east from there, each time zone is one hour later than GMT; moving west from there, each time zone is one hour earlier than GMT. For example, at 12 p.m. GMT (noon), it is five hours earlier (7 a.m.) in Washington, D.C., which is five time zones to the west.

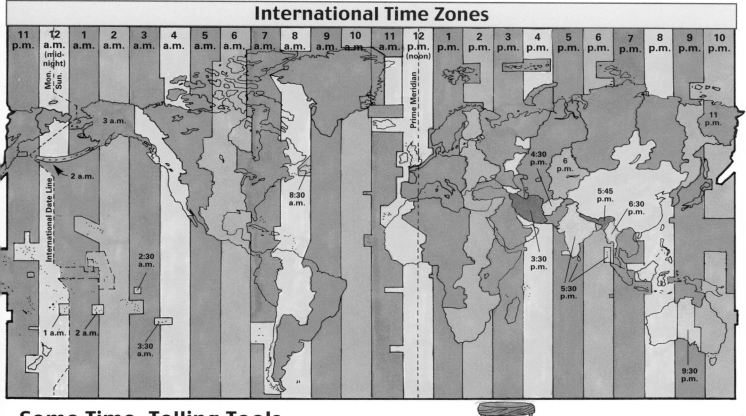

International Time Zones

Some Time–Telling Tools

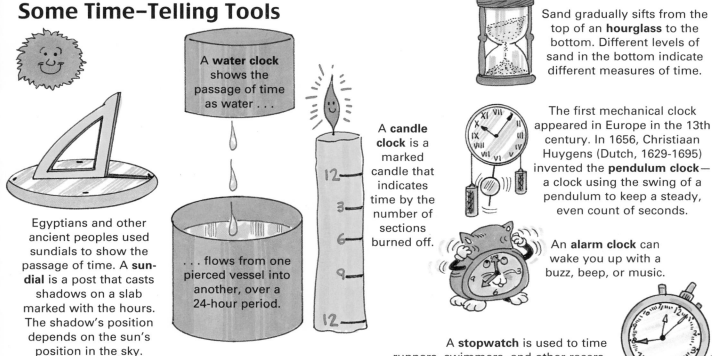

Egyptians and other ancient peoples used sundials to show the passage of time. A **sundial** is a post that casts shadows on a slab marked with the hours. The shadow's position depends on the sun's position in the sky.

A **water clock** shows the passage of time as water . . .

. . . flows from one pierced vessel into another, over a 24-hour period.

A **candle clock** is a marked candle that indicates time by the number of sections burned off.

Sand gradually sifts from the top of an **hourglass** to the bottom. Different levels of sand in the bottom indicate different measures of time.

The first mechanical clock appeared in Europe in the 13th century. In 1656, Christiaan Huygens (Dutch, 1629-1695) invented the **pendulum clock**—a clock using the swing of a pendulum to keep a steady, even count of seconds.

An **alarm clock** can wake you up with a buzz, beep, or music.

A **stopwatch** is used to time runners, swimmers, and other racers.

Transportation

(see also EXPLORERS AND EXPLORATION ● FLIGHT ● INVENTORS AND INVENTIONS ● MACHINES ● SPACE EXPLORATION)

Before the wheel was invented about 6,000 years ago in the Middle East, people traveled on foot, putting heavy items on the backs of their animals. The earliest use of the wheel was as rollers under a platform. Later—more than 4,000 years ago—wheels became part of a cart being pulled by an animal, such as a horse or a donkey. Transportation later developed into the fast-moving cars, mopeds, motorcycles, airplanes, ships, and space shuttles of today. We can now travel halfway around the world in half a day, or explore the ocean's depths in specially built vessels.

Howdah (compartment on an elephant's back), ancient India

Ox-drawn cart, ancient western Asia

Two thousand years ago, Romans and Persians built roads, on which people walked or rode in carts.

WOW! THAT'S BETTER THAN WALKING.

Chariot of ancient Rome

Land Transportation

After the invention of the steam locomotive in 1804, during the Industrial Revolution, a whole new era of travel began—transportation by railroad. The first train locomotives were powered by the burning of wood or coal, which created steam. Most trains now run on electricity or diesel fuel.

In 1885, Karl Benz (Germany) built the first car powered by a fuel-burning engine. By 1903, cars were able to travel up to 70 miles per hour, but they were expensive. In 1908, Henry Ford (U.S.) started the first mass-production factory, making cars faster and more cheaply than ever before. His Model T—nicknamed the Tin Lizzie—made cars affordable to many people.

Cars today: Four-wheel-drive cars can ride over mud, snow, and rock. Family cars are built to carry several passengers in comfort. Sports cars are designed for speed.

The world's fastest passenger trains are France's TGV, Japan's bullet train, and Spain's new *Ave*. The TGV can reach speeds of up to 186 miles per hour.

Seafaring Arabs developed stronger, faster ships. In the 16th century, Europeans adapted those designs and began sailing farther than ever—around the world.

Important Inventions—and Their Inventors—in Transportation History

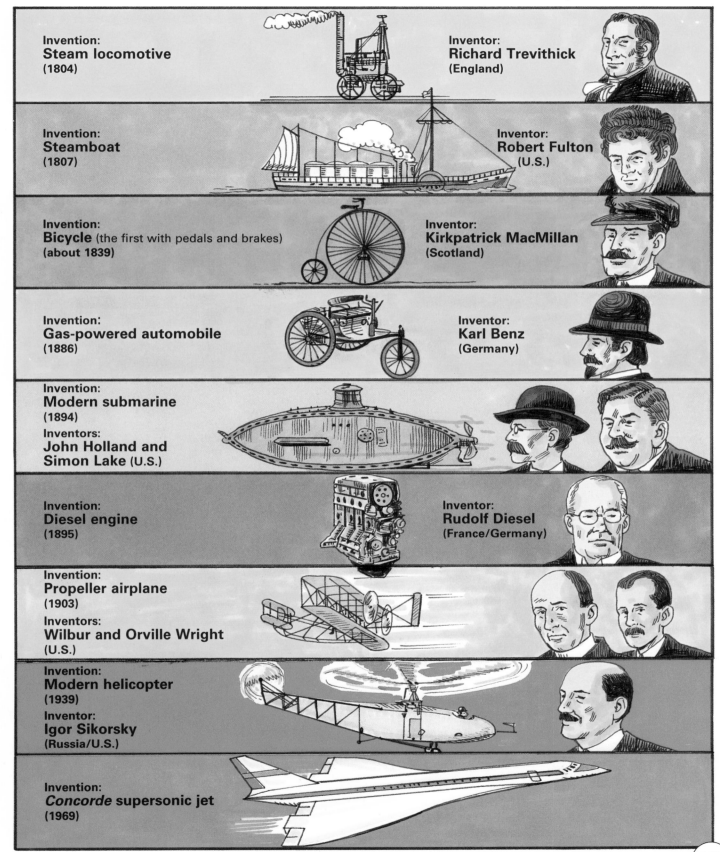

Invention:
Steam locomotive
(1804)

Inventor:
Richard Trevithick
(England)

Invention:
Steamboat
(1807)

Inventor:
Robert Fulton
(U.S.)

Invention:
Bicycle (the first with pedals and brakes)
(about 1839)

Inventor:
Kirkpatrick MacMillan
(Scotland)

Invention:
Gas-powered automobile
(1886)

Inventor:
Karl Benz
(Germany)

Invention:
Modern submarine
(1894)
Inventors:
John Holland and
Simon Lake (U.S.)

Invention:
Diesel engine
(1895)

Inventor:
Rudolf Diesel
(France/Germany)

Invention:
Propeller airplane
(1903)
Inventors:
Wilbur and Orville Wright
(U.S.)

Invention:
Modern helicopter
(1939)
Inventor:
Igor Sikorsky
(Russia/U.S.)

Invention:
***Concorde* supersonic jet**
(1969)

Trees

(see also ECOSYSTEMS ● FORESTS ● PLANT KINGDOM ● RAIN FORESTS)

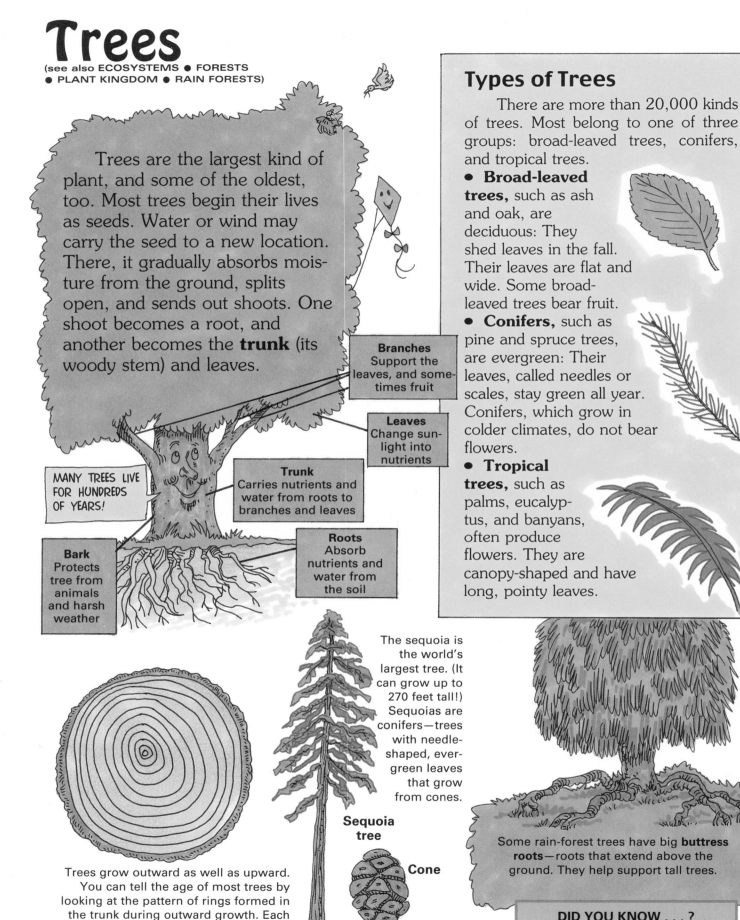

Trees are the largest kind of plant, and some of the oldest, too. Most trees begin their lives as seeds. Water or wind may carry the seed to a new location. There, it gradually absorbs moisture from the ground, splits open, and sends out shoots. One shoot becomes a root, and another becomes the **trunk** (its woody stem) and leaves.

MANY TREES LIVE FOR HUNDREDS OF YEARS!

Branches
Support the leaves, and sometimes fruit

Leaves
Change sunlight into nutrients

Trunk
Carries nutrients and water from roots to branches and leaves

Bark
Protects tree from animals and harsh weather

Roots
Absorb nutrients and water from the soil

Types of Trees

There are more than 20,000 kinds of trees. Most belong to one of three groups: broad-leaved trees, conifers, and tropical trees.

● **Broad-leaved trees,** such as ash and oak, are deciduous: They shed leaves in the fall. Their leaves are flat and wide. Some broad-leaved trees bear fruit.

● **Conifers,** such as pine and spruce trees, are evergreen: Their leaves, called needles or scales, stay green all year. Conifers, which grow in colder climates, do not bear flowers.

● **Tropical trees,** such as palms, eucalyptus, and banyans, often produce flowers. They are canopy-shaped and have long, pointy leaves.

The sequoia is the world's largest tree. (It can grow up to 270 feet tall!) Sequoias are conifers—trees with needle-shaped, evergreen leaves that grow from cones.

Sequoia tree

Cone

Needles

Trees grow outward as well as upward. You can tell the age of most trees by looking at the pattern of rings formed in the trunk during outward growth. Each pair of rings represents one year. The first ring shows early-season growth; the second ring, late-season growth.

Some rain-forest trees have big **buttress roots**—roots that extend above the ground. They help support tall trees.

DID YOU KNOW . . . ?
Some bristlecone pines in California are 4,000 to 5,000 years old!

United Nations
(see also GOVERNMENTS ● LAW ● WAR)

Official seal of the United Nations

The United Nations (UN) was established in 1945 to develop friendly relations between nations and to try to solve international disputes without war. Its first members were the 50 countries that met and signed the **charter** (written list of goals and duties) in 1945. This international organization discusses world problems and seeks solutions. It has played an increasingly important role in world affairs. In 1999, 185 of the world's 192 independent countries were members.*

*The seven nonmember independent countries were Kiribati, Nauru, Switzerland, Taiwan, Tonga, Tuvalu, and Vatican City.

Below: United Nations headquarters in New York, New York. *At right:* The General Assembly.

There are six main parts of the UN. Each has a different duty:

● The **General Assembly** meets once a year for three months, as well as for emergency sessions. This body discusses and votes on many types of issues that concern the world, including poverty, war and peace, economic improvement, health, and education. All member countries of the UN serve in the General Assembly; each has one vote.

● The **Security Council** is responsible for seeking and maintaining international peace and security. The Security Council has five permanent members (from China, France, the United Kingdom, Russia, and the U.S.), plus ten members elected for two-year terms.

● The **Secretariat** is the administrative wing of the UN. It is headed by the Secretary General, whose staff oversees and organizes the day-to-day operations of the UN.

● The **International Court of Justice (World Court)** solves legal conflicts among countries.

● The **Economic and Social Council** addresses world problems in health, education, human rights, and trade. This branch works closely with other UN-related organizations, such as the World Health Organization (WHO) and the United Nations Children's Fund (UNICEF).

● Whenever necessary, the **Trusteeship Council** monitors people living in territories that are temporarily placed under UN **trust** (care, possession, or control).

United States

(see also NORTH AMERICA ● PRESIDENTS, U.S. ● UNITED STATES HISTORY ● WORLD)

The United States is the world's third-largest country in land area (after Russia and Canada), is a world leader in technology, and has the strongest economy of any country in the world.

Alaska

Arctic Ocean

Barrow

MT. McKINLEY

Juneau

Atka

Pacific Ocean

CANADA

Pacific Ocean

Olympia

Washington

Columbia River

Salem

Oregon

Boise

Idaho

Snake River

Helena

Montana

Missouri River

Yellowstone River

North Dakota

Bismarck

South Dakota

Pierre

Wyoming

Cheyenne

Nebraska

Sacramento

Carson City

Nevada

Salt Lake City

Utah

Colorado River

Denver

Colorado

California

Arizona

Phoenix

Santa Fe

New Mexico

Rio Grande

The Land

The U.S. is made up of 50 states—the 48 **contiguous** (connected) states, plus two (Alaska and Hawaii) set apart from the rest. The contiguous states can be divided into different regions: the Northeast, the Middle Atlantic states, the Midwest, the South, the Southwest, the Mountain states, and the Pacific states. Alaska is separated from the contiguous states by part of Canada; Hawaii is in the Pacific Ocean, 2,090 miles west of California.

Each state has its own capital city. The nation has many types of land: grassy prairies (the Great Plains), forests, rocky and sandy seacoasts, bustling cities, deserts, swamps, and mountains.

Honolulu

Hawaii

Hilo

Note: On this map, dark-green areas represent national parks; beige areas represent mountain ranges.

- **Highest point:** Mount McKinley, Alaska (20,320 feet above sea level)
- **Lowest point:** Death Valley, California (282 feet below sea level)
- **Longest river:** Mississippi (2,350 miles)
- **Deepest lake:** Crater Lake, Oregon (1,932 feet)

The People

Every 10 years, the U.S. government takes a census—a count of the country's population. The 1990 census found that 80 percent of people in the U.S. identified themselves as white, 12 percent as African American, and 9 percent as Hispanic, with Asian Americans, Native Americans, and others forming the remaining 8 percent. (The total does not add up to 100 percent because Hispanics can be of any race.) Eighty percent of the American people live in cities or suburbs.

A Nation of Immigrants

In the 19th and 20th centuries, millions of Europeans came to the U.S., fleeing from persecution, escaping from famine (such as the Irish), or searching for better lives. For many of these new immigrants, a memorable sight on arrival was the Statue of Liberty in New York Harbor, which they passed on their way to Ellis Island. Ellis Island was the U.S. government's chief immigration center from 1892 until 1954.

NEW YORK CITY HAS THE LARGEST POPULATION IN THE U.S.

DID YOU KNOW . . . ?

Since the 1980s, the largest numbers of U.S. immigrants have come from Asia and Central America. There are many large new or growing rapidly communities of Chinese and Spanish-speaking people in East Coast and West Coast cities, and of Spanish-speakers in Texas and the Southwest.

- **National capital:** Washington, D.C.
- **Northernmost city:** Barrow, Alaska
- **Southernmost city:** Hilo, Hawaii
- **Easternmost city:** Eastport, Maine
- **Westernmost city:** Atka, Alaska

United States History

(see also AFRICAN AMERICANS ● GOVERNMENTS ● HOLIDAYS ● LAW ● NATIVE AMERICANS ● NORTH AMERICA ● PRESIDENTS, U.S. ● UNITED STATES ● WAR)

The land that is now the United States was first inhabited by people who crossed from Asia and spread through North and South America. Native Americans (Indians) are their descendants.

In 1607, European settlers established Jamestown, Virginia, the first permanent British settlement in North America. The Pilgrims (English Puritans) reached Plymouth, Massachusetts, in 1620, seeking religious freedom. In the 16th and 17th centuries, Spanish explorers staked claims to parts of present-day Florida, New Mexico, and California. On the East Coast, 13 English colonies were formed, each with its own laws. Great Britain controlled the colonies until 1775, when rebellion by colonists erupted into the American Revolution. In 1781, the Revolution ended and a treaty, signed in 1783, recognized the new nation of the United States of America. In 1787, George Washington and other Founding Fathers signed the Constitution, a document that established the structure of the federal government. The Bill of Rights and other amendments to the Constitution guarantee the rights of citizens.

Native Americans helped Europeans survive their first winters in America.

On July 4, 1776, colonial leaders signed the Declaration of Independence.

George Washington, later the first U.S. president, led American troops in the American Revolution.

In 1803, President Thomas Jefferson doubled the size of the country when he completed the Louisiana Purchase—828,000 square miles for $15 million.

1776
1803
1783

During the War of 1812 (U.S. vs. Britain), Francis Scott Key wrote "The Star-Spangled Banner," the poem that became the national anthem.

Francis Scott Key

In 1845, the U.S. acquired Texas. The 1846 Oregon Treaty extended the nation to the Pacific Ocean. More territory was added in 1848 and 1853.

1846
1848
1803
1845
1853
1819

By the 1850s, the question of whether slavery should be allowed in new U.S. territories had grown into a hot national debate.

The Civil War began in 1861 when Confederate troops fired on Fort Sumter, South Carolina.

The North's victory at the Battle of Gettysburg (1863) turned the tide of the Civil War.

The South surrendered in 1865, ending the war. That same year, approval of the 13th Amendment abolished slavery in the U.S.

Following the Civil War, industry grew rapidly in much of the nation.

The transcontinental railroad was completed in 1869, speeding travel and further opening the West.

The U.S. has always been a land of immigrants, but in 1905-1914, the number of new arrivals soared.

In 1917 and 1918, U.S. troops fought in World War I, which began in Europe in 1914.

American lifestyles made a great shift during the post-war 1920s, known as the Roaring Twenties; also as the Jazz Age.

The worldwide Great Depression of the 1930s put millions of Americans out of work. President Franklin Roosevelt's New Deal programs and World War II brought relief by creating jobs.

APPLES 5¢

OUT OF WORK

In 1941, after Japan attacked U.S. naval bases at Pearl Harbor, Hawaii, the U.S. joined the fighting in World War II, which had begun in Europe in 1939.

While men were fighting in World War II, many U.S. women took jobs for the first time, building planes and ships.

Since World War II ended in 1945, the U.S. has been a world superpower—a leader in business, technology, and popular culture.

After World War II, many Americans began moving from cities to suburbs—a new kind of community.

In the 1950s, tension between the democratic U.S. and the Communist Soviet Union grew. This tension, known as the Cold War, affected politics around the world.

The civil-rights movement of the 1950s and 1960s knocked down many barriers that had kept African Americans from exercising their full rights as citizens.

"WE SHALL OVERCOME!"

In 1964-1973, U.S. troops took part in the Vietnam War. During the 1970s, a growing death toll inspired many citizens to join a peace movement, splitting Americans between supporters and opponents of the war.

In the late 1980s, the Cold War ended. So did the arms race, in which the U.S. and the Soviet Union had spent millions of dollars on weapons. The 1990s was a time of prosperity for the U.S.

$TOCK MARKET OAR!

173

Universe

(see also EARTH ● SUN AND SOLAR SYSTEM ● SPACE EXPLORATION)

The universe is not just Earth and its solar system. The universe refers to all light, energy, and living things in the vast reaches of space.

The universe is enormous. It includes many galaxies—including the Milky Way, which is our home galaxy—and all the stars, moons, planets, comets, and suns. The Milky Way galaxy alone is 72,000 light-years from its center to the most-distant stars and gas clouds!

Many scientists think that the universe began with a huge explosion of matter 10 billion to 20 billion years ago. This matter flew all around, creating different galaxies. The universe is slowly, constantly expanding—swelling like a balloon. Many scientists think that the universe will expand forever. Others think that it will collapse someday, due to gravity.

BLACK HOLE

Black Holes

Scientists think that when a star collapses or explodes, it leaves behind nearby matter. This matter has such a powerful pull of gravity that everything around it—even light—gets sucked into it.

THINK ABOUT IT!

➦ Earth is one of nine planets in our solar system.
➦ Our solar system is one of billions in our galaxy.
➦ Our galaxy is one of an estimated 50 million galaxies in the universe.

OUR GALAXY (The Milky Way Galaxy)

The Andromeda galaxy—the galaxy closest to our Milky Way—is two million light-years from Earth.

Spiral galaxies—like our own Milky Way galaxy—are pinwheel-shaped. They have arms (made up of countless stars and solar systems) that spiral out from the center.

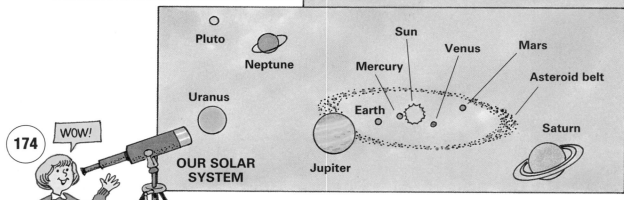

OUR SOLAR SYSTEM

Pluto · Neptune · Uranus · Mercury · Sun · Venus · Mars · Earth · Asteroid belt · Jupiter · Saturn

The Milky Way galaxy is home to about 200 billion stars, but only about 2,000 of them are visible to us without instruments.

174 WOW!

Stars

New stars constantly come into being while others age and eventually die. The life cycle of a star is a very slow process; it takes billions upon billions of years—far too long for us to see it happen to any one star!

THAT'S THE KING OF STARS!

Nebula

Protostars

Star

Red giant

White dwarf

Sometimes, outer parts of a star drift off into space. A **white dwarf** is what is left.

When the protostar gets hotter, it becomes a **star**. As the star ages, nuclear reactions change its hydrogen . . .

. . . to helium, and it swells, becoming a **red giant**.

Gravity pulls parts of the nebula into a ball of gas, which becomes a **protostar**.

Clouds of gas and dust, called **nebula**, exist all over the universe.

Galaxies

Galaxies are made of billions of stars held together by gravity. There are an estimated 50 million galaxies in the universe. Galaxies, which contain dust and gas clouds, come in three main shapes: spiral, elliptical, or irregular.

Elliptical galaxies are rounded, with no arms. Most galaxies are elliptical.

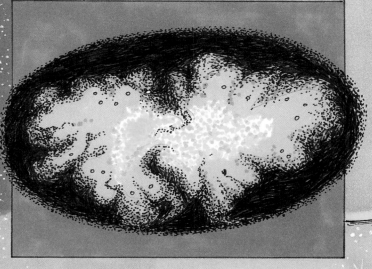

Irregular galaxies have no distinct shape or pattern. Some, for instance, look like huge clouds.

War

(see also ARMS AND WEAPONS ● UNITED NATIONS ● UNITED STATES HISTORY)

A war is a conflict between two or more forces, involving weapons. Some wars are fought between two or more nations, others are conflicts between organized groups within a single nation.

Many wars begin when one group or nation tries to control another, to gain territory or natural resources controlled by the other group. Some wars—such as the Crusades, fought between Christians and Muslims during the Middle Ages (A.D. 1096 to 1291)—have been fought between people of different religious beliefs.

During wars, terrible things often occur—including the loss of many innocent lives, and the destruction of buildings and other property. World War II, the most widespread and most destructive war in history, took 40 million to 50 million lives.

The first-known armies began in Mesopotamia around 5,000 B.C.

Roman legions conquered many lands for the Roman Empire, which lasted from about 27 B.C. to A.D. 476.

Muslim warriors fought "holy wars" to spread the religion of Islam in the 7th and 8th centuries.

In the Middle Ages, European noblemen led their personal armies into battle.

In the Hundred Years' War (1337-1453) between England and France, France's countryside was devastated, and England lost nearly all of its French lands.

Britain and France fought the French and Indian Wars (1754-1763) over which empire would control colonies in what is now Canada and the U.S.

In the American Revolution (1776-1783), Britain lost its American colonies, and the United States won independence.

The Napoleonic Wars (1803-1815) were a series of wars between France and the countries that were trying to keep Napoleon I, France's ruler, from expanding his empire. Britain and Russia were the main opponents. Many battles in these wars were fought at sea, as well as on the European mainland.

More Americans died in the Civil War (1861-1865) than in any other U.S.-involved war.

In the 1800s, Native Americans fought the U.S. government to defend their homelands.

Zulu warriors defeated the British in a major battle in South Africa in 1879. The British eventually won the war.

World War I (1914-1918) claimed 10 million lives and shattered Europe. It was fought between the Central Powers (Germany, Austria-Hungary, and Turkey) and the Allies (France, Britain, Russia, the U.S., and Italy).

World War II (1939-1945), the most destructive war of all time, was fought in Europe, Asia, the Pacific islands, and North Africa.

The atom bomb, dropped by the U.S. on Japan during World War II (1939-1945), led to a long "cold war"—a period of high tension without actual fighting.

The Korean War (1950-1953) was the first conflict in which the United Nations sent troops into battle. The UN aided South Korea; Communist China aided North Korea.

In the Vietnam War (1954-1975), South Vietnam fought to keep North Vietnam from extending Communist rule into the South. U.S. troops aided the South from 1961 to 1973.

Rules of War

In modern wars, countries are supposed to follow rules of conduct. The Geneva Convention of 1864 (revised in 1906, 1929, 1949, and 1977) spells out rules about how prisoners of war should be treated. They must not be tortured and cannot be forced to work for their captors' war effort. The leaders of countries that break these rules may be tried in international courts. The first war-crimes trials were held from November 1945 to October 1946 in Nuremberg, Germany. There, Nazi leaders were convicted of crimes committed against humanity during World War II. In 1945, the United Nations (see p. 169) was founded in the hope of preventing future wars.

Water

(see also DESERTS ● EARTH ● ENERGY ● ENVIRONMENT ● MATTER ● OCEANS AND SEA LIFE ● POLAR REGIONS ● SCIENCE AND SCIENTISTS ● WEATHER)

Water is the most common substance on Earth—71 percent of Earth's surface is water. Most of Earth's water—97 percent of it—is saltwater (oceans and seas). The other 3 percent is freshwater. Most of that freshwater (about three fourths) is frozen in glaciers or in antarctic and arctic ice packs; the rest is what flows in lakes, rivers, ponds, and other bodies of freshwater.

Without water, there would be no life. Every plant and animal needs water to survive.

Water is made of hydrogen and oxygen. Each water molecule has two hydrogen atoms and one oxygen atom. The scientific formula for water reflects this: H_2O.

Drinking Water

The water that we drink starts out as rain. Rain is collected in lakes and rivers, or stored in reservoirs. Then it is **purified** (germs and bacteria are removed), filtered, and pumped into homes, offices, and schools. Waste water is often repurified and reused.

Rain cloud

Lake

River

Reservoir

Purification plant

Holding tank

User

Waste water being repurified

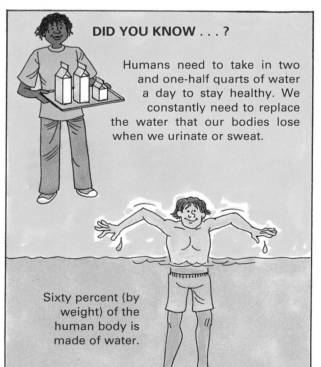

DID YOU KNOW . . . ?

Humans need to take in two and one-half quarts of water a day to stay healthy. We constantly need to replace the water that our bodies lose when we urinate or sweat.

Sixty percent (by weight) of the human body is made of water.

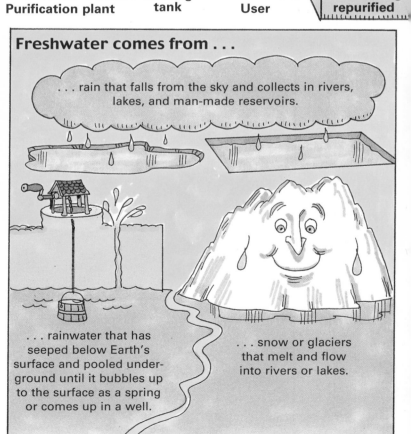

Freshwater comes from . . .

. . . rain that falls from the sky and collects in rivers, lakes, and man-made reservoirs.

. . . rainwater that has seeped below Earth's surface and pooled underground until it bubbles up to the surface as a spring or comes up in a well.

. . . snow or glaciers that melt and flow into rivers or lakes.

A Powerful Force

Most of Earth's surfaces have been sculpted by the pressure of flowing water. Glaciers carve out canyons, valleys, and lakes. Rivers also change the landscape by washing soil away to the sea, which pushes it back again, changing the shape of shorelines.

Save It!

Clean water is precious and difficult to come by, so try to conserve it. For instance, don't let the faucet run while brushing your teeth.

Washing machines and dishwashers use a lot of water. Waiting until you have a full load before turning one on is a simple but effective way of saving water.

One large bathtub holds 50 gallons of water. Taking quick showers instead of baths saves water—more if you use a water-saver shower head.

- Each person uses 80-100 gallons of water per day. (The largest use is flushing the toilet.)
- Most toilets have constant, small leaks. A small leak can waste about 22 gallons in a day—or 8,000 gallons in a year!

The Three Forms of Water

Solid
When water freezes (at 32° F), it becomes ice.

Liquid
At medium temperatures (when ice melts or gas cools), water is a liquid.

Gas
When water is hot enough to boil (at 212° F or above), it turns into vapor.

Weather

(see also AIR ● DESERTS ● EARTH ● ECOSYSTEMS ● ENVIRONMENT ● WATER)

Conditions in the lower layers of Earth's atmosphere are constantly changing: It might be cloudy, sunny, snowy, rainy, or windy. This everyday activity is called weather. Weather is determined by **wind** (circulating air), temperature, **humidity** (moisture in the air), and **air pressure** (the force of Earth's atmosphere). Knowing what the weather will be helps people plan their days—especially farmers and fishing-boat crews, whose livelihoods depend on the weather.

Scientists who study weather are called meteorologists.

Climate is the average weather over long periods of time in a certain area.

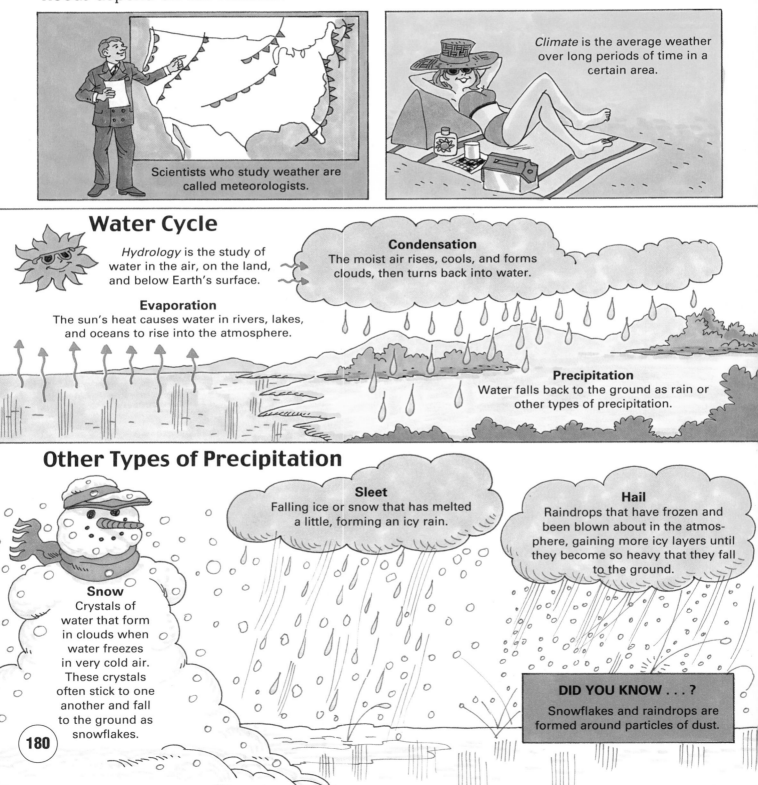

Water Cycle

Hydrology is the study of water in the air, on the land, and below Earth's surface.

Condensation
The moist air rises, cools, and forms clouds, then turns back into water.

Evaporation
The sun's heat causes water in rivers, lakes, and oceans to rise into the atmosphere.

Precipitation
Water falls back to the ground as rain or other types of precipitation.

Other Types of Precipitation

Sleet
Falling ice or snow that has melted a little, forming an icy rain.

Hail
Raindrops that have frozen and been blown about in the atmosphere, gaining more icy layers until they become so heavy that they fall to the ground.

Snow
Crystals of water that form in clouds when water freezes in very cold air. These crystals often stick to one another and fall to the ground as snowflakes.

DID YOU KNOW . . . ?
Snowflakes and raindrops are formed around particles of dust.

Clouds

Warm air holds more moisture than cold air. As warm air rises, it cools and the water forms a vapor—droplets that hang in the air as clouds. There are many types of clouds. A few are:

▲ **Cirrus:** white, wispy-looking clouds; usually the highest; many at once is often a sign of rain

▲ **Cumulus:** mid-level clouds; flat-bottomed with high, puffy tops; usually a sign of fair weather

▲ **Stratus:** low-lying, layered clouds; usually related to stormy weather

COMBINATION CLOUDS

▲ **Cumulonimbus:** also known as thunderheads, these are the clouds of thunder-and-lightning storms

▲ **Cirrostratus:** high, layered clouds; often a sign of precipitation

Stormy Weather

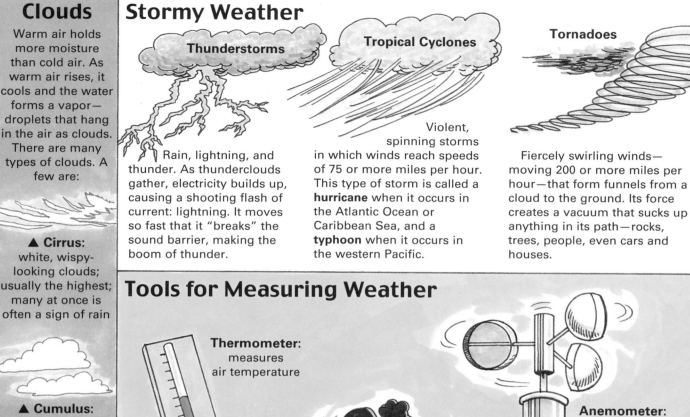

Thunderstorms

Rain, lightning, and thunder. As thunderclouds gather, electricity builds up, causing a shooting flash of current: lightning. It moves so fast that it "breaks" the sound barrier, making the boom of thunder.

Tropical Cyclones

Violent, spinning storms in which winds reach speeds of 75 or more miles per hour. This type of storm is called a **hurricane** when it occurs in the Atlantic Ocean or Caribbean Sea, and a **typhoon** when it occurs in the western Pacific.

Tornadoes

Fiercely swirling winds—moving 200 or more miles per hour—that form funnels from a cloud to the ground. Its force creates a vacuum that sucks up anything in its path—rocks, trees, people, even cars and houses.

Tools for Measuring Weather

Thermometer: measures air temperature

Anemometer: measures wind speed; used to judge the rate of approaching weather

Rain gauge: measures rainfall (in inches or centimeters)

Weather vane: shows the direction in which the wind is blowing

Barometer: measures **atmospheric** (air) pressure

The highest temperature ever recorded . . . was 136° F, at Al Aziziyah, Libya, on September 13, 1922.

The lowest temperature ever recorded . . . was -128.6° F, at Vostok, Antarctica, on July 21, 1983.

WEATHER WISDOM

Lower atmospheric pressure means that the air is warming and rising. (Warm air is lighter than cold air.) Higher atmospheric pressure means that air is cooling and sinking. Wind moves into areas of low pressure. When the air pressure drops rapidly in a short time, a storm is coming!

Women, Famous

(see also AFRICAN AMERICANS ● ART AND ARTISTS ● LITERATURE AND WRITERS ● NATIVE AMERICANS ● OLYMPICS ● SCIENCE AND SCIENTISTS ● SPORTS)

Women's contributions to society and women's importance in history have often been overlooked. However, women have ruled empires, fought battles, invented useful products, and influenced history, religion, and culture. Recently, more historians have made note of the accomplishments of women, past and present, throughout the world.

Politics and Government

Cleopatra VII
(Egypt, 69-30 B.C.)
Ruled Egypt from 51 B.C. until 30 B.C.

Joan of Arc
(France, 1412-1431)
Led the armies of France during a war against invaders from Britain

Queen Elizabeth I
(Britain, 1533-1603)
One of England's greatest and most powerful monarchs

Queen Liliuokalani
(Hawaii, 1838-1917)
Last queen of independent Hawaii (ruled 1891-1893); was also a songwriter

Jeannette Rankin
(U.S., 1880-1973)
First woman elected to the U.S. Congress; served there 1917-1919 and 1941-1943

Golda Meir
(Russia/Israel, 1898-1978)
Powerful leader in Middle East politics; prime minister of Israel from 1969 to 1974

Indira Gandhi
(India, 1917-1984)
Two-time prime minister of India (1966-1977, 1980-1984); a controversial figure; assassinated while in office

The Arts

Sappho
(Greece, about 610-580 B.C.)
Poet of ancient Greece

Sarah Bernhardt
(France, 1844-1923)
Most famous actress of the 19th century; known as "The Divine Sarah" for her voice and emotional style

Grandma Moses (Anna Mary Robertson Moses)
(U.S., 1860-1961)
Famous for primitive paintings of rural America; did not begin painting till in her 70s

Martha Graham
(U.S., 1894-1991)
Dancer and choreographer; a ground-breaking developer of modern dance

Margaret Bourke-White
(U.S., 1906-1971)
Photographer/editor known for her photo essays on World War II and many countries

Billie Holiday
(U.S., 1915-1959)
Jazz singer; her distinctive style influenced generations of singers and musicians

Toni Morrison
(U.S., 1931-   )
Novelist; first African-American woman to win the Nobel Prize for Literature (1993)

Education and Reform

Susan B. Anthony
(U.S., 1820-1906)
A pioneer in the campaign to secure voting rights for all U.S. women

Jane Addams
(U.S., 1860-1935)
Social worker and reformer; awarded the 1931 Nobel Peace Prize for her work

Eleanor Roosevelt
(U.S., 1884-1962)
First Lady (wife of Franklin D. Roosevelt, 32nd U.S. president) who campaigned for human rights worldwide

Mother Teresa
(Albania/India, 1910-1997)
Catholic nun who founded an institution to help the sick and poor; awarded the 1979 Nobel Peace Prize

Rigoberta Menchú
(Guatemala, 1959-)
Reformer; won 1992 Nobel Peace Prize for her efforts to protect the rights of Indian people

Science

Elizabeth Blackwell
(England/U.S., 1821-1910)
Physician; first woman to earn a medical degree in the U.S.

Dian Fossey
(U.S., 1932-1985)
Animal-behavior researcher and the leading authority on mountain gorillas; also a noted author

Margaret Mead
(U.S., 1901-1978)
Anthropologist and author known for her studies of peoples of South Pacific islands

Business

Victoria Woodhull
(U.S., 1838-1927)
One of the first women to run a successful stock-brokerage firm; first woman to run for U.S. president (1870)

Madame Sarah Walker
(U.S., 1867-1919)
Businesswoman; the first black woman—and one of the first women ever—to become a millionaire

Athletics

Wilma Rudolph
(U.S., 1940-1994)
Runner; overcame paralysis of childhood polio to become the first woman to win three gold medals at one Olympics (1960)

Billie Jean King
(U.S., 1943-)
Tennis champion; a key influence in winning public attention for women's sports

Exploration

Nellie Bly
(U.S., 1867-1922)
Journalist known for her record-breaking journey around the world (in 72 days, 6 hours, 11 minutes)

Amelia Earhart
(U.S., 1897-1937)
First woman to fly a plane across the Atlantic Ocean (1928); disappeared during a round-the-world flight (1937)

Valentina V. Tereshkova
(Soviet Union, 1937-)
Cosmonaut; first woman in space (1963)

World

(see also AFRICA ● ASIA ● AUSTRALIA AND OCEANIA ● EARTH ● EUROPE ● GEOGRAPHY ● GEOLOGY ● NORTH AMERICA ● POLAR REGIONS ● SOUTH AMERICA ● UNITED STATES ● WAR ● WEATHER)

Water covers most of the world—about two thirds of it. Most of this is ocean: the Pacific, Atlantic, Indian, and Arctic. The other third is land, which is divided into seven continents—Africa, Antarctica, Asia, Australia, Europe, North America, and South America. The continents are split into more than 190 independent countries, as well as a number of territories and other areas.

Eastern Hemisphere

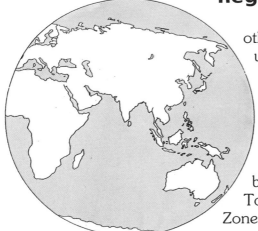

Regions and Other Divisions

Countries and territories are political divisions, but we have other ways of talking about parts of the world. For instance, we use the equator (an imaginary line across Earth's middle) to divide the world into Northern and Southern Hemispheres. (*Hemi* means half; a *sphere* is a 3-D circle, or ball.) We can also split the world into Eastern and Western Hemispheres.

Sometimes, geographers divide the world into five zones. The North Temperate Zone is the area between the Tropic of Cancer and the Arctic Circle. The South Temperate Zone is between the Tropic of Capricorn and the Antarctic Circle. The Torrid Zone lies between the two Tropics. There are two Frigid Zones, between the poles and the polar circles.

Western Hemisphere

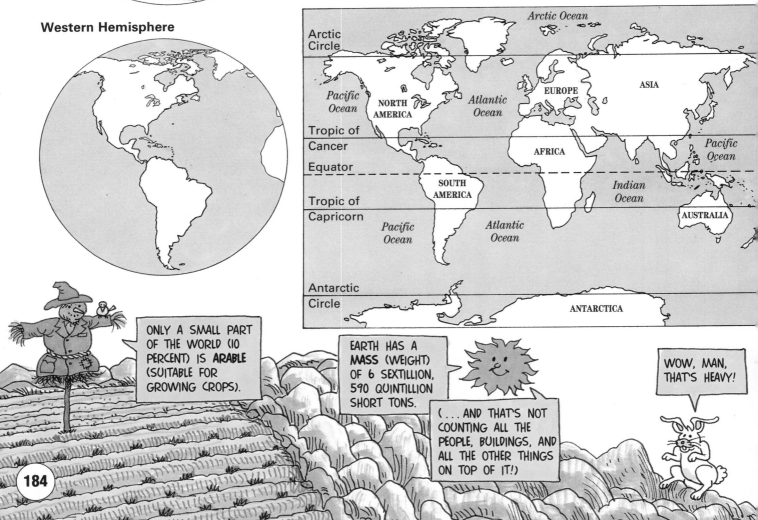

ONLY A SMALL PART OF THE WORLD (10 PERCENT) IS **ARABLE** (SUITABLE FOR GROWING CROPS).

EARTH HAS A **MASS** (WEIGHT) OF 6 SEXTILLION, 590 QUINTILLION SHORT TONS.

(...AND THAT'S NOT COUNTING ALL THE PEOPLE, BUILDINGS, AND ALL THE OTHER THINGS ON TOP OF IT!)

WOW, MAN, THAT'S HEAVY!

People

In 1900, the world's population was three billion. In the 20th century, it rose rapidly. (By 1999, it was rising by about one million persons every week!) By the end of the century, the estimated world population was six billion.

China and India are the most populous countries. Nearly half of the world's people live in towns or cities. The largest urban area is Tokyo, Japan; the most rapidly expanding cities are in Asia and Africa.

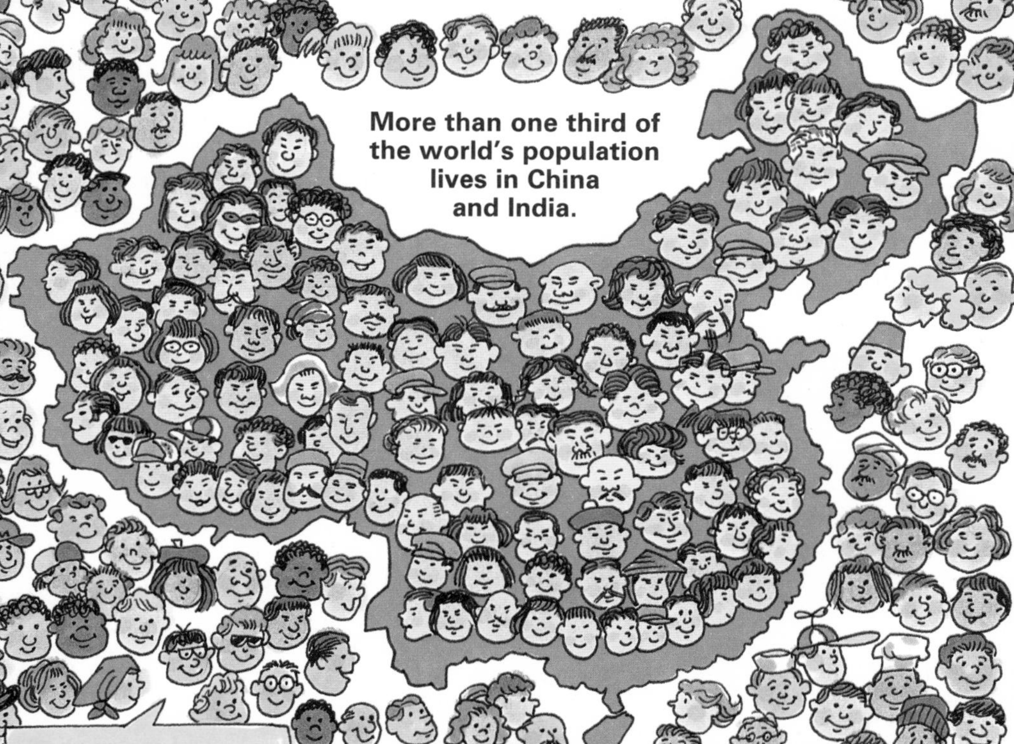

More than one third of the world's population lives in China and India.

THE AVERAGE LIFE EXPECTANCY WORLDWIDE IS 66 YEARS (64 YEARS FOR MALES, 68 YEARS FOR FEMALES).

QUITE A CROWD!
In 1950, the world had 82 independent countries. Since then, many former colonies have gained their independence—a large number of them in Africa during the 1960s. In 1991, the Soviet Union broke apart, giving rise to 15 independent countries. In 1999, the world had 192 independent countries!

PSST! I HAVE A TWIN HIDDEN SOMEWHERE ON THIS PAGE. CAN YOU FIND HER?

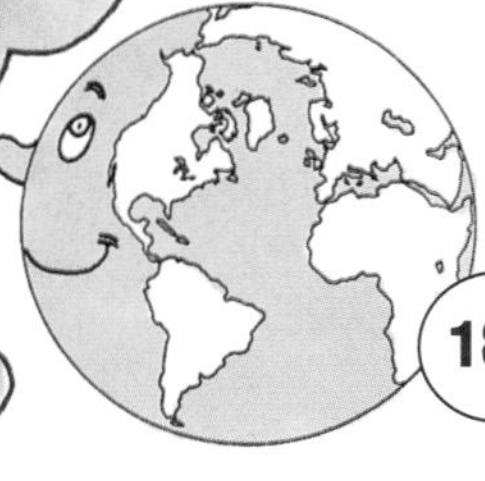

World Superlatives

Longest river:
The Nile (Africa)
4,160 miles

Highest mountain: 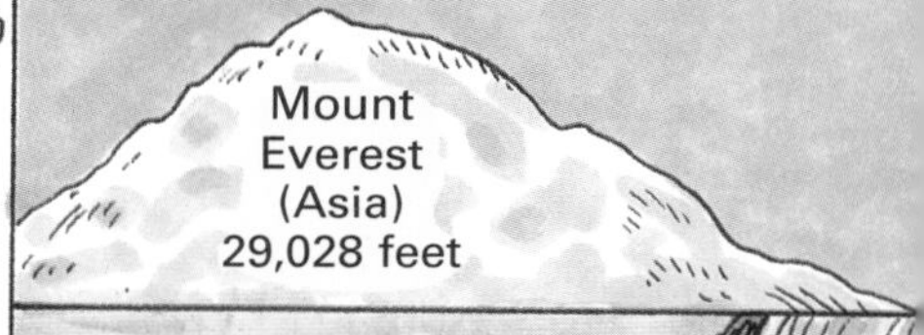
Mount Everest (Asia)
29,028 feet

Highest waterfall:
Angel Falls (South America)
3,212 feet

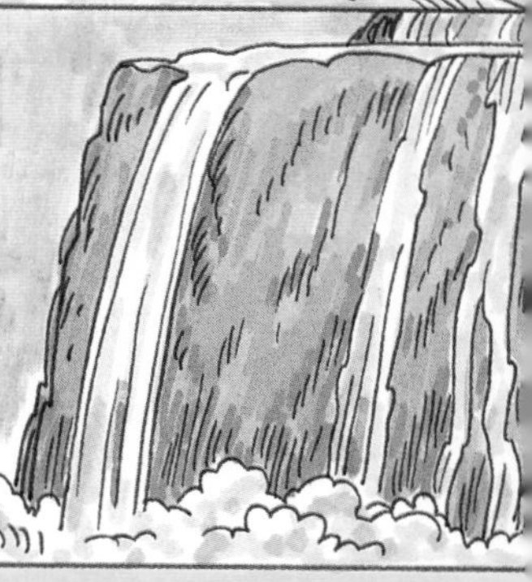

Largest ocean:
The Pacific
63.8 million square miles

Smallest independent country:
Vatican City (Europe)
108.7 acres
(about 0.17 square miles)

Largest independent country:
Russia, 6.5 million square miles

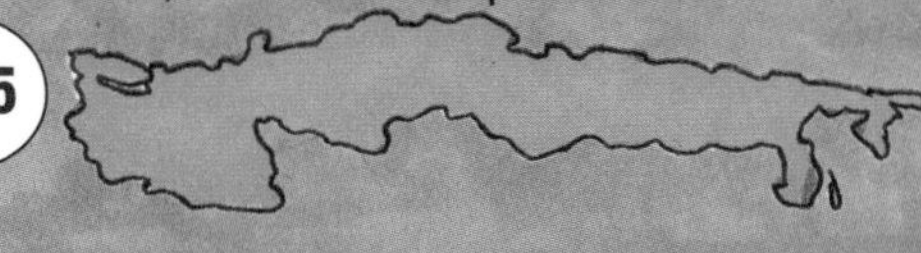

185

Two-toed sloth

Zoos

(see also ANIMAL KINGDOM ● ECOSYSTEMS ● ENVIRONMENT
● NORTH AMERICAN WILDLIFE ● OCEANS AND SEA LIFE ●
SOUTH AMERICAN WILDLIFE)

Zoos are public or private parks where animals are kept so that people can observe and learn about them. Zoos educate the public about animal behavior and about conservation. Few people have the chance to see wild animals in their natural surroundings (such as monkeys in tropical rain forests or zebra in the African savannas), so zoos help us understand and appreciate the variety of life on Earth. They also help in protecting animals that are in danger of extinction.

Aquariums are zoos designed for aquatic animals—animals that live in water. Seals, dolphins, and whales are some of the animals you can observe at an aquarium.

Aardvark

Zebra

Giraffe

Panda
This animal is now rare in the wild. Some zoos are breeding and caring for them, to keep the species from dying out.

AT A CHILDREN'S PETTING ZOO, YOU CAN SEE ANIMALS UP CLOSE—EVEN PET THEM OR FEED THEM.

THE WORLD-FAMOUS SAN ANTONIO ZOO HAS 3,000 ANIMALS IN A NATURAL SETTING, WITH THE SAN ANTONIO RIVER AND LIME-STONE CLIFFS.

Rabbit **Deer**

Beaver

Wallaby

Gopher

Skunk

Zoos, Yesterday and Today

Zoos have been around for thousands of years. Ancient Romans and Egyptians had zoos, and the Chinese had an enormous zoo called the Gardens of Intelligence around 1000 B.C. In the past, zoo animals were kept in cages or other small, enclosed areas. In most modern zoos, however, animals can roam in spacious areas that are similar to their natural habitats. Animals of different species may live in the same area, as they would in the wild. For instance, lions, antelope, birds, and zebras might all live in a zoo area set up like the Serengeti region of Africa, with special trenches to keep the species from attacking one another.

DID YOU KNOW . . . ?
The word *zoo* is short for "zoological garden." *Zoology* is the study of animals and of various types of life in the animal kingdom.

Index

(Main entry topics are listed in **bold** type.)

Animal Kingdom

Computers

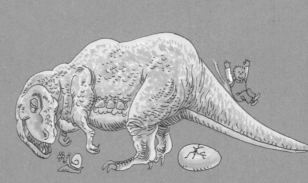

Dinosaurs

Inventions

Literature

Mummies

Rain forests

Sports

Technology